DO THE
FUNKY PICKLE

**Look for these other great books
by Jerry Spinelli**

Fourth Grade Rats
Report to the Principal's Office
Who Ran My Underwear Up the Flagpole?
Picklemania
The Library Card

DO THE FUNKY PICKLE

JERRY SPINELLI

SCHOLASTIC INC.

New York Toronto London Auckland Sydney
Mexico City New Delhi Hong Kong Buenos Aires

ISBN 0-590-45448-X

26 25 24 23 22 21 20 19 18 17 16   4 5 6 7 8 9/0

Printed in the U.S.A.   40

For Jim and Eileen Nechas

DO THE FUNKY PICKLE

1

A t precisely 2:35 P.M. the last bell rang through the hallways and rooms of Plumstead Middle School. At precisely 2:35 plus seven seconds, the main door flew open and five eighth-graders tried to be the first to leave. The eighth-graders pulled each other from the doorway and fought like jackels until huge Mr. Hollis, social studies teacher and school bouncer, grabbed them all in his massive mitts and hauled them off to Detention Room. By the time they were seated, the rest of the student body had poured through the doorway.

One of the last to leave was Salem Brownmiller. Long hair and black scarf flying, she pushed and veered and lurched her way through the crowd until, on the sidewalk, she spotted the person she was looking for. "Sunny! Sunny, wait up!"

Sunny Wyler, whom Salem described as her best friend and worst enemy, halted. Salem came rushing up to her, breathless, her eyes wide with excitement. "Sun — " she gasped, and just as quickly Sunny was gone, racing across the street toward a mob of kids yelling on somebody's front lawn.

Salem gave a scornful sigh. As the yelling grew louder, more kids surged forward, practically knocking Salem off her feet. Within moments she was alone on the sidewalk.

Salem had no intention of crossing the street. She folded her arms over her book bag and glared at the revolting spectacle. After a minute or so an old man came out of the house banging on a drum-sized pot with a wooden spoon. No one seemed to notice. Then a second-story window shot open, an old lady leaned out and like a cuckoo started tweeting furiously on a whistle.

That did the trick. The mob broke up, and within seconds the students were once again streaming toward home. The only evidence they left behind was a white scrap of clothing in the middle of the lawn.

Salem did not move. She waited and glared until Sunny trotted over. Now it was Sunny's eyes wide with excitement. "Wow! Great fight. You shoulda seen it."

"No," said Salem stiffly, "I should *not* have seen it. And neither should you. Don't you have any class? Why do you have to join that herd of animals?"

Sunny was baffled. *"Why?* How can you not? Whoever heard of somebody who *doesn't* like to watch a fight?"

"I heard of somebody. *Me!* Why is everybody around here so big on violence? It seems like there's a fight every day. Whatever happened to peace?"

"Peace?" Sunny sneered. "Peace is no fun."

"Oh, really?" said Salem. "Now that's an intelligent thing to say. I guess it's better to watch two hoodlums ripping each other to shreds."

Sunny grinned. "Don't knock it if you haven't tried it."

Salem's lip curled. "You're disgusting."

"You're weird."

"You're revolting."

"You're unnatural."

"You're bloodthirsty."

"You're nice."

"You're — " Salem blinked. "Huh?"

"Gotcha." Sunny started walking.

Salem stood still, sputtering. Sunny always did that, got you all hot and bothered, then — *zap* — she turned it off. It was infuriatingly impossible to win an argument with her, and just as impossible to stay mad at her. In spite of herself, Salem grinned.

3

She made sure to wipe the grin from her face before she caught up to Sunny. "So," she said, "do you want to hear the big, fantastic, stupendous news or not?"

Sunny merely shrugged. "I already know."

2

Salem's jaw dropped. "You do?"

"Sure," said Sunny. She pulled a Kit Kat mini bar from her pocket and unwrapped it. "I ate sixteen of these for lunch." She popped the bar into her mouth.

Salem stomped. "Get serious."

"I *am* serious. It's a new record."

Salem turned away. "Fine. Then I won't tell you."

The two girls walked on in silence, except for Sunny, who now and then whistled a tune. One block passed. Two blocks. Salem couldn't stand it any longer. She blurted, "Willow Wembley's coming!"

Sunny turned. "What's *that*?"

"The word is *who*. Willow Wembley. The famous author."

Sunny squinted, searching her memory bank. "She write for *Mad Magazine*?"

"Of *course* not!"

Sunny shrugged. "Then I wouldn't know her."

Salem squeaked, "Not *know* her? How can you not know her? She writes the best books anybody ever read. She's world famous."

Sunny sniffed, "Never heard of her."

"You never heard of the Klatterfields? Her famous fictional family?"

"Nope."

"You're lying. Tell me you never heard of Clyde Klatterfield."

"Never heard of him."

Salem swooned. "I think I'm going to faint."

"I think I'm going to vomit."

They walked another block in silence. Salem kept staring at Sunny as though she were an alien life-form.

At last Salem took a deep breath and tried again. "Well, anyway, here's what happened. I was walking past the teachers' lounge on my way out of school when I bumped into Miss Comstock. I thought she was just going to say hi, you know, but she took my arm and sort of pulled me over to the side, like this." She pulled Sunny's arm.

"Then she gets this little grin on her face, and she says, sort of whispery, like she doesn't want anybody else to hear, she says, 'Salem, I have a little item of news that might be of interest to you.' She sort of sang it, you know, her voice going up all singsongy?

" 'What is it?' I asked. I was practically dying.

6

"She says, *really* grinning now, 'Willow Wembley is coming to Plumstead.'

"I almost did die. I almost absolutely laid down and croaked right there in front of the teachers' lounge. 'What did you say?' I said.

"She said it again. 'Willow Wembley is coming to Plumstead.'

" '*Here*?' I said. I was hysterical. '*This* Plumstead? Plumstead Middle School?'

"She said yes, in one month. She said there was more news, which I would find even *more* interesting. 'What?' I said. 'What? What?' She said she would announce the rest to her English classes tomorrow. She was just whetting my appetite for now, she said. I *begged* her. 'Please, *please* tell me.' I pleaded. I groveled. But all she would do was smile and pat me on the head and say, 'Just be in class tomorrow,' and then she disappeared into the teachers' lounge. I just stood there, in a coma. I mean, of course, I know why she did it. Miss Comstock knows I'm going to be a writer, so — "

Salem stopped. She sucked in deep breaths, as though she had been underwater. She looked about. She blinked. "What are we doing? Where are we?"

They were standing in a small square room with a tilt-back chair, a gurgling fountain, and a familiar swinging apparatus that made Salem wince just to look at it.

"Doctor Morley's dentist office," said Sunny. She was grinning impishly. In another room could be heard the tiny, pointed siren song of a high-speed drill.

Salem gasped. *"What?"*

"Well," said Sunny, "you know how you get when you're worked up. You don't even know where you are. So I figured I'd lead you in here, what the heck."

At that moment a young woman in a starchy white pantsuit appeared in the doorway. "Can I help you girls? I don't believe you have an appointment, do you?"

"Nah," replied Sunny, pulling Salem along. "We were just checking out the place, case we ever got a cavity." She led Salem, whose face was now burning red, past a row of grinning plaster jaws, through the waiting room and outside.

"I don't believe you did that," said Salem.

Sunny made a thoughtful face. "Next time I think I'll take you to the back room of the dry cleaners, check out all those hanging pants and shirts."

Suddenly a noise rang out, like the squawk of a wounded moose: *Ooguh! Ooguh!*

Both girls turned to see Pickles Johnson and Eddie Mott tooling up the sidewalk on the Picklebus, Pickles' green, six-wheeled, surfboard-size skater.

3

The Picklebus slowly circled the girls.

"Hey, Mottster," said Pickles, putting a leer in his voice, "what do you think of these two? Think we ought to offer them a ride?"

"I don't know," said Eddie, playing along. "What if they have boyfriends? We could get beat up."

Pickles looked amazed. "Boyfriends? You kidding? Who would want these two warthogs?"

At that Sunny and Salem charged, knocking the boys from the bus, which went rolling across the dentist's parking lot and into the right front tire of a patient's car. Within moments they were all laughing and Picklebusing down the street.

Salem told the boys of her encounter with Miss O'Malley and of Willow Wembley's upcoming visit.

"*Willow?*" said Eddie. "What kind of name is that? Is she a tree?"

"Does she have a loud bark?" asked Pickles.

"Fun-nee," sneered Salem. "That's what I expected of you two ignoramuses. You're probably still trying to get through *The Little Engine That Could.*"

"Is an ignoramus like a hippopotamus?" Eddie inquired.

From the helm Pickles' voice came washing back, "Clyde Klatterfield."

For several seconds there was no sound but the whir of the wheels and their *clack clack* as they crossed the sidewalk cracks.

"Well, well," said Salem, at last, "he reads."

Pickles was always surprising her.

"Hey," said Sunny, "did you guys see the fight?"

"Nah," said Eddie, "we got there too late. Was it good?"

"It was great, man! They were going *bam! pow!*" Sunny jumped from the bus, put up her fists, threw jabs — *"Pow pow pow!"* Threw crosses and uppercuts, punches in flurries — *"Powpowpowpowpowpowpow!"* She ended with an overhand, pummel-fisted, sledgehammer blow to the top of her imaginary victim's head: *"POW!"*

Eddie groaned, "Ohhh, man." He staggered off the bus, wobbled, whirled, and toppled to the ground on his back, arms and legs radiating like wheel spokes.

Pickles stood over him, pumping his arm. ". . . nine . . . ten . . . yerrrrr OUT!" He hoisted Sunny's hand. "The *winnah* . . . and new cham-*peen* . . . from Plumstead Middle School . . . the Plumstead Porkbelly . . . Sluggin' . . . Sunny . . . WWWWWWW*yler!*"

Three kids cheered and clapped. One kid folded her arms. "Savages," said Salem.

Sunny informed the boys. "Little Miss Muffet is against violence."

Pickles recoiled in mock horror. "Against violence? Nobody's against violence. That's un-American."

Salem stood tall. "Make love, not war."

"What would life be without war?" posed Pickles. "People clobbering each other. Blood and guts. Be honest — wouldn't you like to see an eyeball rolling across the sidewalk right about now . . . like . . . *there.*" Something round and blue and glassy fell from Pickles' hand and rolled across the sidewalk.

Salem screamed. The others laughed.

Pickles picked it up. "My lucky marble." He returned the imposter to his pocket.

Salem scowled. "I gave you more credit, Dennis Johnson. I never thought you were bloodthirsty like the rest of them."

Pickles bared his teeth, rolled his eyes, snickered hideously. "Just call me . . . Drrrrracula." He lunged for Salem's throat. Salem screamed, lurched backward, toppled over the Picklebus and took a hard, sudden seat on the cement.

11

Pickles and Eddie helped her to her feet. "See that," said Pickles, "even the Picklebus is violent."

Salem was too furious to see the twinkle in Pickles' eye.

The four Pickleteers rode on home. First off was Salem. Then it was Sunny's turn. As she hopped off the bus and started for her house, Pickles called, "Sun, wait up."

Sunny turned just as Eddie let out a yelp. She did not see the quick kick from Pickles' foot to Eddie's shin that caused the yelp.

"What?" said Sunny.

"Eddie forgot to ask you something."

Sunny turned to Eddie. "So, what?"

Eddie just stared, mouth open, eyes agape, fishfaced.

Sunny waited a few more seconds, then said, "Maserati."

"Huh?" chimed Eddie and Pickles in chorus.

"He was going to ask me what I want for my next birthday, right? I want a Maserati." She ran for her house; at the front door she turned — "Red!" — and went inside.

Pickles shook his head sadly. "You failed, Mottster."

Eddie stared vacantly at the sidewalk. "I can't do it."

"You can do it."

"No, I can't."

"Yes, you can."

"I'm a chicken."

Pickles sighed. "You're a chicken."

He pushed off. The Picklebus rolled down the sidewalk.

4

When they got to Eddie's house, they parked the Picklebus and sat down on the front steps.

"It's not gonna just happen, you know," said Pickles. "You gotta make it happen."

Eddie nodded heavily. "I know . . . I know."

"It's like people say about learning to swim, you just got to dive in and do it. Just do it. Don't think about it."

"I know."

"You think too much."

"Right."

Right, indeed. Think — that's about all Eddie had been doing lately. Think. About Sunny. About how he had met her on the bus on the first day of school and hadn't been able to get her out of his thinker since.

Think: about Sunny in her beloved DEATH TO MUSHROOMS T-shirt.

Think: about Sunny in her Plumstead purple-and-white cheerleader outfit, before she got kicked off for attacking a spectator.

Think: about Sunny in her hamster mascot suit, before she got kicked off that, too, for tackling an opposing football player.

Think think think. Sunny Sunny Sunny. Morning, noon, and night. Rain or shine, the forecast was always the same: Sunny.

And now, with the school dance coming up, Eddie felt a deep push toward action. Before, he had been pretty much satisfied to think about Sunny, dream about Sunny. But now, thinking was not enough. He had to act, do something about it.

He had to ask her to the dance.

But he didn't. He flunked.

"What are you afraid of?" said Pickles. "What do you think she's going to do to you?"

"Do to me?"

"Yeah. I mean, are you afraid she's going to stick her thumbs up your nostrils and pull your nose apart?"

Eddie giggled. "Not really."

"Stick you in boiling fat until you become the world's first french-fried sixth-grader?"

Eddie was laughing too hard to answer.

"So," said Pickles, "if you asked her to the dance, what's the worst that could happen?"

"The worst?"

"Yeah. Seriously."

Eddie thought about it. "Well . . . I guess . . . she could say . . ."

"Say what?"

". . . say . . . no?"

Pickles snapped his fingers. "Bingo. She could say no. Is that going to kill you?"

Eddie knew that here he was supposed to say, *Nah, of course it's not going to kill me.* But the fact was, if she did say no, it *would* kill him.

Pickles read this in Eddie's face. "That bad, huh?"

Eddie shrugged.

Pickles was silent for a while. "Want me to ask her for you?"

Eddie perked up. "Would you?"

"If you want."

Eddie thought, Wow, why didn't I think of that? Sure, why not? He said, "Okay."

Pickles nodded. "Okay." He pushed off on the board. "Gotta go." He rolled out to the sidewalk and turned up the street. He was three houses away when Eddie called, "No!"

Pickles stopped, swung his head. "Don't," called Eddie. "It's not your job. It's mine."

Pickles gave a sharp nod and a thumbs-up sign and pushed off. The wheels sang to him. He smiled. He was proud of his buddy.

Eddie lingered on his front steps, thinking. Tomorrow. It had to be tomorrow, that was clear. Get it over with. Like Pickles said: Dive in.

How do I say it? What words? Hi, Sunny. Would you like to go to the dance with me? Or be cool. Yo, babe. Wanna boogie? And when? At her locker? Coming out of English class?

Something smacked the door behind him. He felt sprinkled on. Rain? He brushed the top of his head; chocolate crumbs flew. The remains of a chocolate cupcake lay at the foot of the door, and out front, at the end of the walkway — where had they come from? — were a handful of nickleheads. As always, the sight of their polka-dot haircuts — the little bald circles — and earrings and leather jackets did queasy things to his stomach.

They were laughing. They had been laughing at him and tormenting him since the first day of school.

"Yo, Mott," one of them called, "come on out and play."

"Bring yer little dollies out. We'll play house."

"Yeah — you can be the mommy and we'll be the daddies!"

"Hah-hah-hah-hah!"

Eddie got up. His knees didn't seem to want to support him. He wished Pickles were here.

"Hey, Mott — look!"

One of them, the one called Cueball, was pulling a yellow marigold out of the little triangular patch

17

at the end of the walkway, pulling it out real slowly, grinning, as though it might scream. He held the flower up by its roots, dangling it, grinning. "You gonna go tell Mommy on me? Huh?"

Eddie went inside, shut the door, threw the bolt. But he could not shut out the grin. It was still there, with him, in his own living room.

5

Salem was far and away the first student into Miss Comstock's English class the next day. The endless hours of last night and this morning had been agony. She pinned her eyes on Miss Comstock, now erasing the blackboard, now sharpening a pencil, now paging through papers on her desk. So casual, so cruel. You would never know by looking at her that she possessed one of the world's great secrets: the rest of the news about Willow Wembley's visit to Plumstead.

The class hadn't even begun, and already Salem wanted to stand up and scream at Miss Comstock: "Stop! I can't take it any longer! Tell me now!" She squirmed and twitched and fidgeted in her seat like a first-grader. If she had her way, she would be running laps around the classroom to ease the tension. She was a balloon swelling with impatience . . . swelling . . . swelling . . .

Pop!

She yelped, "Yaaa!" She looked. It wasn't a pin,

it was Pickles' finger, poking her shoulder, Pickles saying, "A little wound-up there, Brownmiller?"

Salem snarled, "Maybe you'd be a little wound-up, too, if the next couple of minutes were going to be the most important minutes of your life. Now beat it."

Pickles backed away. He looked at Sunny and Eddie. He pointed at Salem, pointed to his own head and made circles with his finger: loony.

The bell rang. Miss Comstock, callously cool, ambled over to the door, looked up and down the hall, and closed the door. She ambled over to her desk, stood in front of it, leaned back against it, gazed over the class, and smiled.

And told them.

She told them that Willow Wembley was coming to Plumstead in one month. Salem heard gasps of surprise. Someone squeaked, "Wow!" Salem felt a burst of pride, since she had already been told, in private.

Miss Comstock went on: "When Miss Wembley comes to our school, she will need someone to accompany her from place to place, someone to guide her and answer questions about the school, and help out if she needs anything. In other words, she will need an escort for the day.

"I have spoken with Ms. Jeffers, the librarian, and we decided that there should be three escorts, not one, and that the escorts should be students."

Her arm, her eyes swept the class. "You. After all, it's your school, you're her readers. So — " Miss Comstock paused, smiled faintly; her eyes seemed to land on Salem for the briefest of moments. "So, here's what we're going to do. This will be a perfect tie-in with our writing program. Everyone will write a short story, no less than three pages, no longer than ten. The judges will choose one story from each grade — sixth, seventh, and eighth. The authors of the three chosen stories will be Willow Wembley's escorts for the full day of her visit to Plumstead Middle School."

Salem slumped in her seat, overcome, knocked out. To be Willow Wembley's escort, her personal escort for the whole day — it was too good to be true, a fantasy. And yet it *was* true, Willow Wembley *was* coming to Plumstead, and one sixth-grader *would* be chosen. Somewhere in the building, in some classroom, at this very moment, was the sixth-grader destined to be blessed above all others. Salem closed her eyes and pressed her writing scarf between her fingers and she knew, absolutely knew, that it had to be her.

The rest of English class was lost on Salem. While the teacher's voice droned on dimly in the background, Salem pictured herself guiding Willow Wembley about the school. ("This is the library, Miss Wembley." "This is the cafeteria, Miss Wembley.") Seeing to her every need. ("Can I get you a cup of coffee, Miss Wembley?") Chatting with her writer to writer. ("So, Miss Wembley, what do you think of flashbacks?")

Somewhere a bell was ringing. People were moving. Class was over. Salem gathered her books and drifted out with the crowd, quite unaware of her friends Sunny and Eddie as she passed them in the hallway.

"Look at her," said Sunny. "A zombie."

Eddie nodded. "Yeah."

"She's really going goofy over the Willow Wembley stuff."

"Yeah."

"Probably ought to stay away from her. Safer."

"Yeah."

Sunny turned to Eddie. She stared at him. "So what do you want?"

Eddie flinched. "Huh?"

"You're acting weird."

Eddie shrugged. He looked away from her. He felt his face getting warm, his nose getting itchy. *Do it. Just do it.* He shrugged again. "Well uh . . . I uh . . . I was just . . . uh . . . wondering . . . something." He shrugged. "That's all."

Sunny swung a finger in his face. "Aha! I knew it. You want to ask me something, right?"

Eddie stared at her fingertip. "Well . . ."

"You want to ask me, but you're afraid, right?" She was leaning toward him.

"Well . . ."

She grinned. "I know what it is."

Eddie gaped. "You do?"

"Sure. You want to ask me for one of these. Maybe two." She pulled a plastic sack of Kit Kat mini-bars from her schoolbag.

Eddie stared at the sack of bars swinging before his eyes. The longer he stared, the less sure Sunny felt she was right. She said, "That's not it?"

He winced. He shook his head.

Sunny frowned, thinking. "Hmmm." She looked at Eddie, she looked away, and somewhere in the mob of bobbing heads she seemed to find it. She grinned, she nodded. "So *that's* it."

Eddie stared straight ahead.

"You want to ask me to the dance."

Eddie stiffened, flash-frozen as a fish.

"Well," said Sunny, "go ahead. Ask."

Eddie swallowed. His throat felt like a walnut. *Dive!*

He dived. "Would you go to the dance with me?"

"No," said Sunny brightly and zipped into her next class.

6

There was another fight after school that day, just beyond the last bus waiting in the driveway.

"Be right back," said Sunny, heading for the mob.

Salem lunged, grabbed her. "No!"

Sunny whirled. She stared unbelievingly at the hand grasping her sleeve. "No?"

Salem pleaded, "Sunny, here's your chance to break the habit. Just say no. You don't have to join the rest of the animals. Be an individual."

"I'll be an individual," said Sunny, "an individual animal. Now if you please." She shook her arm. It remained in Salem's grip.

"Sunny, you need help. I'll help you. That's what best friends are for. I'll help you become a decent, nonviolent person."

"If you don't let go," growled Sunny, "*I'll* help *you* become a decent, nonviolent punching bag."

"Sunny, we have more important things to do. We have to talk about my story for Willow Wembley Day."

The mob was screaming.

Sunny drew back her fist. "Let go or I'll slug ya."

Salem laughed. "Be serious."

"On the count of three. One — "

"Sunny — "

"Two — "

"I'm not letting go. I know you would never hit — "

"Three."

She let go.

The two friends stared at each other. Salem's lip was quivering, her eyes gleaming. The mob roared. Sunny turned, looked back at Salem, and took off. After ten steps or so she slowed to a jog, then a walk. She stopped. Her whole body heaved in a single expulsion of breath. She snapped about and came storming back to Salem. "Are you faking it?"

"Faking what?"

"This little blubber act."

Salem sniveled, "No, I'm not faking it. It just so happens I'm an emotional person, especially when my best friend threatens to hit me. Excuse me, I meant to say *slug* me."

"Yeah?" sneered Sunny. "I'm gonna slug you

anyway if you're just trying to make me feel bad so I won't go see the fight."

"Look," said Salem, defiance in her voice. "It's *real*." She squeezed her eyes shut. After several seconds, from the corner of her left eye trickled a solitary tear. She opened her eyes. "See?"

Sunny gave a smirk, winced at the sound of another roar from the mob, and started walking home. Salem came alongside. She looked at Sunny but could not find words. At last she said, "I know that was a really big sacrifice for you to make. You gave up watching a fight for me."

Sunny stared dead ahead, and said nothing.

"I want to say thank you."

Silence from Sunny.

"You must really love me to do that for — "

Sunny snapped, "Brownmiller, if you don't shut your trap, you're still gonna get it."

Salem shut up.

As they neared Sunny's house, Pickles and Eddie rolled up in the Picklebus.

"Hey," said Pickles, "you two see the fight?" He saw the frost in Sunny's eyes. "Don't tell me you missed it. Probably the best fight all year."

Sunny shot all three a final frozen glare and marched into her house.

"What's with her?" said Pickles.

"Oh, nothing," said Salem breezily. "She just decided to give up watching fights. She's against

26

violence now." Pickles and Eddie looked at each other. "Really. She did it because of our great friendship." Salem cast a fond look toward Sunny's front door. "She doesn't want to lose me. Just shows you what can be done."

Pickles and Eddie traded glances that said: *Right.*

Pickles tapped the bus with his green sneaker. "Want a ride?"

"Sure," said Salem. She hopped on and off they went.

When they reached Salem's house, Eddie got off, too. "Gotta talk to Salem about something," Eddie explained. "See you later."

"Later." Pickles waved and was gone.

Salem led Eddie into her house and up to her room. Salem's room looked like Paris. Specifically, the Left Bank of Paris, famous for its artists and writers. Salem had decided that since she could not go to the Left Bank, the Left Bank would come to her. Surrounded by posters and flags and magazines, pictures and berets and, in one corner, a plastic replica of the Eiffel Tower, Salem hoped to draw inspiration for her own writing.

But Eddie was not here to talk of writing. "I need help," he said.

"What with?" asked Salem.

"*Who* with."

"Ah." Salem nodded knowingly. "Sunshine Wy-ler, alias Sunny."

Eddie sat on the side of the bed, slumped, nodded.

Salem wanted to giggle, for she loved to give advice; but seeing Eddie's dejection, she kept her face serious, counselorlike. She sat on her study chair, crossed her legs, picked up her notepad and pencil and leaned forward. "Tell me about it."

7

Eddie told her about Pickles' advice, and how he had followed it in the hallway after English class, and how Sunny had turned him down. "Turned me down flat," he said, clubbing the mattress with his fist. "So now I'm thinking maybe I shouldn't listen to Pick. Maybe a girl can help me better. Maybe you can figure her out better than a boy and tell me what to do."

It was all Salem could do to keep from shrieking with joy. She jotted down a few thoughts. She looked up at Eddie, arranging her face in an encouraging, confidence-inspiring smile. "Well," she began, "first of all, you're right. Pickles gave you the wrong advice. But that's not surprising. He's only a boy. He doesn't understand women. You can't just go up to a girl like that, out of the blue, and expect her to fall all over you."

Eddie protested, "I wasn't asking her to fall all over me. I was asking her to the dance."

"But you surprised her," Salem pointed out.

"You" — she searched for the word, found it — "*ambushed* her."

"I *asked* her to the *dance!*"

Salem sighed and shook her head. "I know that, but it's *how* you asked her. You went too fast."

Eddie thought about that. "I should talk slower? Like . . ." he spoke as slowly as he could, allowing full seconds between words, even syllables. "Sun . . . ny . . . would . . . you . . . like . . ."

Salem stomped her foot. "No, no, that's not what I mean. I mean you have to, like, build up to it. I mean — " She thought of the love stories she had been reading lately. "I mean romance."

Eddie's face went sour. "Romance? That's grown-up stuff. I'm just a kid. She's just a kid."

Salem launched her finger into the air. "Aha! *That's* the problem. You think of her as a kid."

"Well, isn't she?"

"Compared to a twenty-five-year-old, maybe. But compared to you, no. You ought to be thinking of her as a woman."

Eddie's face was a blank. "A woman?"

"Right."

Eddie turned from Salem and stared vacantly at the wall. In his mind's eye he tried to picture Sunny as a woman. He pictured her with lipstick on, but then he remembered her pretending to flick a boogie ball at him in math class. He imagined her wearing high heels, until he remembered her DEATH TO MUSHROOMS T-shirt.

He turned back to Salem, shook his head sadly. "I can't do it."

Salem reached out and patted him on the hand. "That's okay. I understand. It's not your fault."

"What are you talking about?"

"I mean, it's not your fault that you're a boy, and there are some things that boys can't understand."

"We're stupid?"

"No, just immature. Girls mature much faster than boys. It's a scientific fact."

"It is?"

"Sure. Why do you think little girls play with dolls?"

Eddie was stumped. He knew that's what little girls did, but he had never asked himself why they did it.

Salem answered her own question. "Because they're getting ready to have families. Even when they're only two years old. And what do you suppose boys are doing when they're two?"

Eddie thought, tried to remember all the way back to when he was two. "Dump trucks?"

Salem folded her arms and grinned with great approval, as though she were a teacher and he had just given the perfect answer. "Exactly. See?"

No, as a matter of fact, he didn't see, but obviously Salem saw, plus probably the rest of the world, so he nodded. He made a mental note to ask his father some day what was wrong with dump trucks.

"You see," Sunny went on, "it takes boys a long time to grow up. Much longer than girls. You boys . . ." She wagged her head and smiled in faint wonder. "You boys . . ." She stared at him, squinting as if through a telescope over the pink eraser end of her pencil.

Eddie began to feel uncomfortable. Was his fly open? He checked. No. "What are you looking at?"

"Oh," she mused, "you. In the future."

"Huh?"

"I'm seeing you, oh, about two years from now. Eighth-grader."

"Really?"

"Yep."

"What do you see?"

She squinted, squinted. "An earring."

Eddie squawked. "Never!"

Salem nodded matter-of-factly. "Oh yes. You'll see other stud boys wearing them and you'll have to play follow-the-leader and get one yourself. Typical immature boy behavior."

Eddie asked, "What else?" not sure he really wanted to know.

Salem ticked them off on her fingers. "Oh, you'll turn into a bully, squashing little sixth-graders like you get pushed around now. Then you'll start acting like a big macho he-man. You'll call girls chicks. You'll smoke a cigarette. You'll say bad words. You'll get your driver's license and pester your parents for the car, and then you'll crack it up. You will write stuff on bathroom walls."

"What stuff?" said Eddie.

"Hah!" Salem snorted with contempt, cleverly disguising the fact that she had no idea what he might write. She sneered distastefully at him. "You'll find out soon enough."

Eddie felt overwhelmed, smothered, drowning in a tidal wave from his own future. How did she know what lay ahead for him? And Sunny, in the hallway that morning, she had said, "You want to ask me to the dance." What was it with these girl people? He had heard about a mysterious some-thing called women's intuition. Was this it? He felt weak, empty, small, powerless, dumb. He saw before him a lifetime that had already been pre-dicted by the females around him. Like at every step into the future, they would already be there, waiting for him, snickering, wagging their fingers.

It was all too scary, too heavy to think about, so he turned his back on it and found himself star-ing at the question he should have asked in the first place: "What's all that have to do with me asking Sunny to the dance?"

Salem stared at him. Frankly, she didn't know either. She consulted her notes. Ah, there it was, the word of words. "Romance, of course," she said, her arched eyebrows daring him to ask another silly question.

At that moment a call came from Salem's mother downstairs: "Salem! Dinner!"

Eddie glanced at the clock radio. Dinnertime for him, too. He popped up from the bed and clattered down the stairs behind Salem.

On the way home Eddie felt more baffled than when he had entered Salem's house. That night, while taking his bath, he stared at the pink square tiles above the tub. *You will write stuff on bathroom walls.* He closed his eyes. He searched his innermost self, trying to detect the beginnings of an urge to write there. But all he could feel was the soft crinkle of Mister Bubble soapsuds against his skin.

8

When Sunny boarded the school bus next morning, she still looked grumpy from missing the fight the day before. She took a seat way up front and never even looked back at Eddie.

Meanwhile, Eddie was forced to watch a pair of eighth-graders kissing in the seat directly in front of him. Eddie was sitting on an aisle seat, so he couldn't just look out the window. He had little choice but to stare straight ahead, and when he did so there were these two faces about twelve inches away. Only half of each face was presented to him: one eye, one ear, half a nose, half a mouth. It reminded him of those paintings on Egyptian tombs, where everybody is shown from the side, in profile.

To make matters worse, they were nicklepeople. He was a nickelhead, she a nicklechick, as the girlfriends of nickleheads were called. Eddie would have felt safer if the seat were occupied by a fifteen-foot alligator.

The nickelhead wore a skull and crossbones earring. The nickelchick wore a nose ring, a little gold thing poked right through the flared flap of her nostril. It made Eddie cringe, and yet he could not take his eyes from it. He wondered if there was another ring on the far side of her nose.

As with all nickelheads, the boy's haircut featured quarter-sized bald circles polka-dotted over a teddy-bear-cut scalp. He also featured about the fattest, ripest zit Eddie had ever seen. It squatted an inch from the side of the kid's mouth, like a miniature, yellow-headed volcano about to erupt.

The girl's hair was bluish-green. To Eddie it looked as if she had dunked her head in Easter egg coloring. The style was two inches tall flattop — flat enough to lay a tablecloth on — except for the back center. There a stiff, gloppy spike pointed straight at the ceiling, like an aqua javelin. Her lipstick was the same color as her hair.

They smooched and snuffled and nuzzled and whispered things that Eddie, close as he was, could not make out. Suddenly, in the middle of a nuzzle, the nickelhead's one visible eyeball shifted all the way to the left, till it was staring straight at Eddie. The nickelhead pulled back, turned full-face, and snarled, "Wadda *you* lookin' at?"

"Nothing," said Eddie. His eyes reached out and clutched the back of a boy's head two rows up and across the aisle.

"You lookin' at us?"

Eddie shook his head briskly. "No."

The nickelchick giggled. "He was."

The nickelhead looked at her, looked at Eddie. He grinned. He nodded. "Yeah. You *was* lookin', right?"

Eddie slammed his head from side to side. "Not me."

The grin vanished. "Yeah, you was lookin' okay — at *her*."

An icepick of terror pierced Eddie's heart. "No!"

The nickelhead flinched backward, he frowned. "No? Waddaya mean no? You wasn't lookin' at her?"

"No."

"Why not?" His face came over the seat top, inches from Eddie's. "She too ugly for ya to look at?"

Eddie tried to speak; nothing came out. He cleared his throat, he swallowed. "No . . . no . . ."

"No what?"

"No . . . she's not ugly."

The girl was giggling.

"Look at her," commanded the nickelhead.

"Huh?"

"*Look* at her."

Eddie's head stayed still while his eyeballs

37

crawled to the far corners of his eyes. They saw her face loom larger and her lips purse and pucker until she looked like some giant painted tropical guppy. The blue-green lips blew him a kiss.

"My chick ugly?" came the nickelhead's voice.

"No."

"What is she then?"

"Not ugly."

"Tell her."

"Huh?"

"Tell her. Look at her" — Eddie felt his head sandwiched by a pair of hands and swiveled till he was facing the tropical fish — "and tell Angelpuss what she is."

Anglepuss puckered and blew him another kiss. She batted her long black eyelashes. She reached out and tweaked his cheek. "Hiya, cutie."

Eddie gulped, gulped again. "She's . . . uh . . ."

"No, *no*," snapped the nickelhead. "Tell *her*. Say *you're*."

"You're — " The word came out like the squeak of a rusty mouse. Eddie cleared his throat. "You're . . . uh . . . buh . . . beautiful."

Angelpuss squealed. "Ouuu!" She tweaked his cheek again. "Thank, you, cutie."

Eddie relaxed a little, thinking, It's over. But the girl's smile became suddenly a scowl. She turned to the boy. "He's lying. I'm not beautiful."

She stroked her spike, she batted her lashes. "I'm *gorgeous!*"

They laughed. Eddie stopped relaxing. His peripheral vision revealed the other riders sitting nearby, many of them fellow sixth-graders, all of them ramrod rigid, staring straight ahead. No one to mess with a nickelhead, no one to save him.

"So, Puss, what's the punishment for lying?" The nickelhead was speaking to the nickelchick but was grinning at Eddie.

"Gee, Weasel, I don't know. Let's think about it."

The two of them put on frowns, thinking. Suddenly the girl piped, "Ah!" She grabbed her boyfriend's chin and turned his face toward her. Her eyes lit up. "Yes. Firing squad." She tugged on the nickelhead's head till he was leaning well over the back of his seat. She positioned his face a mere six inches in front of Eddie's face.

"Ready"

She fine-tuned the nickelhead's face so that Eddie was staring dead into it.

"Aim."

By the time she yelled "Fire!" Eddie was gone, racing down the aisle. He might well have crashed through the front of the bus had it not just then come to a stop and opened its door to the school. Eddie flew outside, past the goggled eyes of

Sunny Wyler. He did not stop till he was safely at his desk in homeroom.

Later that morning, on the way to English class, Eddie still felt a little shaky. Salem breezed up to him and said, "I have something for you." And he knew, by the lilt in her voice and the twinkle in her eye, that it had to be good.

9

Salem slipped the piece of paper to him while Miss Comstock was reading aloud to the class a chapter from Willow Wembley's latest book about the Klatterfields, *The Owl Hoo Came to Dinner*. Eddie unfolded the paper. It was a letter, typed very neatly, a grown-up-looking job. He read it:

Dear Sunny,

Please forgive me if I offended you by asking you to the dance. I did not mean to offend you or make you angry.

Nevertheless, I accept full responsibility for my actions, and if you are upset in any way, then I am to blame.

But what else am I to blame for? Ah, that is the question!

Am I to blame for thinking about you morning, noon, and night?

Yes.

*Am I to blame for all the wild and
peerless feelings that swirl through my
being like a whirlpool of emotion whenever my eyes behold you?*

Yes.

*Am I to blame for wanting to take you
in my arms and sweep you across the
dance floor to the melodies of love songs
and swirling lights at the school dance
on Friday, November 16th, at 7:30 P.M.?*

Yes! Guilty as charged!

Yes! Yes! Yes!

*When I see you walking down the
hall . . .*

It went on and on like that, three full pages,
single-spaced. The bell was ringing as he reached
the end:

> *Most truly yours,*
> *Your Faithful Admirer*

Salem nudged him on the way out. Her eyes
were bright. "Well?"

Eddie looked at her. "Well what?"

She tapped the three pages in his hand. "What
do you think of it?"

Eddie stared at the letter. In truth, he did not
know what to think. With all its twists and turns
and flowery words, the letter itself was a swirling

whirlpool. One thing for sure, Eddie could never have written it. Nor, he guessed, could Pickles.

But then, he didn't really have to understand it, did he? All he had to do was put himself in Salem's hands. She was the one who understood girls. She must know what she was doing. So he nodded and said, "Pretty good."

Salem beamed. "Yep. I think so, too, if I do say so myself. The secret is romance. Remember that word. Never forget it." She stared at him, confirming that he was remembering. "Okay, now, the first thing you do is sign it, in your own handwriting."

"Then do I mail it to her?"

Salem thought. She shook her head slowly. "No, I don't think so. I think it would be more romantic for her to find it. You know, where she least expects it."

"So where's that?"

Salem thought some more. "How about a book?" She tapped Eddie's math book. "Wouldn't that be something? She's in math class and she opens her book and what does she see — a letter. From a boy." Salem's eyes rolled upward, picturing it. "Yes! That's it."

Eddie slipped the letter between the pages of his math book. "Then what?"

"Then we wait and see. If you want my personal opinion, I think she's going to be in the throes of rapture."

Eddie frowned. "What's that?"

Salem tossed her hand. "Oh, just a romantic phrase. It means she'll probably start calling you on the phone and walking past your house and writing stuff in her looseleaf."

This was interesting. "Yeah? Like what?"

"Oh, like your name, about a million times. Like hearts that say 'S.W. Loves E.M.' Like 'Mrs. Edward A. Mott.'"

Eddie reacted as if he had been slapped. "Hey, who said anything about getting married?"

Salem patted his hand. "Calm down, boy. Listen, you hired me to help you, didn't you?"

"Yeah."

"Okay. Number one, I'm a writer, so it's my job to understand human nature. Number two, even before I was ever a writer I was a girl, which is why you came to me in the first place. Right?"

Eddie nodded.

"Okay. So trust me. Okay?"

Eddie nodded again.

Kids were running. Next class was about to start.

Salem waved. "After she gets the letter, we'll have a meeting." She darted into a classroom.

The hall was almost empty. Eddie hurried. He reached math just as the bell rang.

Doors closed up and down the hallway. A single student remained. It was Cueball, the nickelhead. He had been walking behind the shrimpy Mott kid and the girl. He had intended to hassle Mott when he noticed the sheets of paper sticking from his book. So instead he pulled the sheets out. And now, in the silent hallway, he stopped to read them.

10

"It's gone," said Eddie. His eyes were wide with disbelief, his face in pain. "It's *gone*."

"How?" said Salem. "I saw you put it in your book."

"I don't know. It's not there now. I don't know."

They were outside the building for gym. It was a mixed class: boys and girls, sixth-, seventh-, and eighth-graders.

"Well, you look until you find it," Salem grumped.

"What if I don't? You can write me another one, can't you?"

Salem stopped, put her hands on her hips. "Eddie, do you know what it took to write that? I was inspired. It was like the muse of romance was dictating it to me. My fingers were flying."

"Didn't you save it on your computer?"

"No. I didn't *do* it on my computer. Whenever my subject is romance, I use an old-fashioned pen, the kind you have to keep dunking in an inkwell.

I only typed it up because Sunny would recognize my handwriting."

The gym teacher blew his whistle, time to start. The game was football, tail football. The teacher handed out bright red strips of cloth. Each student stuck one end into the back of his or her gym shorts, so everyone had a "tail." The idea was to pull the tail from the ball carrier.

"Here," said Salem to Eddie, "you take it." She was holding out her red strip.

"It's your tail," said Eddie. "Put it on."

Salem snickered. "Are you kidding? I don't wear tails. Do you really think I'm going to go running around with a red tail sticking out behind me? It's bad enough I have to wear these dumb clothes in the first place."

"But it's only gym class," said Eddie. "That's all it is."

Salem lifted her chin. She thrust the cloth strip at Eddie. Eddie sighed, shook his head, and accepted it. He balled it up and stuffed it into one of his shorts pockets.

Salem and Eddie were on the same team. The other side started out with the ball. On the first play the quarterback threw a pass to a girl, who came running with the ball straight toward Salem. Salem stepped aside, and the girl dashed on by for a touchdown.

A girl came charging over. It was Angelpuss, the nickelchick. Her hair spike was orange now.

"Hey!" she yelled at Salem. Salem turned. The nickelchick jammed her face up to Salem's. "Waddaya think you're doing?"

Salem's eyebrows rose. "I beg your pardon?"

"Why didn't you stop her? Why didn't you pull her tail."

Salem sniffed. "I do not *wear* tails, and I do not *pull* tails."

"Yeah?" snarled Anglepuss. "Well, pull *this*." She reached behind, yanked out her own tail and flapped it in Salem's face.

Eddie stepped forward. "Hey!"

Somebody called, "Fight!" The gym class converged.

"Hey *what*?" came a familiar voice behind Eddie. He turned. It was Angelpuss's boyfriend, whom she had called Weasel.

Weasel took the red tail from Angelpuss and dusted Eddie's face with it. "You got a problem?"

Eddie backed off, spread his arms. "No . . . no problem here."

At that point the gym teacher waded into the crowd. "All right, break it up. You can fight when we get to boxing."

The game resumed, with Eddie, Salem, and Angelpuss on one team, Weasel on the other. Whenever Weasel's team had the ball, they would run plays straight at Salem. Time after time Salem stepped aside, like a matador waving a bull by. Angelpuss was getting madder and madder.

Eddie had his own problems. Offense or defense, wherever he lined up, there was Weasel, squarely opposite him, grinning. He kept trying to goad Eddie into a confrontation. Weasel was the only member of his team who did not carry the ball straight for Salem. Instead, he ran straight at Eddie, and Eddie ran the other way. "Come on! Come on!" called Weasel. He even turned his rear end toward Eddie and flapped his tail. "Here I am. Stop me."

Eddie wasn't biting. A long time ago he had decided to steer clear of all nickelheads. When Eddie's team was on offense, he refused to be a ball carrier, and he never ran out for a pass. Meanwhile, Weasel brayed across the line, "Give it to Mott! Give it to Mott!"

Since the gym teacher was always hanging around nearby, things never really got out of hand. But then the teacher was called into the school building to answer a phone call. "I'll be right back," he told the class. "Don't kill each other."

Weasel sidled up to Eddie and whispered, "He didn't say don't injure each other."

Eddie's team had the ball. The quarterback threw a pass to Angelpuss. Eddie settled back to watch the nickelchick dart this way and that to escape the tail chasers, all the while laughing and shrieking.

Then Eddie noticed something strange was happening. As Angelpuss was fleeing her chasers, she was not running toward the goal line. She was racing in loops and squiggles that, as it happened, carried her closer and closer to Eddie. With the action coming in on him, Eddie started backing away, but he was too late. By the time he realized what was going on, Angelpuss was charging full speed at him and shrieking, "Here — catch!"

The ball came flying. Instinctively — and stupidly — Eddie caught it. And just like that, Weasel was on him.

From the first instant it was clear that Weasel had no intention of bringing the matter to a quick conclusion by pulling out Eddie's tail. He mauled and pawed Eddie, pulling his shirt, his shorts, his arms, his legs, his ears. He kneaded Eddie like a lump of bread dough, twisted him like a pretzel, practically turned him inside out, all the while croaking, "Hey, where's that tail? Can't find that tail!"

Eddie yanked it out himself. "Here it is!" But Weasel just stuffed the red strip into Eddie's waistband and went on mauling him.

Even for a peacemaker such as Salem, this was too much. "Let him go, you brute," she commanded.

Weasel looked up in surprise, but it was Angelpuss who acted. "You calling my boyfriend a brute?" she growled, and with a sideways swipe of her hip sent Salem reeling backward and onto the grass.

Now it was Eddie's turn. With Weasel momentarily distracted, he pulled himself free and headed for the nickelchick. "Hey!"

Angelpuss met him halfway, hands on hips, chin out. "Hey *what*, turtle turd?" She moved so close to him that the tip of her nose was touching his. Her feet were on his sneakers.

Eddie's voice dried up in his throat; he swallowed several times; his nose twitched; his ears reddened. "Hey . . . stop," he rasped.

"Watta you gonna do if I don't?" she said. Eddie had no answer. "You gonna *bop* me?" She took one step back. "Huh?"

Eddie gulped. "I don't hit girls."

She laughed. She looked around at the gaping, expectant faces. She grinned at Weasel. "Okay then — I'll bop you." She dropped her arms to her sides, lowered her head and darted forward. The top of her forehead caught Eddie square in the nose.

Eddie staggered backward. It felt like a pumpkin had been stuffed up his nose. Faces floated in the tears springing from his eyes. He was sure his nose was broken, yet there didn't seem to be any blood.

And now the gym class was erupting, going bonkers, because here was not only a fight, but the rarest fight of all: a girl versus boy fight. Few kids in the history of the human race had been privileged to witness such a spectacle.

"Go, Mott!" they shouted. "Go, Angelpuss!"

They were behind him, pressing him, pushing him forward, toward the girl with the orange spiked hair. And then they were falling away, letting him go, because the teacher was returning, trotting across the field, blowing his whistle, telling them all to get inside *now*! And for a brief second, as the others streamed by, Eddie was left alone with the girl. He blinked and blinked again, trying to clear the blur from his eyes, to see if she was coming at him again. She wasn't, she was just standing there.

He turned and ran into school.

11

After school that day, Sunny headed for the lobby to feed Humphrey, the Plumstead hamster and mascot. Before she even reached the glass tank, she noticed something new inside: a piece of paper. She raised the cover screen and took it out. One edge was ragged from where Humphrey had snacked. She unfolded the paper. It was a letter. Typewritten. To her.

She read it.

Outside, Pickles and Salem were at the Picklebus. Salem was telling Pickles about gym class that day. "Barbarians. That's all I see around me. Even the girls. You should have seen the way that . . . that female, pardon the expression, attacked Eddie. And the rest of them! The bloodthirsty looks on their faces. Screaming for murder. I shudder to think what would have happened if the teacher hadn't come back." She stopped, thought, shuddered. "What's the world coming to?"

Pickles, who had been content to listen, was caught off guard. At the end of a long day in school, he really wasn't ready to think. So he just waited, knowing Salem would answer her own question. She did. "I'll tell you what the world's coming to. It's coming to the end. *Finito*. You know what we're probably looking at here?" Pickles looked around. "We're probably looking at the end of civilization as we know it."

Pickles looked again, seeking clues to civilization's collapse. Just then, not ten feet away, one boy sneaked up behind a second boy and knocked his books to the ground.

"Hey," growled the second boy, "pick them up."

"I'll pick 'em up," grinned the first, "after you pick *that* up." He spit on the ground.

"See what I mean," said Salem, turning away in disgust. "Some day the history books will say it all started right here in Plumstead Middle School."

Eddie showed up.

"How's the nose?" said Pickles.

Eddie touched it. "A little sore, but okay."

"You shouldn't have stuck up for me," Salem told him. "You should have stayed out of it."

"She pushed you," Eddie countered.

"That's no excuse. Just because she was being

54

a barbarian doesn't mean you should be, too."

"But what if she pushed you again? What if she didn't stop?"

Salem gave a dismissive wave of the hand. "That's okay. I believe in nonviolence. I do not believe in striking back."

"Not even if she punched *you* in the nose?" said Pickles.

Salem sniffed. "Not even."

"Not even if she pulled your hair out till you were bald? Not even if she pulled your ears like bubble gum and tied them together behind your head? Not even if she pulled off your shoes and socks and let ten lobsters clamp on every one of your toes?"

Eddie was howling, Salem was scowling. "Some day, Mister Johnson, you'll learn some things are not funny."

"But, Salem," said Eddie, "you did the same thing I did. You stuck up for me."

Salem looked away. "That's different."

"Different? How?"

"I'm a woman. Women don't have to explain themselves." She tossed her writer's scarf over her shoulder and boarded the Picklebus.

The three of them coasted toward the main entrance. Sunny was coming out. She was smiling, but the smile had a tilt to it.

"Yo, Picklepeople," she called brightly. She

waved a plastic bag in the air. "Mini Kit Kats! Who wants some?"

Three kids answered, "I do!"

"Hands out," Sunny directed.

Three hands shot out, palms up.

Sunny dipped into the bag, pulled out a mini-bar, put it in Salem's hand. "One for you." She put one in Pickles' hand. "One for you." A second in Salem's hand. And Pickles' hand. Salem. Pickles. Salem. Pickles.

All eyes but Sunny's were staring at Eddie's upturned hand, still bare.

Sunny doled out the last two bars to Salem. "For you and . . ." — to Pickles — "for you."

No one moved, no one spoke. Only Sunny smiled her tilted smile.

At last Pickles said, "Didn't you forget somebody?"

For the first time Sunny looked directly at Eddie. Her eyes shot open as if in surprise. "By golly, you're right!" She reached into her pocket, pulled out a balled-up piece of paper and dropped it into Eddie's hand. "Here, you can eat this."

"Have a nice day," she said breezily and whisked herself away.

Eddie uncrumpled the paper. He began to read. A bewildered expression came over his face. He looked up. "What's this all about?"

Salem took the letter. She scanned it, then began to read aloud:

Dear Sunny,

I am writing this letter to tell you how beautiful you are. Your eyes are like pools. Cesspools. Your ears are like flowers. Cauliflowers. Your nose is as cute as a button. A bellybutton. Your teeth are like stars. They come out at night. Your lips are like cherries. They're the pits. You have the best shape I have ever seen. On an elephant. As you can see I am just crazy about you. I am also just crazy. Will you go to the dance with me?

Your lover boy,
Eddie Mott

12

The three friends stared at each other.

"I didn't write this," said Eddie.

"It's a fake, " said Salem. "Somebody is framing you."

"The *real* note!" piped Eddie. "*That's* what happened. Somebody stole it and then did this."

"Who?" said Pickles.

Eddie didn't have to think for long. "A nickelhead, I bet. Almost everything bad that's happened to me this year, a nickelhead had something to do with it."

Pickles took the letter from Salem. He looked it over. Sunny was already two blocks away. "Let's go after her."

"All aboard!" called Pickles. Pickles tooted the picklehorn and the green six-wheeler zoomed down the driveway. They caught up to Sunny as she was turning a corner. She kept staring straight ahead. The bus rolled alongside.

"Sunny," said Salem, flapping the letter, "did

you read this thing? You don't really believe Eddie wrote it, do you?"

"Somebody wrote it."

"But not Eddie."

"His name is on it."

"It's forged. That's why — look — his name is typed instead of written, so you can't tell it's not his handwriting."

"That's crazy. Who would write a letter for him?"

Salem hesitated, recalled that's exactly what she had done. "Who knows? Anybody. Somebody playing a joke on him. Somebody trying to get him in trouble."

The wheels of the green board hummed as they kept pace with Sunny. Eddie cleared his throat. "I have enemies."

Salem echoed, "He has enemies."

Sunny snorted. "I'm impressed."

Salem jammed her foot to the sidewalk, halting the bus. "Sunny, stop!"

Sunny took two more steps and stopped. She continued to stare stiffly down the street.

"Sunny, you *know* he didn't write it, because you *know* he likes you. Everybody knows it."

Eddie looked around. He felt his face getting warm. Was Salem right? Did everybody know it?

Sunny turned. Her eyes skipped over Eddie and landed on Salem. "I am not an elephant." She walked on.

Salem jumped from the Picklebus and ran after her. "Sunny, you can't treat Eddie like that."

Sunny smirked. "Really?"

"No." Salem held out a handful of Kit Kats. "If you're not giving these to Eddie, you're not giving them to us."

In the background Pickles uttered, *"Us?"*

"Fine," said Sunny. She held out the empty plastic bag. "Fork 'em over."

Salem gaped. Then she rushed back to Pickles, snatched the mini-bars from his hand and dumped both his and hers into the plastic bag.

Sunny waved the bag and took off. "Have a nice life."

Salem stood stunned. The bus rolled up to her. "Let's walk," said Pickles. A few nights before, Pickles had screwed a metal post onto the front of the board and fastened a length of clothesline to it. Now he unwrapped the rope and started pulling the board behind him like a pet on a leash.

They walked a block and a half before Salem fumed, "Ouuu, that girl. Sometimes I want to . . ."

"Don't sweat it," said Pickles.

"Don't *sweat* it? How can I *not* sweat it? How am I supposed to write my story for Willow Wembley with all this going on? I need to clear my mind. I need peace and quiet. So what do I get? I get nickelheads and loony tunes and bloodthirsty savages and now a best friend who treats me like dirt."

Pickles said matter-of-factly, "She didn't mean it."

Salem's eyebrows went up. "Oh, really?" Being the writer, Salem considered herself the group's expert on human nature. "You have it all figured out, I suppose."

"Sure." Pickles pulled a Kit Kat from his pocket and unwrapped it.

Salem screeched. "I gave them back to Sunny!"

"Not this one." Pickles held it out. "Want it?" Salem just glared. "Guess not. Mottster? Open." Eddie opened his mouth, Pickles stuck it in. "She knows he didn't write the letter."

Salem scoffed. "Is that so, Doctor Johnson? Well, pray tell, explain it to us poor ignoramuses."

"Simple. The letter hurt her feelings. She had to blame someone. Eddie's name was on it. She blamed him. Just his bad luck."

"Oh, sure," snickered Salem. "Sunny getting hurt feelings? Sunny caring that somebody calls her an elephant? May I remind you that this is the person who once went sixteen days without washing her hair. May I remind you that this is the person who wears a DEATH TO MUSHROOMS T-shirt till it rots off her back. And you think she cares what she looks like? You better go back to school, doc-*tor*."

Pickles shrugged. "Just an idea. Anyway, she'll get over it. Probably call you up tonight, like nothing ever happened."

Salem made a mocking laugh. "Hah-hah. Thank you, Doctor. Is there anything else you can do to straighten out my life?"

"Sure," said Pickles casually, "maybe I could help you with your story."

Salem nearly popped. "Hah! That's the funniest thing I've heard all day. Pardon me for not laughing. Good-bye." She crossed the street and headed home.

Salem ate two bites of dinner and went up to her room. She planted herself at her desk to begin making notes for her story. After ten minutes she slammed her ballpoint pen down on a still blank sheet of paper. It was no use.

The phone rang. She picked it up. The voice was Sunny's, bright, snappy. "Yo, pickleperson."

Like nothing had happened.

13

"**I** need moves," Eddie said.

"Moves?" said Salem. "What moves?"

"You know, moves. To get girls."

"Oh. *Those* moves."

It was two days before the dance. They were in Salem's room after school.

"I guess we don't want to try another letter, do we?" said Salem.

Eddie shot back, "No more letters."

Salem paced about the room. "Okay, moves . . . moves . . ."

"I figure this way," said Eddie. "She's not going to the dance with me, no matter what I do. So forget that, right?"

"Right."

"So how about the dance itself? Is she going?"

"If I have to drag her by her hair."

"Okay. So I need some moves I can pull at the dance."

Salem nodded. "Right." She paced, paced.

"Moves . . . moves . . ." She stopped, turned, studied him for a moment. "You have to change."

"Change?"

"Yes. Be different. The dance will be different, for her anyway. I don't think she's ever been to one. Music. Low lights. Boys. It'll be new. You should be new, too."

Eddie thought it over. "One thing for sure, the old me isn't getting anywhere."

Salem clapped her hands. "Exactly! So . . . what can we do?"

Eddie was sitting on the edge of the bed. Salem stood before him, hands on hips, studying him with squint-eyed intensity. She flicked a forefinger. "Stand." Eddie stood. She twirled her finger. "Turn." He turned. "Walk." He walked.

A smile crept over Salem's face. She nodded slowly. "It's the walk."

Eddie, who had reached the far wall, turned. "The walk?"

"Yep. You walk like, well . . . walk some more."

He walked across the room and back.

Salem nodded decisively. "You walk like a wimp."

"But I *am* a wimp," Eddie blurted.

"Makes no difference," she said. "We're not working on what you *are*. It's your image."

She was losing him. "What are you talking about?"

"Impressions. Look, the real problem is, Sunny

doesn't know what a great guy you are. Why? Because all she sees is a wimp. You have to show her somebody else."

"You mean pretend to be somebody else?"

"Sort of."

"Okay, so suppose I pretend to be somebody else. Then she starts to like me, right?"

"Right."

"Okay, so she starts to like me — and *then* she finds out that underneath this new pretend me, I'm still the same old wimp shrimp Eddie Mott I always was. Big deal."

"Maybe so, but this time she'll *like* the same old Eddie." She leaned in and wagged her finger. *"Because she liked your moves."*

Eddie thought about that. He pictured Sunny liking him. He nodded firmly. "Okay. Teach me to walk."

Salem placed him against the wall. She tried to imagine how the men in romantic stories would walk. "Okay, something like this." She demonstrated. "See . . . head up . . . shoulders back . . . no shuffling . . . lift your feet . . . step out, like a man."

Eddie gave it a try.

Salem screeched. "No, no! You look like a walking mannequin. Not so stiff. Be cool. Graceful." She jumped in front of him. "You know what?"

"What?"

"Here's how to think of it. Your walk should

65

talk. It should say, Hey, world, watch out, here I come. I know where I'm going and nothing's going to stop me. That doesn't mean I'm a brute. I'm not. I'm actually very sensitive and caring, not to mention romantic. It's just that I'm confident. I know how to succeed. If you're smart, you'll keep your eyes on me."

Eddie whistled. "That's a lot for one walk to say."

"Pooh," said Salem. "Just do it." She snapped her fingers, fluttered her hand. "Go on, walk."

Eddie walked, or tried to. Suddenly, it seemed so complicated. Head, shoulders, step, cool, graceful, sensitive, romantic, confident. He felt like all sticks and rubber bands. He barely made it to the other side of the room. He almost felt out of breath. It used to be so easy.

"Not bad," said Salem, surprising him. "With a little practice, who knows. Now this time I want you to put a little swagger into it. Take charge. It's like you're the only pro walker around here, the rest of us clods are amateurs. Come on, swagger."

He swaggered.

She laughed. "Whoa! Not that much. Cut back a little."

He cut back on the swagger. According to her directions, he turned up the sensitive, shortened his step, lengthened his step, projected his con-

66

fidence, back and forth across the room, five, ten, fifteen times.

Salem pulled down her window shades, turned out the overhead light, and draped a red sweater over her desk lamp. "That's as close as I can get to making it like a dance. Okay — here I am, Sunny Wyler, standing in the corner with Salem Brownmiller, watching the action, when who comes *walking* by — "

Eddie came walking. Salem nodded. "Yeah, not bad. Now we have to work on the rest."

"What rest?"

"Clothes."

He squealed. "I can't go buying all new clothes." He glanced at Salem's digital clock. "And I gotta be home for dinner in ten minutes." He started backing toward the door.

Salem thought fast, talked fast. "Okay . . . okay. Listen. You don't need all new clothes. You just need something different. To be noticed. Something that makes a statement. Something that says — "

"Oh, great," said Eddie, "now my clothes have to talk, too."

"Shhh!" Salem silenced him. She closed her eyes, balled her fists, clutched her writing scarf. "Think . . . *think* . . ." Her eyes shot open. "I got it!" She squeezed his arm — "Wait here" — and fled the room. She returned with something that, to Eddie, looked like a giant three-foot-long Slim Jim beef stick.

"What is *that*?"

Salem tapped it once upon the floor. "A cane. It used to be my grandfather's. He called it a swizzle stick."

"I don't need a cane," said Eddie. "There's nothing wrong with my leg."

Salem laughed. "It's not for walking, goofy. It's for style. You just carry it."

This time it was Eddie who laughed. "You gotta be kidding."

"I'm perfectly serious," she said, looking perfectly serious. "You want to be noticed, don't you?"

"Not *that* noticed."

"Oh, you conformists. Here." She thrust the cane at him until he took hold of it. "It'll work, you'll see."

"Okay," said Eddie, hurrying from the room before she came up with anything else. Halfway down the stairs he was halted by her call. "Eddie!"

He turned. "What?"

"I almost forgot. This is really important."

"Salem, I'm late."

"Don't speak to her."

"*Huh?*"

"Don't speak to her. At the dance. When you come walking, just walk on by. Don't say anything." She came down one step. "Even *more* important. Don't even *look* at her. Pretend she's not there."

"That's crazy."

"Trust me."

"What if she talks to me?"

"Pretend you don't hear. Pretend you have more important things to do."

Eddie was backing down the stairs. "What if she asks me a question? Right to my face."

"Say — " Salem thought a moment, took another step down. "Say, 'Later, babe.' Whatever she says, you say that, and walk away."

"Later, babe?"

"Right."

By now Salem was halfway down the stairs. Eddie was at the door. He felt for the knob, opened the door, stepped outside.

"And walk away!"

He shut the door. Her last words came through: "And twirl the cane!"

After dinner, on the telephone with Pickles, Eddie told of his session with Salem.

"Come on over," said Pickles. "I'll show you the only move you'll ever need."

14

It was supposed to be a dance, but maybe they should have called it a war. As Pickles and Eddie approached the school on Friday evening, squads of kids, mostly eighth-graders, were stalking and marching and darting this way and that, calling up the alleys, huddling in dark knots.

"Fights tonight," said Pickles.

Eddie nodded. "At the dance?"

"Maybe. Probably after."

"Think we'll see any?"

"Could be."

Salem was right about one thing: There were a lot of fights. But they were hardly the gory massacres that Salem made them out to be. Often they never got past the yelling and threatening stage. If there was action, it often as not began and ended with pushing, accompanied by the word *yeah*, as in:

"Yeah?"

"Yeah."

70

"Yeah?"

"Yeah!"

Once in a while, the pushing became grabbing, and the grabbing became yanking, and the yanking became wrestling. Then you'd have the two warriors grappling and hugging and grunting, at which point the war did in fact begin to resemble a dance. Hopefully, from the other kids' point of view, they would topple to the ground and roll around there for a while. But even this was usually disappointing, since the best thing that happened was that the "fighters" had their shirts pulled up over their heads.

No, when you got right down to it, a fight was not really a fight until a punch was thrown. And the fact was, that rarely happened. Yet the possibility that it might happen was precisely what drew the crowds when someone shouted, "Fight!"

Eddie was no exception. He felt the excitement, the thrill. He would claw his way to the front of the mob to see a fist land on a nose. Did that mean he was a barbarian, as Salem might say? A savage? If he were living in ancient Rome, at the Colosseum watching two gladiators battle to the death, would he be up in the stands cheering and yelling with the rest of them and giving the thumbs-down sign?

Eddie didn't know. He didn't think that deeply about it. All he knew was that he liked to watch

71

a fight, and so did a lot of other kids, and he didn't know how to explain it to Salem. It was just there.

He did know one thing, though. When Angelpuss butted his nose in gym class, he had been as terrified of being the center of attention as of her. He knew now more than ever that there was only one way he would ever be involved in a fight: as a spectator.

The dance was in the cafeteria, though Eddie hardly recognized it. The tables were gone and most of the chairs. What was left was a huge square room. Music poured out of the dark onto a bare linoleum flatness as big as a prairie. People, hordes of them, swarmed around the edges.

Eddie nodded toward the bare expanse in the middle. "That where you're supposed to dance?"

"Yep," said Pickles.

"Nobody's there."

"They will be. When things warm up." Pickles gave him a knowing wink and a grin.

Eddie kind of hoped they never would warm up. In fact, along about now he kind of wished he had just stayed at home, spent a nice, safe night in front of the TV. He had not brought the cane, nor was he walking as he had practiced at Salem's. He was nothing more or less than the usual Eddie Mott.

"I don't know about this," he said.

"You don't have to know," said Pickles. "Just do it."

"I'm nervous."

Pickles fanned him with his hand. "Don't sweat. It's a piece a cake."

"How do we know it'll work?"

"Trust me."

"That's what Salem said."

"It's guaranteed. Girls can't resist."

Eddie scanned the mob. "Think she's here yet?"

Pickles looked. "Don't know. Hard to tell. There's plenty of time."

Kids were still streaming through the door. The noise was beginning to top the music. Eighth-graders, raucous as crows in treetops, called to one another across the room.

Pickles tugged Eddie's sleeve. "Come on."

"Where?"

"There."

Pickles was pointing to the other side of the cafeteria.

"Okay," said Eddie. He started around the perimeter.

"No," said Pickles, "this way." He pulled Eddie into the great open space.

Eddie dug in his heels. "Hold it! Not that way."

Pickles said, "Come on, I think I see her over there," and yanked Eddie along with him.

Eddie felt as exposed as a bug crawling across

a white porcelain sink. Any instant he expected to be flattened by a swatter. He could barely believe it when they reached the other side. He looked around. "I don't see her."

Pickles grinned. "I lied. Just getting you ready for the spotlight."

Suddenly Eddie was bumped sideways, and someone said, "Oh, excuse me."

It was a nickelhead.

"Oh, excuse me," came another voice, from another nickelhead, whose shoulder sent Eddie staggering into yet another bump. "Oh, excuse *me*."

The third bump sent him reeling into a girl, a nickelchick, Angelpuss. "Well, well," she beamed, "we meet again." She gave his cheek a tweak, and then he was gone, swept away by Pickles.

They didn't stop till they reached the refreshment table. Eddie was flushed and panting, his nose twitching like a rabbit's. "I could've died."

"I wouldn't have let you," said Pickles. "Have a soda. I'm buying." Pickles laid money down and took two sodas and a bag of pretzels. He pulled out a pretzel and practically stuffed it into Eddie's mouth. "Eat. Help you get back to normal."

Eddie was munching and sipping and trying to calm down when Pickles said, "There they are."

Eddie looked. Sunny and Salem were heading their way. Eddie almost choked.

Pickles slipped behind him and whispered, "Okay, you know the plan."

"I can't." Eddie said the words without moving his lips.

Pickles poked him in the back and sent him forward. "Go."

The plan called for Eddie to avoid Sunny until he made his move. In the meantime, Pickles would take care of business.

Propelled by Pickles' push, Eddie moved ahead, straight toward Sunny and Salem. Eddie knew that Salem must be wondering where the cane and walk were. He saw them slow down. And suddenly, brilliantly, he found a way to follow both Pickles' and Salem's advice. He walked right on past them — he could feel their astonished eyes — but not before muttering, kind of low and out of the side of his mouth, "Later, babe."

Oh, how he wished, as he blended into the crowd, that he could turn and see the look on Sunny's face!

15

As the girls approached Pickles, Salem was stifling a grin and Sunny was saying, tossing a thumb back in Eddie's general direction, "I think he's finally gone cuckoo."

"Nah," said Pickles nonchalantly, "he's just scouting around."

"Scouting?" said Sunny. "What for?"

Pickles chuckled. He gestured at the crowd. "What else? Girls."

Sunny's snorty laugh was so sudden and forceful that she had to quick blow her nose. "Yeah, right," she snickered. "Romeo Mott."

Pickles shrugged. "Believe it or not."

"I'll not," said Sunny and ordered a soda.

First to start dancing were a half dozen nickelcouples. Within seconds the perimeter flooded inward, and the empty space in the middle vanished for the night.

After finishing her soda plus a bag of pretzels

and a bag of popcorn, Sunny stood for a full minute watching the action. Then she said, "Okay, what now?"

The same question had occurred to Salem. Her whole focus had been to drag Sunny to the dance, partly for Eddie, partly as company for herself. Now Sunny was here, Eddie was gone, and so was Pickles. "Where do you think the guys disappeared to?" she asked, stalling for time.

"I don't know," said Sunny, "but I'm gonna disappear in a minute if somebody doesn't tell me what I'm doing here."

"It's a dance," said Salem. "Want to dance?"

Sunny answered with a long and dirty look.

Secretly Salem herself wished someone would tell her what she was doing here. Though she acted like a veteran of these things, the fact was this was her first dance ever.

Until now, when the word *dance* was mentioned, the first thing that came to Salem's mind was the championship ballroom dancing that she watched every year on the public television station. She imagined herself swirling in a pastel gown in the arms of a dashing man in a tuxedo. She loved the grace and elegance and romance of it all.

Tonight, looking over the cafeteria dance floor, she found neither grace nor elegance. As for romance, well, if there was any out there, it sure wasn't aimed in her direction. Still, she could not help wondering if even now, right here, Cupid was drawing back his bowstring. Was someone watching? Someone fated to enter her life tomorrow, next week, next year? Perhaps to cleverly bump into her around a corner, or to wisely need to borrow a quarter from her in a lunch line. Watching her even now as she stood by the refreshment table sipping soda. The thought of it made her stop swallowing, raise her chin, and produce a faint, alluring smile.

"I don't believe it," said Sunny.

Salem broke from her cobweb of reverie. "Huh?"

"Look."

In the middle of the floor Mr. Brimlow, Plumstead's bow-tied principal, was doing a moonwalk that resembled a backward stumble through a pothole patch. And then he was out of sight, enclosed by a mob of clapping, whistling students.

"Aren't you glad you came now?" asked Salem.

Sunny did not answer, which meant, for the time being at least, yes.

The two girls spent the next hour looking: Sunny for something as entertaining as Mr. Brimlow's pothole walk, Salem for somebody looking at her. Before long, Salem had convinced herself that half the boys in the place were eyeing her. She could feel them checking her out, this sixth-grade girl with the long brown hair and long skirt. Ah, but they were sneaky, those boys, always turning away just before she looked their way, pretending to be looking elsewhere, talking to their friends. She began swaying a tiny bit to the music, bobbing her head to the beat, to show she was available in case any of them worked up the nerve to ask her to dance.

Meanwhile, Sunny consumed three more sodas, two bags of popcorn, a bag of pizza-flavored nachos, and three full-sized Kit Kat bars. When the next mob of clappers and whistlers converged on the dance floor, Sunny pulled Salem away from the sideline. "Sounds like Brim's at it again. Let's get a good view this time."

Both girls were fond of Mr. Brimlow. Along with Pickles and Eddie, they comprised his so-called Principal's Posse, four sixth-graders that he had lunch with once a week. The mob was even bigger and louder this time, totally obscuring the center of attention. They were going wild.

"Maybe he's taking off his bow tie," quipped Sunny.

It was hopeless trying to see over the heads of the cheering mob, many of whom were taller seventh- and eighth-graders. So the girls wormed and squirmed their way between bodies until they found themselves right behind the front row. Neither of them, not if they had traded eyeballs, could believe what they saw.

16

It was Eddie and Pickles.

Dancing.

Even Eddie couldn't believe it.

He had spent the last hour blending in with the crowd, visiting the boys' room, hiding. He knew Pickles would be coming for him, to carry out the plan. But he just couldn't get up the nerve to do it.

The thing was, this was so unlike anything he had ever done before. He had tried to make Pickles understand that the other night, but all Pickles would do was shrug and say, "So? First time for everything."

Lurking from shadow to shadow, Eddie had come to understand what the terms *clammy* and *cold feet* meant.

Of course, Pickles finally found him. "Let's go. Where've you been?"

"Right here. Where've *you* been?"

Pickles scowled. "Forget it. Next song we do it."

The chill from Eddie's feet was rising. He now had cold ankles, shins, and knees. "I don't know."

"You don't need to know. Just do it."

Pickles was casually looking over the dance floor, bobbing his head to the music. Eddie couldn't get over how easy Pickles was about everything, how fearless.

"I don't think I'm ready."

"You're ready," said Pickles, bobbing. "That's why we practiced. You're ready."

"I stink."

Pickles turned, poked him in the chest. "You don't stink. I taught you everything you know. You can't stink."

The music ended. Some dancers headed for the sidelines, some hung where they were, awaiting the next record. Eddie's ears were cold. Next thing he knew, he was out in the middle of the floor, dancing.

It was Pickles' invention. He had taught it to Eddie, and they had practiced it over and over yesterday after school and after dinner. It was all based on skateboarding. The basic step was to keep your left foot still while you paddled with the right, then slide the left ahead, then paddle with the right some more: paddle, slide, paddle, slide. Like driving a skateboard along a sidewalk.

There were all kinds of moves you could make off that: curb jumps, whirlies, high-bank turns. You could even keep both feet still, spread just right, hold your arms out wide, and sort of teeter and sway as though you were zinging down a monster hill at sixty per.

Any other time you were free to do pretty much what you wanted with your arms. Pickles liked to throw one arm straight out ahead and the other behind, making him look like a cross-country skier. Eddie liked to bend his arms halfway, make fists, and do a circular, chugging motion.

The tip of Eddie's tongue was firmly in the grip of his teeth as he concentrated on the music and his own feet. Pickles meanwhile was free-lancing all over the place, improvising moves as he went along. Eddie stayed with the basics: paddle, slide, paddle, slide. He did try a whirlie once and surprised himself that it went so well. His first clue that Pickles had been right came about twenty seconds into the record, when a nearby voice called, "Hey, check this out!"

Pickles heard it, too. Halfway through a U-turn, he flashed Eddie a wink and a grin.

Eddie became aware of motion around him subsiding: Dancers were stopping to watch. And now they were coming, rushing even, from all directions, surrounding them, totally engulfing them, like he had seen them do to Mr. Brimlow earlier on.

Somebody whistled, somebody called "Do it!", somebody clapped. and from then on the mob lent its own percussion and lyrics to the music.

"It's the Pickles kid!"

"Who's the other one?"

"They're only sixth-graders!"

"They're doin' it!"

"Go!"

"Yeah!"

Someone leaned in, cupped his hands, and yelled, "What's it called?"

Pickles whirled twice and shot back, "Funky pickle!"

There was a second of stillness while the mob digested this, then they exploded, cheering, whistling, stomping the floor while shouts of "Funky pickle!" and "Awesome!" filled the night.

Eddie kept expecting to wake up from a dream. But until he did, he had to admit Pickles was right. It was turning out just as he had said. Now there was only one thing left to fall into place.

Was she out there, in that dark, stomping, cheering crowd? Was she watching him, seeing him in a new light, thinking *Hey, that's not the Eddie Mott I know*, feeling something?

Oh, she was, all right. She was out there, among the dark faces, watching, feeling. Only one difference: She wasn't the she that Eddie had in mind.

Not even close.

17

Monday morning in the hallways.

Half the student body, it seemed, was funky pickling down the corridors of Plumstead. Paddle, slide, paddle, slide, *twirl*. Pickles and Eddie couldn't show their faces without somebody calling:

"Hey!"

"Yo!"

"Pickle dudes!"

"Check it!"

Pickles grinned slightly. "Like the dance never ended."

Eddie gushed. "We're famous!"

But he wondered how famous he was with a certain person. Eddie never did see Sunny for the rest of the dance. He and Pickles spent the night putting on exhibitions and teaching the others how to do it. As a matter of fact, Eddie had not laid eyes on Sunny all weekend, and now, as praise rained down upon him in the hallways, he ached to end the suspense.

He cornered Salem in English. "Did she see? Was she watching? Did she say anything? What do you think?"

Salem flinched under the barrage. "Calm *down*."

He calmed down and repeated the questions.

Salem opened her grammar book and sighed. "Yes, she saw you. No, she didn't say anything. And what I think is that I don't have any more time to spare for you and your love life. The stories for the Willow Wembley contest are due this week, and that's the only thing I'm giving my attention to. I must *not* be distracted. I worked on my story all weekend. I eat, sleep, and think my story twenty-four hours a day, and until it's finished you and the rest of the world are *persona non grata*." She turned from Eddie and stared straight ahead as Miss Comstock began the class.

Well, whatever *persona non grata* meant, the nail-biting fact was that next period was math, and Sunny was in the class. As Miss Comstock read from a Willow Wembley novel, Eddie stewed in his questions. How would Sunny act? Would she compliment him on his dancing? Say she was sorry she had turned down his invitation? Would she write him a note? *Did* she write him a note? He riffled through his books, turned them page-end down, shook them. No, there was no note.

Most important of all, would there be a different look to her face? The look that he had seen other girls give other guys. The look that said, *I like you.*

In short: no. None of it happened. When Eddie saw her in math, she was no more or less than the usual Sunny. He tried to convince himself that her eye had a twinkle that hadn't been there before, that her lips curled in a way that meant something. But when, at the end of class, Sunny popped out of her seat and, without so much as glancing at him, flipped her hand and said, "Later, 'gator," well, Eddie knew that Pickles for once in his life had been wrong.

He was still feeling down when lunchtime came around. Instead of seeking out his friends as usual, he walked down the lunch line by himself. He wasn't very hungry, and he didn't feel like being healthy. He picked out a package of peanut butter crackers and a chocolate milk. He was reaching for a bag of potato chips when a voice behind him, female and as friendly as could be, said, "Hi, Eddie."

He turned. Orange hair spike. Purple lipstick. Angelpuss.

She looked at his tray. "Not hungry today?"

"Guess not," Eddie replied. He felt blindly for the potato chips. He was afraid if he took his eyes off her, she would butt him in the nose. He felt very tense being this close to her. He put all his systems on red alert, ready to jump aside if that forehead came darting forward. His nose itched and ached. The spike made her a six-footer.

She reached into the potato chip bin and pulled out two packs. She smiled. "Want one?" Eddie shrugged, half nodded. She put a pack on his tray. "Maybe I'll be a waitress someday," she giggled. Her nose ring gleamed like a tiny, misplaced halo.

Eddie peeked at the line behind her. He didn't see Weasel.

"That was some dance you guys did the other night," she said.

Eddie edged toward the cashier, trying to put some distance between himself and the girl. "Thanks."

She closed the gap. He moved farther. She closed the gap. She stayed close, smiling her purple smile. The leading edge of her tray was smack against the trailing edge of his. "Oh, look!" she squealed, way too loud. "Our trays are kissing!"

Eddie's face boiled. He was sure he must look to all the world like Tommy Tomato. He rammed his tray up to the cashier, paid his money, and headed for the tables. He found an empty one in the corner. He sat down — and so did she, taking the seat to his right.

"Boy," she said, opening a carton of juice, "I'm hungry as a hog." A pair of chili dogs lay on her plate. She picked one up and devoured half of it in one bite. She chewed for a full minute, closing her eyes and going, "Mmm . . . mmm . . ."

"Just think," she said, "it was right here where it started. What's it called, the dance?"

"Funky pickle," Eddie replied. For the first time, the name felt silly on his lips.

"That's it, yeah!" She rapped a fork on the table. "Funky pickle." Then, while Eddie watched helplessly, she jumped up from her seat and did a few funky picklesteps.

Kids at nearby tables applauded. Angelpuss took a bow and sat down. Eddie was mortified. The whole lunchroom was staring at his table. The only good news was that he didn't see Weasel, or any other nickelhead for that matter.

Eddie worked on his potato chips and peanut butter crackers, just to keep busy. He prayed she would go away, but instead she settled back, finished off her first chili dog, and said, "So, you got a girlfriend?"

What kind of a question is that? Eddie wondered. "No," he said, "guess not."

She smiled enormously. "Good."

Now what did she mean by *that*?

Next thing Eddie knew, her hand was coming at him. A punch? He flinched back, but she leaned, and her hand kept coming till it landed on his nose, softly. Her fingertips patted it. His eyeballs moved around his sockets like slugs in a pinball machine.

"Sorry I butted you," she said. Her voice was

full of sympathy. And her face — Eddie couldn't believe it — had the look he had been hoping to find on Sunny. "Maybe I should kiss it to make it feel better." She was coming closer: the face, the orange spike, the purple lips.

Eddie recoiled with such force that both he and his chair toppled backward onto the floor. The place exploded in laughter. The bell rang, adding its own ridicule. Eddie left all as it was — the chair, the lunch, the girl — and sprinted for the safety of the hallway.

18

Eddie had been dreading it, and sure enough it happened. He was walking innocently down the hall to his last class when suddenly he was walking on air. Hands had grabbed the shoulders of his shirt, lifted, and now he was floating down the hall like Peter Pan, except Peter Pan was never hung between two nickelheads. And they were two of the biggest of all, pure giants.

"In there," came a familiar voice from behind.

As he continued to skim over the floor, Eddie wrenched his neck to look. It was Weasel. He sailed through a boys' room door. "There," said Weasel, and Eddie was deposited on top of a sink. His feet dangled in air. His mind flashed back to a high chair, himself in it. But this was not home, and the face before him was not his mother's.

Weasel had a sharp, triangular face. His haircut could not fit as many polka-dot bare spots as other nickelheads because his nickelhead was on the small side. He was rolling a jawbreaker around in his mouth. It was making his tongue green. "What's this about you and my chick?" His sugary jawbreaker breath poured the words into Eddie's face.

"Wh — " Eddie tried to speak, but all that came out was a gravelly croak. He tried again. "Wha — " Getting better. The third time he nailed it. "What do you mean?"

"I mean at lunch. I mean sitting with my chick. I mean trying to lay lips on my chick."

Eddie gasped. "Who?"

"You." As punctuation, Weasel poked Eddie until he was sitting in the bowl of the sink. It happened to be a perfect fit.

The best Eddie could do was babble: "Me . . . huh . . . no . . . who . . . her . . . huh . . ."

Weasel placed the tip of his index finger between Eddie's eyes. "You go near her again, you're dead meat." He pushed Eddie's head as he backed away. Eddie's backward motion carried him into the cold water knob, which turned just enough to bring water from the faucet. Eddie leapt from the sink — too late — the seat of his pants was soaked. The three nickelheads went out the door in stitches.

Eddie tried fanning his fanny with his hand to dry his pants. He tried blotting them dry with paper towels. Realizing then that only time would dry him, he remained in the boys' room. He did not go to his last class. He did not go to homeroom.

He did not sneak out of the building until 4:30 that afternoon.

After dinner Eddie phoned Pickles and told him what happened. "He said I was dead meat."

"Don't worry," said Pickles. "He's not going to kill you. Maybe beat-up meat, that's all."

Eddie shrieked. "Oh, great!"

Pickles chuckled into the receiver. "Just kidding. Hey, I told you that dance was powerful stuff, didn't I?"

"Yeah?" Eddie retorted bitterly. "Well, it didn't do nothing to the one it was *supposed* to do something to."

"Maybe she just won't admit it."

"Maybe I'm dead meat."

"Hey, get off that. He was just trying to scare you."

"Trying? He did."

"Listen, if you're worried, all you have to do is stay away from her. And anyway, she was probably just joking around. You probably saw the last of her."

Eddie wished.

Next morning, on the way to get his books, there she was, waiting at his locker. He did a quick U-turn, ran up the steps, along the hall, down another stairway, and darted into homeroom from the other side. In every class that morning he got into trouble because he didn't have his book.

At lunch he hooked up with Pickles, figured he was safe. She wasn't in sight. Halfway through the line he heard, "Hi, Eddie." He bolted, leaving Pickles with two trays. He spent lunch period in the darkness of the music room's instrument closet, aching for tacos and burgers among the trombones and clarinets.

After school, sure enough, she was at his locker. He ran straight home.

"I couldn't go to my locker all day," he complained to Pickles over the phone. "I didn't have any books. I didn't eat lunch. I'm a wreck."

"What can I say?" said Pickles. "You're irresistible to the opposite sex."

"Funny. And two times I passed Weasel in the halls. He gave me this look, I can't even describe it. And you know what else?"

"What else?"

"He makes his hand like a gun, with his finger out, you know?"

"Yeah?"

"And he, like, aims with one eye shut and goes, 'Pow.' "

"So? He's playing cops and robbers."

"And I didn't even tell you the worst thing yet."

"Tell me."

Eddie paused. He lowered his voice. "I'm being watched."

Pickles suppressed a chuckle. "Yeah? By who?"

"The nickelheads, who do you think? I can feel their eyes on me. Everywhere I go. I'm afraid even to go to the bathroom. If they ever catch me in there again . . ." Eddie left the unspeakable thought unspoken.

"No sweat," said Pickles. "Just make sure you go to the bathroom before you leave the house in the morning, and don't drink water all day."

Eddie didn't answer, unsure if Pickles was kidding or not.

"And anyway," Pickles added, "things will probably cool off tomorrow."

Eddie groaned into the phone. "No *way*! That's the *really* worst thing of all."

"It is?"

"Yeah. Tomorrow I have gym class, and Angelpuss and Weasel are both in it."

19

Salem had her own problems, number one being how to keep the rest of the world away while you're trying to write the story that will determine the success or failure of the rest of your life.

In recent days Salem's future had begun to show itself. It looked something like this: Salem wins Willow Wembley contest. Along with seventh- and eighth-grade winners, Salem escorts the great author around the school on Willow Wembley Day. Miss Wembley is dazzled by Salem's knowledge and vocabulary and maturity and refinement and elegance and all-around *savoir faire*. In fact, they even speak a little French to each other.

But most of all, Willow Wembley is impressed with Salem's story. She asks to see more of Salem's work, which Salem pulls out of her book bag (having cleverly anticipated such a request). Once Miss Wembley begins reading, she cannot stop. She drags Salem into a vacant room and reads and reads. Her eyes bulge in wonder. She wags her head and says things like, "This is incredible!" and "Are you sure you didn't copy this?" and "Are you sure you're only in sixth grade?"

Then she rushes to a telephone and calls her publisher and says, "I have just discovered the next great writer of our time. Send her a contract." And Salem signs a contract and writes a five-hundred-page book, and it's a smash, it's bigger than *Gone With the Wind*, it's made into a movie, and Salem writes the screenplay and swoops onto the stage in Hollywood to accept the Academy Award . . .

Or something like that.

Wrapping her writing scarf about her, Salem experienced the week as if in a cocoon. Home, school, day, night — all was a gray, muffled blur beyond the fierce concentration with which she bore down on her story.

Every minute away from her Left Bank garret was a minute lost. Only there, with the door closed and the Eiffel Tower looking down, did her artistic soul feel at home. From handwritten notes to computer keyboard to laser printer, she wrote and rewrote, corrected and deleted and added and clarified and simplified and polished and repolished until, at precisely 9:46 Thursday evening, the last page of the second correction of the ninth improvement of the third version came sliding from her father's Hewlett Packard LaserJet.

The relief, the exhilaration, the occasion of it brought tears to her eyes. Ten pages. Two thousand one hundred and thirty words. So light to hold, nearly weightless, and most of that was paper. Take away the paper, she fancied, and the LaserJetted letters, the powdery, unmoored words would probably rise like thistledown against gravity, hang forever in the cosmos. Ten little pages: one future, her world to be.

Salem keyboarded and printed out a title page. She drilled tidy holes in the pages with her three-hole punch. She inserted and fastened them in a sky blue, fresh-from-the-drugstore binder.

She took off her writing scarf and draped it over the back of her chair. She turned out the light. She toppled into her bed like a felled tree. Forget brushing, forget pajamas. But exhausted as she was, she could not sleep. Though she had dismounted, the steed that had borne her still raced on, mane flying, foaming at the bit. She turned on her twelve-inch TV, kept the volume at a whisper, and saw shows at hours she had barely known to exist.

Next morning she handed her story to Miss Comstock.

Coming out of class, she gave Eddie a playful shoulder bump. "Good morning, Mister Mott."

Eddie looked at her like something he found between his toes.

"What's the matter?" she inquired cheerily.

"What's the matter?" he squawked. "What's the *matter*? Now you ask. I'm a dead man, I'm a slab a salami, *that's* what's the matter. I'll never see twelve. I'll never be a teenager. I'll never drive a car. I don't even know what I'm doing in school. I might as well go straight to the cemetery and start digging my own grave." His eyes were flashing, his nostrils flaring. "Yeah, that's where I'll go. You got a shovel? Anybody got a shovel?"

Salem had seen him like this before. He tended to go overboard when upset, not unlike herself. She touched him gently on the arm. She looked into his wild eyes. "Hey — hey — it's me. Salem. Calm down. Tell me what happened."

He calmed down and told her. He told her about the day in gym class. About Angelpuss chasing him all over the field and grabbing him and pulling out his red tail and tying it around her neck and strutting around yapping, "Eddie Mott loves me!"

"What did that Weasel creature do?"

"He wasn't there. He was absent that day."

"So what happened then?"

Eddie fished a piece of paper from his pocket, uncrumpled it. "This." There were two words in black marker:

DEAD MEAT

Above the words was a tiny hole in the paper.

"This was tacked to my front door when I left for school next day. His spies must have told him about it. Good thing my parents didn't see it."

Salem cringed just to look at it. "Why didn't you tell me about this before?"

Eddie's eyes bulged. "*Tell* you? What do you think I've been *trying* to do?"

The bell rang. Eddie ran for his class, leaving Salem with the paper. She could not take her eyes from it, this evidence from the violent world around her. It seemed to grow hot and burn evilly in her fingers. She tossed it to the floor and rushed for class.

Later that day Salem was talking with Pickles.

"So what is it with this Angelpuss creature anyway? Why is she being this way with Eddie?"

Pickles shrugged. "Love, I guess."

Salem scoffed, "Oh, right, sure. She's in eighth grade, he's in sixth. Not to mention that Eddie looks like he only belongs in fourth or fifth. And double not to mention that she's one of these nickelcreatures. I thought they all stick together."

Another shrug from Pickles. "Love conquers all."

"I'm going to kick you if you don't get serious."

"Kick? I thought you were against violence." Salem folded her arms and glared in silence. "All I know," said Pickles, "is what she tells Eddie."

"Which is?"

"Which is, she has the hots for him."

"Hots? You've got to be kidding."

"That's the word."

Salem stared, blinking. "Why?"

"I guess it started with the funky pickle. She says ever since she saw him doing it at the dance, she can't stop thinking about him."

"And Eddie, what about him?"

"He tries to stay away from her, but she catches up to him once or twice a day."

"And the Weasel creature?"

"He put a note on Eddie's front door."

"He showed me."

Pickles looked surprised. "Well . . ."

They fell silent for a while.

"So," Salem resumed, "what now?"

Pickles shrugged. "Fight, I guess."

Salem stomped her foot. "Oh, really. Fight. Like that's the answer to everything. Little Eddie? That's the most ridiculous thing I ever heard in my life."

"Tell that to Weasel."

Salem marched off, marched back. She shook her head, still trying to make sense of it all. "I thought this Angelpuss was supposed to be this Weasel's girlfriend."

"She was."

"And now she doesn't like him anymore? She

likes Eddie Mott? Our Eddie Mott?"

"Looks that way."

Salem paced some more. "Okay, so, if it's true, ridiculous as it sounds, the girl actually likes Eddie, why doesn't this Weasel character go find himself another girlfriend?"

"You'll have to ask him. All I know is, Eddie's scared stiff. He's been, for a couple of days now." He said this looking straight into Salem's eyes.

Salem blinked. "You're mad at me."

"I didn't say that."

"But you are, aren't you?" Pickles looked away. "You're mad because I wasn't paying attention to all this, because I was busy writing my story."

"So were we."

"It was just an assignment for you."

He said nothing.

"Pickles, that story is the most important thing in the world to me. My whole future could depend on it."

Pickles nodded, hands in pockets.

"Ohhh!" Salem stomped. Many feelings bubbled inside her, but only guilt boiled over. It oozed across every bright meadow of her being until she felt as rank and lifeless as lettuce in a gutter, as vile as a virus. It was not only an unwelcome feeling, it was most untimely; for on the eve of her greatest triumph, there was simply no room in her life for a rotten intruder. And so she got rid of it, expelled it, replaced it with a feeling of her own making, an old familiar feeling.

"Well," she sniffed primly, turning to Pickles, "I tried to stop you all from being savages. This is what happens when you live by the sword. It serves him right."

And off she marched.

20

On Monday Eddie found another note tacked to his front door. It said:

FRIDAY AFTER SCHOOL

"I have five days to live," he told Pickles as they raised the flag at school that morning.

Pickles finished playing reveille on his battered and ancient bugle. He put his arm around Eddie's shoulders. He smiled. "Don't worry."

Don't worry?

How could Eddie not worry? Tell that to his hand, which sweated so much all day that it practically shrunk his pencil. Tell that to his nose, which twitched from first period till last.

Following Pickles' advice, he avoided drinking fountains and lavatories. Nevertheless, in spite of consuming nothing more liquid than honey-lemon cough drops, he barely made it home in time to go to the bathroom, after which he guzzled down two glasses of cranapple juice and a can of cherry cola.

Salem stayed after school. She joined several other volunteers, under the direction of Miss Comstock, in creating a Willow Wembley display in the glass case in the lobby. It featured copies of the author's books along with artifacts of her most famous characters, the Klatterfields: a wooden pipe, such as Clyde Klatterfield continually smoked while taming a spot in the wilderness for his family; a pressed dandelion, such as thirteen-year-old Tara Klatterfield might have created; and a teacup and saucer, for even in the wilderness, never did the Klatterfields fail to have high tea at four o'clock by the homemade sundial.

And, of course, there was a photograph of Willow Wembley herself. It was bigger and better than any of her dust jacket photos. The great author was shown in profile, gazing out over a harbor from a dramatically high promontory. Her skirt was full and long, like Salem's; her sleeves were flouncy. She was the very portrait of elegance, the crowning jewel of humankind's long and fitful reach for perfection.

To think that in four days Salem would be in Willow Wembley's presence was almost too much to bear. She caught herself daydreaming numerous times throughout the day. This was no problem in class, but when, on the way home from school, she awoke to the squeal of brakes and discovered herself inches from a car bumper in the middle of a street, that was something else. She literally slapped herself for almost committing the most unspeakable blunder of all time: getting herself killed before Friday.

That evening Eddie Mott, instead of doing homework, wrote out his will.

21

Tuesday morning Eddie awoke to a golden glow. It was the window shades. He had awakened in this room approximately four thousand times in his life, yet never, until now, had he noticed how the dull pale of the shades became magically transformed by the morning sun behind them. He lingered in bed, he smiled, he bathed in the warm, butterscotch blessing.

Vanished were the frightful hours of the night, when he had been visited by memories of the time he came closest to a fight. He was in fourth grade, innocently playing basketball on a dusty park playground, when a burly kid he didn't know started pushing him and pushing till he'd slammed back into a chain link fence. As the kid reached out, Eddie ran, ran like he had never run before, ran till there was nothing but clear pavement and the echoes of his own footsteps behind him. He was safe. He headed for home. He cried. He didn't want to, but the tears just came. And for the first time he saw, and had seen ever since, that he was a coward.

For two years he had secretly hated this about himself. He had seen other kids go swinging into battle with one another. He marveled at their zest for combat and cursed himself for having none. His way was to make a smile, not a fist. While he thrilled to the brawl of others, for himself he relished peace. He asked only to be safe and unafraid.

And now his worst nightmare had come true. The call that used to bring him running — "Fight!" — now chilled his bones. In three days he would be standing somewhere outside Plumstead Middle School, maybe on a patch of grass, maybe on a blacktopped parking lot or driveway. Across from him would be Weasel Munshak. Surrounding the two of them would be a ring of spectators, kids, hundreds of them. Classmates who had sat beside him minutes before would now be yelling for his blood. Weasel would move closer, and the only question, the most terrible question in all the world was: Would he start to cry after he got hit in the face, or before?

In any case, Eddie figured that by five o'clock Friday afternoon, as the rest of the town was quitting work and heading home to their families, he would be a croaker on a cement slab.

In the golden glow of the window shades, it all seemed a bad dream. Even his will on the dresser seemed like some leftover from a game he must have played. He read the opening words — "I, Edward Albert Mott, do leave behind to my parents . . ." — and chuckled and tossed the paper aside.

Forty minutes later, as he stepped outside to find a note tacked to the front door:

THREE DAYS

he knew again that it was no dream.

In English class, Salem avoided Eddie's eyes and locked into Miss Comstock's. She had handed in her story on Friday morning. It was now Tuesday morning. The judges — three English teachers, one of them Miss Comstock — must surely have read all the entries by now. Were they still making up their minds? Had they narrowed it down to five or ten finalists from each grade? Had they already decided? Were the winners' names in a sealed envelope somewhere?

Miss Comstock read two chapters from *The Owl Hoo Came to Dinner*. She was pacing the reading in order to finish on Thursday, the day before Willow Wembley's arrival. Salem searched her eyes, her face, her body language for clues. No fewer than four times did the teacher's eyes come up from the book to meet Salem's. Twice her lips seemed to hold a faint smile. Was Miss Comstock sending a signal? Was the faint smile saying, "Yes,

Salem, you did it. I knew you would"?

When class ended, Salem lingered at her desk, pretending to rearrange her books. Within seconds the two of them were alone in the room.

Salem kept her eyes down. She took her breath in silent sips. She was aware of Miss Comstock fussing at her desk. Any moment she expected to hear: "Salem, now that we're alone . . ."

It didn't happen. When Salem finally dared to look up, Miss Comstock was breezing out of the room with a briefcase and a cheery, "See you tomorrow, Salem."

Maddening!

When the first person said "Good luck" to Eddie midway through the day, he wondered what the kid was talking about. When the second kid said it, he knew. Apparently the word was out. By Friday they would be panting for action. The crowd would be huge indeed.

More than the words, Eddie felt the eyes. They were no longer only nickelhead eyes. They watched him in the hallways, the classrooms.

Heads turned. Voices whispered.

It was one thing to count yourself a goner. It was something else to have others agree. The funeral, it seemed, had already begun.

No matter how hard he tried to avoid Angelpuss, she always found him at least once a day, always cooing at him, no matter how many people were around. "Eddie, do the funky pickle once. Come on. Just for me?"

After school Eddie did not meet the Picklebus. He walked the streets of Cedar Grove. As far as he knew, he wasn't heading anywhere in particular, just wandering. Yet in fact something deep within was steering him, guiding him back to a place of happier times, of days that glowed like morning window shades. He turned a corner and walked no more. He was at Brockhurst Elementary, his old school.

His eyes watered up. The playground was nearly deserted, just a few little kids on the swings. How many recesses had he raced and screamed away on that playground?

He worked up his nerve and went inside. The hallways were empty. He peeked into one room, another. Empty. From somewhere came the sound of laughter. For an instant he thought he recognized the voice. Could it possibly be Mrs. Lewis?

Oh, how he had loved her! Once, on a note on his report card, she had called him my little ray of sunshine. If only she knew what can happen to little rays when they reach middle school.

He found his old second-grade room. He went in, looked around. He giggled out loud — there was the Child of the Day button, big as an all-day lollipop. How proud he had been to wear that giant yellow button when he was Child of the Day.

Eddie picked up a piece of chalk and wrote on the blackboard:

Dear Mrs. Lewis,
You are the best teacher I ever had.
A Former Student

He wiped his cheeks dry and went outside. The little kids were gone. He sat on a swing. It seemed so small now, he wondered if he would break it. He felt a little foolish, but he didn't care. He pushed off slightly, swinging just slightly back and forth, dragging his sneaker heels. In second grade he had needed to straighten his legs to touch the ground. He pushed off a little harder, then harder, and he felt that flying feeling and he knew then, no, it would not break, and so he went on swinging and swinging.

22

Sitting in homeroom Wednesday morning, Salem knew this was the day. The electronic three-note intro to the intercom announcements speared her breath. Her eyes fixed on the square charcoal speaker above the blackboard, she heard Principal Brimlow blather on about tryouts for this and practice for that and sign-ups for this and Parents' Night and teachers' in-service and keeping the lavatories clean and bringing a note from the doctor when you're absent for three days or more.

And then he talked about the visit of "one of your favorite authors and mine, Miss Willow Wembley." He talked about what an inspiration she was to kids all over the country. He charged everybody, "students and faculty alike, to be on our best behavior." He told everyone (for the millionth time) that Plumstead was a brand-new school, whose doors first opened in September, and therefore this was "an historic occasion" because Miss Wembley would be the first famous person ever to visit the school. "So let's show her," he practically yelled, "what it means to be the Plumstead Fighting Hamsters!"

Silence then. Is that all? feared Salem.

"And now," resumed the voice in the charcoal box, "the announcement you've all been waiting for. The results of the story-writing contest to determine who will personally escort Miss Wembley around the school on Friday." There was a pause, a rustle of paper. "May I have the envelope, please . . . ha-ha . . . just kidding, Hamsters. Okay, three winners, one from each grade . . . from grade six, Miss Wembley's personal escort will be . . . Dennis Johnson . . ."

Salem did not hear the rest of the announcement. She sat in numbed, stunned stillness. When her mind returned, it came in fragments.

Pickles.

Pickles?

Did I hear right?

Did he make a mistake?

Pickles?

There *must* be a mistake.

Pickles?

On the way to first class, Salem stopped by the main office. "May I see Mr. Brimlow?" she asked the secretary, Mrs. Wilburham.

Mrs. Wilburham, ever protective of her principal, asked in return, "What would you like to see him about?"

Salem's tongue felt dusty. "I . . . uh . . . just wanted to ask him something about one of the announcements today."

"And what — " Mrs. Wilburham was saying when Mr. Brimlow himself came out. His usual beaming face changed the instant he laid eyes on Salem. He knew very well of Salem's ambition to write, and the change in his face, slight as it was, gave Salem her answer: There had been no mistake. He was raising his hand to his red bow tie and opening his mouth to speak as Salem fled the office.

Later, in English, kids were mobbing Pickles, congratulating him. Through a thicket of back-slapping hands he looked her way, a funny smile on his face. Salem turned away.

When the bell ended class, Miss Comstock asked Pickles to stay for a minute.

After school Eddie visited Humphrey in the hamster tank in the lobby. Sunny was cleaning the tank and feeding the furry Plumstead mascot.

Watching the tiny brown rascal, Eddie fervently wished he were a hamster. "I'll bet Humphrey is the only one not at the fight," he said.

"What fight?" said Sunny, pushing the salt wheel under Humphrey's nose.

Eddie was shocked. "My fight. Friday."

Sunny shrugged indifferently. "Oh, that one." She carried the water bottle off for a refill.

Eddie couldn't believe it. Pickles had been acting the same way, saying things like, "Don't worry" and "No sweat." How could two of his best friends be so casual at a time like this?

When Sunny returned with a full bottle, he said, "Well you *are* going to be there, aren't you?"

Fixing the bottle to the glass wall of the tank, Sunny replied lazily, "Oh, probably not. I got stuff to do that day."

Meanwhile, four blocks from school, Pickles coasted his green six-wheeler alongside Salem. "I waited for you outside school," he said. "Give you a ride?"

Salem kept walking, her eyes straight ahead. "I'm fine."

"Come on, hop on."

"I said I'm fine."

Pickles coasted with her past several houses. "Where's your writing scarf?"

Salem stopped cold. She glared. "You're not funny."

Pickles spread his arms. "Who's trying to be funny?"

"You're rubbing it in. It's not enough that you won, now you're rubbing my face in it." She marched on.

Pickles caught up. "I'm sorry. I wasn't trying to rub it in. I wasn't even trying to win."

"Right." Even as Salem scoffed, she knew he was telling the truth. Pickles seldom tried to win at anything. He just did things because he felt like it. First or last never seemed to mean much to him, which made his victory in this case all the harder to take.

"Really," said Pickles. "You were right, it was just an assignment to me. Beginner's luck. What do I want with Willow Wembley?"

Salem picked up her pace. The wheels of the Picklebus hummed higher. Her eyes were stinging. She felt like screaming a million things. "Just leave me alone," she said.

He stopped. He let her walk another ten feet. Then he said, "Salem, I told Miss Comstock I didn't want to be an escort. She said if I really meant it, I should ask you if you would like to. Your story was next best."

Salem continued on several more steps. She stopped and turned. She leaned as if into a wind and screamed, "I am *not* anybody's *substitute*!"

For Eddie, this night was the worst yet. His nerves totally got the best of him. At dinner, he buried his burger in an avalanche of catsup. When he brushed his teeth, the toothbrush slipped out of his mouth and smeared his cheek with Colgate. Steering his feet into the leg holes of his pajamas

116

was like trying to thread a needle. He finally accomplished it only to discover that he had put them on backward.

He checked over his will. He had left most of his worldly possessions to his parents. There was something for each of his grandparents. Finally there was Pickles, Sunny, and Salem. The fact that Pickles and Sunny were taking his tragedy so lightly and Salem was ignoring him did not change the more enduring fact that they were his best friends in all the world.

To Pickles he had bequeathed his baseball glove and his pocket knife featuring a corkscrew and a tiny pair of tweezers. Tonight, that didn't seem enough to leave the very best of his best friends. So he threw in his lifetime collection of pennies, gathered from sidewalks, gutters, and floors in every corner of town. There was something special about a penny found. He never spent one. A hundred and twenty-one of them in the stomach of a fat glass frog on his dresser.

To Salem, the writer, he left the silver ballpoint pen he had received for Christmas and had never used.

To Sunny, after much thought, he had given maybe his most prized possession of all: the original eight-by-ten glossy print of a photograph from last summer. It showed him crossing first base in a Little League game, the first baseman stretching to receive the throw, the umpire calling him out. The picture had appeared next day on the front sports page of the Cedar Grove *Gazette*.

Eddie added one final item to his will — a tennis ball for Humphrey the hamster — and sealed it in an envelope. He placed it in the top drawer of his dresser, beneath his stack of undershirts.

He went to bed then, but not to sleep. Even leaving the bedside lamp turned on did not calm his nerves. At 11 o'clock he was still awake. At 11:05 a small smile appeared on his face, then a grin, then an ear-to-ear beamer. He had just thought of something. He could live to see Saturday after all. All he had to do was fake a stomachache on Friday morning. His mother would call him in sick. Edward Mott, absent.

Yeah!

He leapt to his dresser, tore up the will, and let the pieces snow into the wastebasket. He turned out the light and went straight to sleep.

23

When Pickles got to English class next day, he found a scrap of paper on his desk, folded four times. He unfolded it. It was a note. A short note.

OK
S.

Pickles glanced over to Salem's desk. She was sitting erect, staring straight ahead. He put the note in his pocket. He smiled to himself.

At her desk two aisles away, Salem clung fiercely to what little self-respect she had left. A night of dilemma had led her to a simple question: How will I feel the rest of my life knowing I blew my only chance to spend a day with Willow Wembley?

End of dilemma.

Halfway through class she risked a quick peek at Pickles. He was giving Miss Comstock his full attention. There was one thing Salem felt good about. She knew Pickles would not gloat, would never remind her that she had reversed herself. Some day she would thank him. But not today.

In the same class, while Miss Comstock read the final chapter of *The Owl Hoo Came to Dinner*, Eddie rewrote his will from memory.

By the time he had stepped off the school bus that morning, he had come to realize that he would not stay in bed tomorrow. It was not that he had changed his mind, for his mind still told him "be sick, be sick." No, there was something else inside him, something that had shouldered aside his common sense and commandeered his steering wheel. It ignored the notes found daily on his front door, this morning's saying "ONE MORE DAY." Whatever it was, it certainly hadn't been around when the bully chased him from the basketball court. As far as Eddie could tell, this something else was stupid and useless. It had done nothing more than leave him back where he had started: scared stiff.

It had taken Salem till the end of classes to work up the nerve to say something. She came up behind Sunny at her locker. "Did you hear what Pickles did?"

Sunny turned. She raised her eyebrows. "Well, well, it speaks."

Salem glared. "Okay, so I get wrapped up sometimes. Are you going to answer my question?"

Sunny shut her locker door. "He won the contest. That what you mean?" She gave Salem a funny look, then started down the hallway. "Gotta feed Humphrey."

Walking along, Salem said, "He told Miss Comstock he doesn't want to escort Willow Wembley. He said I should."

Sunny stopped. "So? Are you?" Again she looked at Salem funny.

Salem nodded. "I guess so." Sunny started walking. "What do you think?"

"I think that's pretty nice of him, is what I think."

Salem smiled fondly. "I think so, too."

When they reached Humphrey's tank, Sunny turned to Salem and stared at her. "What's that on your neck?"

Eddie had never been so aware of time. Each minute that blinked from the red LED display on his clock seemed to reel him in closer to the gallows.

He went to the window, looked out at the moon. For the last time? he wondered. He turned out his light so he could see outside better. The moon seemed to have a calming effect on him, seemed to beckon him into the vastness of a future in which the next twenty-four hours were a mere blip. He began to see himself immortalized. Perhaps they would change the name of his old school to Edward A. Mott Elementary. They did things like that when kids died. Or name a street after him. Or a cupcake. He could see his tearful mother saying to reporters, "Oh, how he used to love those cupcakes."

The mood lasted only as long as he looked out the window. Turning back to the room, he felt nothing but a black and immense loneliness. He turned the light back on.

He knew he needed help to make it through the night. He found it in a corner of his closet, in the old computer paper box that held his father's collection of Bugs Bunny comic books. He brought them out, he laid them on the bed, and for hours he giggled at Bugs and Yosemite Sam and Elmer Fudd, and he could not remember ever being so happy in his life.

24

"CHICKEN POX?" Salem shrieked. "I *can't* have chicken pox!"

"You can," her mother replied evenly, "and you do."

Salem looked again at her red-speckled stomach. She yanked down her pajama top. "Well that's too bad. I'm going to school." She got up from her bed.

Her mother stood directly in front of her. "Lie. . . . Down."

"Mom, I *have* to go to school."

"You're not going anywhere. You're sick. Lie down."

"Mom, this is the day I escort Willow Wembley."

"She'll have to manage without you."

Salem implored, "This is the biggest day of my entire *life*. My *career* is at stake."

"Your heinie's going to be at stake if you don't lie down."

Salem gaped unbelievingly into her mother's face and saw that she would never win. She threw herself onto the bed. With both hands she pounded her pillow. She rolled into a fetal position, clutching her pajamas and wailing in agony.

Eddie took unusual care in dressing and grooming himself that morning. It had occurred to him that if he were destined to be laid out in an emergency ward sometime after school, with doctors and nurses peeling off his clothes and searching for a pulse, well, he had better be presentable. So he took extra time brushing his teeth, dug out dirt from under his fingernails, rubbed his father's deodorant all over his body, and picked out his cleanest, newest underwear.

After breakfast he went upstairs to touch his old Daffy Duck pin for the last time. Back downstairs, he kissed both his mother and father — something he hadn't done in a long time — and left them gawking and speechless when he said, "You were the best mom and dad a kid could ever have." He then gave them what he hoped would be remembered as a brave little smile and departed.

Sunny and Pickles were on his doorstep. Pickles had a briefcase.

"What are you doing here?"

Pickles tapped the long green six-wheeler with

his green sneaker toe. "Figured you should go to school in style."

Just the way Pickles said it, and the way Sunny looked at him, Eddie knew he had been wrong. They *were* concerned, they *did* care. They just acted as if they didn't.

The three of them boarded the Picklebus and pushed off. Eddie glanced back at his front door. There was no note. He guessed that if he searched his fellow riders, he would find a crumpled piece of paper in one of their pockets.

As they rolled along toward school, he realized that even their arrangement on the board — Pickles in front, Sunny behind, himself in the middle — was no accident. He was the ham in a loving sandwich.

Thanks to the visit by Willow Wembley, every student at Plumstead got out of at least one class. There were three assemblies in the auditorium, for the eighth-, the seventh-, and finally the sixth-graders.

In the last period, the author also conducted a workshop for those especially interested in writing. After each session she autographed copies of her books, not to mention a few backs of hands and one plaster cast. She survived lunch in the cafeteria with the students, an interview with the editor of the school newspaper, and her sixth-grade escort — an awestruck, practically hysterical girl — who at one point ushered her into a broom closet.

Eddie drifted on the currents of the day. There was little sense of time or place, only a vague wandering as if in a liquid dream. Faces floated by like jellyfish.

One belonged to the famous visiting author, Willow Wembley. Eddie saw her once breezing by in the hallway, once at lunch, and of course on the auditorium stage. She dressed a lot like Salem, especially the long skirt. Eddie had expected gray hair, but hers was brown, again reminding him of Salem.

But she was different from Salem, too. She seemed very open and chummy, chatting and laughing and even horseplaying with the students. Except for her size, she would have made a pretty good sixth-grader. Salem, too, could be chummy and even goofy, but only her close friends saw that side of her. To most others, she often appeared more grown-up than kid. In the lunchroom someone gave Willow Wembley a FIGHTING HAMSTERS T-shirt. To the cheers of the students, she pulled it right on over her blouse.

From the moment Willow Wembley arrived that morning, there was an awareness of her presence throughout the school, a sense of something special, a constant buzz of excitement shared by students and teachers alike. There was also a second, competing buzz, this one sensed only by the students, felt as a tremor in the bones that dove-tailed by noon into the midsection, crept up the windpipe and, at precisely 2:35, the end of school, erupted from a hundred adolescent tongues:

"FIIIIIIIGHT!"

Eddie put all his books in his locker, plus his looseleaf and pencils. Everything. For once, no books to carry home. He hadn't bothered to write down his homework assignments. He closed his locker and spun the combination. They would have to saw it open.

He started down the hallway. Before he had taken five steps he was joined by several class-mates. Rounding the corner, he picked up more. By the time he reached the door, he was the eye of a swirling gale, calling:

"Get 'im, Eddie!"

"Show him the funky punch!"

"Go, Mott!"

Eddie heard them only as background static. While his legs carried him numbly forward, his mind ferried him back to playground days at Brockhurst, to birthday parties, and Saturday morning cartoons. Eddie was back at his favorite birthday party of all time, the one at Dumbo's with five of his friends, kicking off their shoes and diving into the fat, red, billowing, air-filled mat-tress and laughing and jumping and screaming and jumping. He found himself alone, the mob peeling away. And before him, arms folded, scowling, was Weasel Munshak.

In the first rank of the encircling crowd was Angelpuss, her mouth open, her eyes wide, her orange hair spike looking taller than ever, as if growing with excitement. Eddie did not see Pickles, or Sunny, or Salem. In fact, he hadn't seen Salem all day. Apparently she wanted no part of a gladiator on his day at the Colosseum.

Eddie wondered where he was, where had the mob led him. He looked around, but all he could see above the heads of the crowd was blue sky. When his eyes returned to earth, he found Weasel extending his arm, crooking his index finger, wagging it: Come on. Eddie just stood there, looking, blinking. Weasel wagged. Eddie stood.

Weasel stepped forward. Girls screamed. Boys laughed at the girls, some making mock, falsetto screams of their own.

Another step.

The crowd went bonkers. The gap was now five feet. Eddie could have taken one step and scratched Weasel's nose.

Another step . . . and above the bonkers, splitting it like a spiked shaft, a scream so dazzling that it froze every movement, every breath. Weasel's eyes shifted, his head turned. Eddie didn't have to turn. He was already looking at the right place, past Weasel's polka-dotted hairdo to Angelpuss, her mouth still open, the moussy glop of her orange spike firmly in the grip of Pickles' right hand. On the other side of her stood Sunny. Sunny's arms were raised. She held a pair of hedge clippers. The open blades of the clippers formed a V, with the orange spike between them.

In the cold stone silence, Pickles leaned in to Angelpuss's ear. He appeared to whisper something. He pulled away.

Angelpuss screeched. "Don't touch him!"

Pickles leaned in again to whisper. The clippers were poised between the top of Angelpuss's scalp and Pickles' hand.

"I was just messing around. To make you jealous!"

Pickles whispered.

"I don't like him! I never liked him! He's a jerk!"

Pickles whispered.

"A little twerp!"

Another whisper, longer this time.

"If you touch him they're gonna cut my hair off! They *will*! They'll do it! Don't *ever* touch him! Or they'll find me and do it!"

One last whisper.

"In my *sleep*!"

Weasel took a long time to turn back to Eddie. He looked him up and down. He gave a sneering grin and walked away.

25

When the bedside clock turned to 2:35, Salem groaned and scratched and buried her face in the pillow. "It's over . . . it's ooooover." All day long, hour by hour, she had been picturing what she would be doing had she been in school.

Every five minutes she had lifted her pajama top to check her stomach, hoping each time to find that a miracle had occurred, that the red dots were gone, and she would leap from bed and be at school in five minutes flat. Now, not even a miracle would help. The opportunity of a lifetime: gone, poof.

A mere week ago the future had been so bright with promise. Since then she had lost the story contest, missed a day with Willow Wembley, mistreated Eddie, alienated Sunny and Pickles, and caught the chicken pox. Could life get any worse? She had read that great literature often comes out of great tragedy. If that was true, well, Shakespeare better move over.

In the meantime she buried her face deeper in

the pillow and scratched and groaned some more. It was about a half hour later when she heard the doorbell ring. Her mother answered . . . voices . . . the door closing . . . footsteps on the stairs . . . one voice, a man's, familiar. ". . . heard she was absent . . ." Mr. Brimlow! Salem sat up, stuffed the pillow behind her, scratched. Wasn't that nice of him. He knew how devastated she was.

The door opened, her mother's face appeared. Her eyes were twinkling. "Salem, someone to see you."

Salem forced a smile, for her principal's sake. "Okay."

Her mother stepped aside for the visitor. It wasn't Mr. Brimlow. It was someone Salem had seen a thousand times on the dust covers of a dozen novels. *Willow Wembley!*"

Beaming as if greeting a long-lost daughter, Willow Wembley strode straight for the bed, hand extended. "Salem Brownmiller, I presume? The young author?"

Salem could not move except to repeat hoarsely, "Willow Wembley."

The great author laughed. "Don't wear it out." She grabbed Salem's hand and shook it. She sat on the bed, holding Salem's hand in both of hers, smiling in a way she never did on her dust covers. "I'm sorry I missed you today."

Salem blurted, "I have the chicken pox!" And

then she was sobbing against Willow Wembley's shoulder, wrapped in the author's arms.

"I know, I know. I remember when I had them. They just ruin one's life, don't they?"

Salem pulled back, amazed at the author's insight. "They *do!*"

"Yes, but only until Doctor Wembley shows up. Thanks to Mr. Brimlow. Aren't you glad you have a principal who cares so much?"

Mr. Brimlow grinned sheepishly and waved from the foot of the bed.

"Thank you, Mr. Brimlow."

Miss Wembley stood and looked around. "Left Bank, huh?" She nodded approvingly. "Well, I'm *wearing* my inspiration." She spread her jacket. "Like it?"

The elegant, the exquisite Willow Wembley was wearing a FIGHTING HAMSTERS T-shirt. Salem nodded, incredulous.

The author fished into her shoulder bag. "It should be here . . . somewhere . . . ah!" She pulled out a thin black ballpoint pen. "In my motel room last night, I wrote a couple pages of the next Klatterfield book, with this." She held out the pen. "Would you like to have it?"

Salem wanted to cry. "Oh, thank you." She cradled the pen lovingly in both hands, then was seized by an itching fit. Her frenzied scratching brought laughter from everyone, including herself.

"My mother put washcloths dipped in tea on me," said Willow Wembley. "Didn't stop the itch, but I got a great tan!"

Gales of laughter filled the room. In the lull that followed, Salem's voice came timidly. "Miss Wembley?"

The author turned to her the gentlest face she had ever seen. "Yes?"

"Miss Wembley, I just . . . I . . . can't believe you're really here. I mean, you're so busy writing books and all."

The author smiled. She stroked Salem's cheek. "Yes, writing is important, but people are more important." She lightly pressed the end of Salem's nose. "Don't you agree?"

Salem hesitated.

The doorbell rang. Mrs. Brownmiller hurried downstairs, and moments later Sunny, Pickles, and Eddie burst into the room.

Only now, seeing Eddie, did Salem realize how much she had feared for his safety. "You're okay," she marveled. "What happened?"

Her three friends laughed. Pickles patted a large briefcase he was carrying. "It's a long story."

"Put it this way," said Eddie, wincing, "I'll never do the funky pickle again."

Salem turned to Willow Wembley. "The answer," she said firmly, "is yes."

About the Author

Jerry Spinelli is the author of several novels, including *Fourth Grade Rats*, *The Library Card*, *Picklemania*, and the Newbery Medal–winning *Maniac Magee*. He lives in Phoenixville, Pennsylvania, with his wife and fellow author, Eileen Spinelli, and their children.

PICKLEMANIA

**Look for these other great books
by Jerry Spinelli**

Fourth Grade Rats
Report to the Principal's Office
Do the Funky Pickle
Who Ran My Underwear Up the Flagpole?
The Library Card

PICKLEMANIA

JERRY SPINELLI

SCHOLASTIC INC.

New York   Toronto   London   Auckland   Sydney
Mexico City   New Delhi   Hong Kong   Buenos Aires

ISBN 0-590-45447-1

Copyright © 1993 by Jerry Spinelli.
All rights reserved. Published by Scholastic Inc.
SCHOLASTIC, APPLE PAPERBACKS, and associated logos
are trademarks and/or registered trademarks of Scholastic Inc.

17 16 15 14 13 12 11 10 9 8 7 6   4 5 6 7 8 9/0

Printed in the U.S.A.   40

For Frank Hodge

PICKLEMANIA

1

The bus horn was going bonkers, the windchill felt like three hundred below, and forty-eight students were bored or freezing or both.

Oblivious to it all, the man in the white pants and long blue coat and funny three-pointed hat droned on and on: ". . . not enough coats for the whole regiment to drill at once, so while some would wear coats on the parade grounds, others were back at the fires. Even officers had to lead drills in their dressing robes. An infantry regiment consisted of five hundred and eighty-five individuals: four hundred and seventy-seven privates, twenty-seven corporals . . ."

The scene was Valley Forge National Park.

". . . twenty-seven sergeants . . ."

The occasion was a field trip for Miss Billups' two social studies classes.

". . . nine ensigns, eight lieutenants . . ."

The man in the white pants and funny hat was a park ranger, telling them all about the Continental Army's encampment at Valley Forge during the winter of 1777–78.

". . . eight drums, eight fifes . . ."

The honking horn came from the school bus. The driver, known only as Bobo, featured hairy ears and a stomach big enough to hold a full load of wash. He was pounding on the horn because park rules forbade him from keeping the motor on while parked, so he was cold. And because they were supposed to be finished by three o'clock and it was already three-thirty. And because he had to go to the bathroom.

". . . one drum major, one fife major . . ."

"One frozen sixth-grader," muttered Pickles Johnson.

Pickles' friend Eddie Mott giggled. His friend Sunny Wyler grumbled, "I'm so cold I have green icicles hanging from my nose."

Eddie let out a squawk. Classmates turned and giggled. The teacher glared. The ranger droned on: ". . . one quartermaster . . ."

"Quartermaster?" muttered Pickles. "Why didn't they have a whole one?"

This time Eddie shook silently with laughter, thereby momentarily warming himself.

". . . one adjutant, one surgeon, one surgeon's mate . . ."

Ten minutes and fifty horn honks later, the ranger's story came to a halt. He shouldered his

2

musket, looked over his audience, and said, "Any questions?"

Already half the kids had taken a step backward, edging for the bus. No one spoke until Salem Brownmiller raised her hand. "Yes, I have a question." Forty-seven students groaned. Salem looked up from her notebook, in which she had been writing the entire time. "You said one surgeon's mate?"

The ranger nodded. "That's right."

"You mean he was allowed to bring his wife to war?"

The ranger seemed stumped, then he smiled. "In this case 'mate' means assistant, not wife. It's military language."

Salem nodded. "I see." She made more notes. Her notebook was shaded by the wide brim of her floppy, black felt hat. She had seen a picture of her favorite author Willow Wembley wearing such a hat. Since Salem aspired to be a writer — in fact, considered herself already to be one — she was delighted to discover that she herself owned a similar hat; she had worn it only once, on Halloween. She kept it in her book bag and wore it to and from school and all the time at home, indoors and out. With her hat, black writing scarf, and ankle-length skirts, she got plenty of static from other students, but that didn't bother her. In fact, she kind of liked it. The way she figured, artists were supposed to be eccentric and non-conforming, and static from others was a badge that told you that you were doing it right.

When she finished writing, her hand shot up again. The students, by now leaning so severely toward the bus that they were practically horizontal, made mutinous noises. Sunny kicked Salem in the shin. Salem shot her a glance and asked her question. "You said earlier that one of the things they ate was bone soup. Could you give the recipe?"

The ranger blew warmth into his hands. "I'm afraid I don't know it. Maybe you can find it in your library at school."

Salem nodded and jotted; she spoke while writing. "I guess it's safe to say it starts with a bone."

"Yes," agreed the ranger. His lips were blue. His eyes were pleading, *Don't ask another question, please.*

Salem's hand began to rise once more, but it never got above her head. She found her arms pinned, herself wrapped in a bear hug by Sunny, whose voice hissed in her ear, "Say another word and you're dead."

Pickles seized the moment. "Everybody run for the bus!" he shouted, and forty-eight students stampeded for the parking lot.

2

Bobo saw them coming. The bus roared to life, the door swung open, the fans delivered cold air along the seats.

Salem Brownmiller and Miss Billups were the last aboard. The moment Miss Billups climbed onto the first step, the door snapped shut, nudging her in the backside and tipping her forward. The students laughed. Miss Billups stepped onto the platform, adjusted her glasses, and scowled at the driver. "I'll thank you to wait until I am *completely* inside before you close the door."

Bobo worked his cigar butt to one side of his mouth, growled, "You're welcome" out the other, and jerked the gearshift into reverse. The bus lurched backward, then forward — fast — with no letup as it careened out of the parking lot and onto Outer Line Drive. By now Miss Billups was sitting in Eddie Mott's lap, and the bus was rocking with laughter.

The teacher stood, spread her feet for balance,

grabbed the seat backs on either side, and declared with as much dignity as possible, "Mr. Bobo, you will be reported to the principal." She took a seat.

Bobo said nothing, only worked the cigar butt from side to side. The butt was cold. Out. Dead. Another rule: No smoking on the job. Well, how about a dead butt? That against the rules, too? Let 'em take him to the Supreme Court.

Most of the teachers at Plumstead Middle School hated Bobo. He was obnoxious, cantankerous, and grumpy. He drove recklessly and too fast, yet half the time he was late. He fought with the students and was always complaining. He was a slob. He shaved only once a week. The hair sprouting from his ears was long enough for a Weed Eater. And that brown, chewed on, masticated, smelly stump was forever sticking out of his face.

For the very same reasons, the students loved him. Some even walked across town every morning so they could be picked up along his route.

As the bus flashed past a row of cannon forever pointed toward the British redcoats in Philadelphia, a boy called from the rear, "Hey Bobo, you're going too fast!"

Others joined in:

"Yo Bobo, slow down!"

"Where's the fire?"

"Bobo!"

The students expected two things to happen: (1) The bus would go faster, and (2) Bobo would holler at them, probably tell them about all the mouths he had to feed, and if they were lucky maybe even lay one of his famous curses on them.

"Buh-buh-buh-buh-*Bobo*!"

Sure enough: (1) The bus speeded up, and (2) he hollered at them. "Shut up, back there! I'll slow down when you speed up. Look at this. It's almost four o'clock. I'm gonna be late for work. This ain't my only job, y'know. I got three mouths to feed. Four counting me. I got better things to do than driving you nosepickers around."

This only encouraged the kids to goad him on more.

"Hey Bobo, this air's cold coming outta here!"

"Hey Bo, you're going too slow!"

"Hey yo hobo Bobo!"

Bobo hung a sharp right and the bus squealed into the parking lot of Washington's Headquarters. Ignoring the area reserved for buses, he parked across seven automobile spaces and turned off the motor. He stood and faced the long rows of students. "May a squirrel the size of an elephant sit on your birthday cake," he said and left the bus.

The kids roared for a full minute. Bobo patterned his curses after the old *Tonight Show* with Johnny Carson. They seldom made any sense, but that only made the kids love them more.

When they finally stopped laughing, they began to wonder where he went. "Maybe he finally did it," said Eddie Mott. Everyone knew what he meant. Bobo was always threatening to walk off the bus and let the kids drive it, if they thought they were so hot.

"I don't think so," said Pickles. "I think he's going to the bathroom."

While Miss Billups cringed, the students debated: Were they abandoned for good, or just for a bathroom call?

3

A cheer erupted from the bus as Bobo was spotted coming out of the snack and souvenir shop. He climbed aboard and fired up the motor. The parking lot was confusing, with several entrances. He went out the one he thought he had come in, only to realize he was heading back the way they came.

"Hey Bobo," someone shouted, "you're going the wrong way!"

Bobo never admitted to a kid that he was wrong. "I'm taking a shortcut," he called and gunned the gas.

For the next ten minutes the yellow bus barreled about the park, zooming past soldiers' huts and cannon and markers and monuments. At one point the bus found itself atop Mount Misery ("Yo Bobo, what're we doing up here?"), with no place to go but back down.

As they approached the statue of Mad Anthony Wayne, Bobo coughed several times and pulled the bus to a stop. He opened the door and, never leaving the driver's seat, reared back, thrust forward, and sent a spitball out the door.

"Oh, gross!" forty students yelled as one.

Miss Billups looked faint.

Bobo closed the door and drove on. Suddenly Salem Brownmiller was at his side. "You should be ashamed," she told him.

"You should be in your seat," he said. "Go sit down."

"I will when you apologize."

"To who?"

Salem gazed at the rolling hills, bare and brown with grass as dead as the tobacco in Bobo's cigar butt. She pointed. "Them."

Bobo looked. "Huh?"

"The dead," said Salem. "The valiant men who died here so that the United States could be born. This is hallowed ground. This is the birthplace of a nation. They froze and got sick and ate bone soup and died for you, and you spit on them."

"I spit on the street."

"You spit on their memory. You spit on history."

"I'll spit on you if you don't sit down."

Salem tightened her lips; she took a long, loud breath through her nose. "Are you going to apologize?"

Bobo shifted the cigar butt till it pointed at the brown-haired sixth-grader. Then he removed it from his mouth and pronounced the word as though he were blowing a smoke ring: "No."

Salem glared at the bus driver. Her nostrils flared. "Then you may let me out."

"Go sit down," he said.

"You have insulted my country. I will not ride with you."

From her seat Miss Billups reached out to Salem's book bag. "You'd better sit down now, Salem."

Salem turned. "Miss Billups, he's against everything you've been teaching us. He has no respect. This" — she sneered in the driver's direction — "is the reason our country is in trouble."

Before Miss Billups could respond, the bus came to a sudden stop. Car brakes squealed behind. The door flew open. Bobo swept his arm toward the open door and said to Salem, "Have a nice walk. Hold onto your hat."

Shocked at first, Salem quickly recovered. She sniffed, lifted her head high, and walked off the bus.

"Salem!" screeched Miss Billups, but Pickles was already out the door. A half minute later he returned with Salem. With one hand around her wrist, he said to Bobo, "Say you're sorry."

The bus was silent. Miss Billups' eyes and mouth made a trio of ovals on her face. The look on Bobo's face, whatever it was, no one had ever seen before. For a full minute, as traffic backed up and cars honked and swerved past the bus in the middle of the road, Bobo never twitched, never took his eyes from the green-sneakered kid before him. Then, with no apparent movement on his part, the bus door closed with a gasp, and they were rolling again.

4

When the yellow bus finally left the students off at school, Salem, Sunny, Eddie, and Pickles climbed aboard the green one — the pickle-bus, Pickles' green, surfboard-size skateboard-for-four. As they coasted away from the school grounds, Pickles called back to Salem, "I feel a spit coming on. You want to get off and walk?"

"Funny," said Salem. "I can't believe all of you didn't protest with me. That man is a disgrace. He should be fired. If Miss Billups doesn't report him, I think I will."

"He's got three mouths to feed," said Pickles. "You want his kids to starve?"

Salem snorted. "Probably be doing his kids a favor. Then the Board of Health would take them away from him. They'd be better off in an orphanage. How would you like to have that beast as a father?"

"I wouldn't mind," said Sunny. "I think he's funny."

"He probably lets his kids do anything they want," said Eddie.

Pickles said, "You're just jealous, Salem. Because his ears are so hairy he doesn't even need earmuffs in the winter."

Everyone but Salem laughed.

The picklebus wobbled for half a block as the friends laughed and fought for balance.

"Well anyway," said Salem, still wanting to make her point, "it would be one thing if he was in a zoo. He belongs in a cage, not a house. I get the creeps just thinking about being married to him. I don't blame his wife for running away."

"Where is she now?" said Eddie.

"I heard she went to California," said Pickles.

"I heard she's a lady boxer somewhere," said Sunny.

"But really," said Pickles, "if she took off and left him with three mouths to feed, doesn't that make her worse than him?"

Everyone pondered the question as the six wheels hummed over the sidewalk.

Eddie was next to speak. "You know, I was just thinking. I never heard him call them kids. He always just calls them three mouths to feed."

Pickles pulled the bus to a sudden stop. He turned. He nodded. "Hey, you're right. Just mouths to feed. Has anybody ever seen the mouths?"

14

Three kids stared back at Pickles.

"Maybe they're three monkey mouths," said Sunny.

"Or goldfish," said Eddie.

"Whatever they are," said Salem, "I'll bet they're not human."

The picklebus rolled on.

Sunny said, "I think I'm gonna start wearing a mask when I ride this bus."

"Why?" said Eddie.

"So nobody will recognize me."

"Why do you want to do that?"

"So nobody'll know it's me riding on the same bus with a stupid hat."

Eddie and Pickles cracked up. Salem snipped, "Then maybe I'll wear a mask, too. I feel the same way about your abominable DEATH TO MUSH-ROOMS T-shirt."

"At least everybody wears a shirt," Sunny said.

"Maybe I don't wish to be everybody."

"Maybe you don't wish anybody to see your hair. Maybe it's turning green from mold."

"Maybe she has cooties!" Eddie laughed.

"Maybe someday you'll all be begging for my autograph," said Salem. "Maybe you'll be bragging to your children about how you used to be friends with the famous author Salem Jane Brownmiller. And how she used to wear a hat and you used to make fun of her. And how you grew up and amounted to nothing, and you'll wish to your dying day that you had been more like her."

"Goosepoop," said Sunny.

The picklebus rounded a corner. The green-sneakered driver called, "Uh-oh. Trouble ahead."

The three passengers leaned out to look.

5

"Tuh-Tuh-Tuh . . ." Eddie tried to speak but couldn't get far.

"Tuna Casseroli," said Pickles.

"You sure?" said Salem.

"Who else is that wide?" said Sunny.

The body with its back to them a half block ahead was indeed as wide as the sidewalk.

"Looks like he did it," said Pickles.

"He said he would," said Salem.

"What a jerk," said Sunny.

Tuna Casseroli had joined the nickelheads, which meant he had a nickelhead head: hair cut down to a fraction of an inch, with shaved, bald circles all over, a polka-dot effect. Despite the cold, he wore nothing above the waist but a sleeveless T-shirt. Huge red letters spelled the word TUNA across the front and back.

At first it seemed that Tuna was alone. Then he veered to walk along the curb and three other nickelheads appeared; they had been obscured by his bulk.

"Maybe you should turn off," said Eddie.

"Too late," said Pickles.

The first rule of Eddie's life since arriving in middle school was Beware of Nickelheads. The second rule, dating from the time the mammoth eighth-grader dangled him upside down by his ankles, was Beware of Tuna Casseroli. Now that rules one and two had merged, Eddie felt like a fly in Spider Web City.

One of the nickelheads turned. "Hey, Tuna," he called, "look who's coming."

Tuna turned and stopped. He smiled. His cheeks puffed up like two small bellies. "Well, well." He stepped back into the middle of the sidewalk.

The picklebus came to a halt. Four sixth-graders, four grinning nickelheads.

"Howdy," said Tuna. He strolled around the picklebus, took his time doing it. "Nice board you got there. Sure wish I had one."

"Save your pennies," said Pickles.

Tuna stopped strolling and smiling. The other nickelheads circled the bus. Tuna stared at Pickles. He wasn't used to kids staring back at him, but then Pickles Johnson wasn't an ordinary kid. The nickelheads had never been able to scare Pickles, or catch him, or figure him out. And that made them a little unsure of how to deal with him.

But Pickles was not the only passenger who was not afraid of Tuna. "Outta the way, lardbutt," growled Sunny.

This gave Tuna an excuse to forfeit the staring duel to Pickles. He cranked up his grin. "Say please."

Sunny leaned forward and made a pleading face. "Please . . . drop dead."

Tuna laughed. Beneath his shirt, his body shook like a huge, water-filled balloon. He held out his bare arms. "Hey, what's the matter with you wimps?" He reached behind Pickles to where Eddie was trying unsuccessfully to vanish. He felt the thickness of Eddie's winter jacket. "Can't you take a little cold?"

"We don't have all that blubber to protect us," said Sunny.

Tuna smiled like a crocodile. He pointed to Sunny. "If you weren't a girl, I might have to drop you on your head to teach you a lesson."

"If you weren't so ugly," said Sunny, "maybe the zookeeper would stop feeding you."

Pickles laughed first. Then Tuna, then the rest of the nickelheads. While he was laughing, it occurred to Tuna that he had come to the end of the line with this group. He had several choices. He could continue to stand here and let this snot-nosed girl work him over (no); he could hit somebody (tempting, but no); or he could get himself gracefully out of this (okay, but how?).

As if in answer to the question, his eyes directed him to the other girl, the one who kept her mouth shut, the one wearing . . . He snatched the black floppy hat from her head, yelled, "Hiyo, nickelheads!" and took off.

For a two-hundred-and-forty-pounder, Tuna Casseroli could move. Before Salem was finished shrieking, "Give me my hat, you bully!" the nickelheads were turning the corner at the end of the block. Also, a fully loaded picklebus was slow to get going.

By the time Pickles had the nickelheads in view, they were racing and hooting past the storefronts of Winter Street. Suddenly, Tuna stopped, looked back, waved the hat grandly in the air, and flipped it over his head. It disappeared onto the roof of a one-story building as the nickelheads went on their way.

Sunny jumped off the bus and ran into the building. In less than a minute, she appeared on the roof. She tossed the hat down to Salem.

When Sunny returned, an obviously relieved Salem said, "I thought you didn't like this hat."

"I don't," said Sunny. "I hate the hat."

"So why did you save it?"

"Because for some stupid reason, you like it. I'm allowed to hate it." She sneered in the direction Tuna had departed. "He's not."

Salem got teary. "Nobody ever had a better best friend." And then she was hugging Sunny.

Sunny put up with it for a few seconds, then said, "Enough already," and disengaged herself. She spoke to all of them. "Did you see what this place is?" She pointed to the large front window. The sign painted across it said KUNG FU ACADEMY. Inside, kids and grown-ups, boys and girls alike in pajamalike white outfits and bare feet, were doing a variety of stylized arm and leg movements.

"I'm going back in," Sunny said and went inside.

6

When Sunny came out, she had a brochure telling all about the Kung Fu Academy. "I'm going to join up," she announced. "I'm taking lessons. I'll be our bodyguard. Nobody'll mess with us then."

No one tried to talk her out of it. Even Salem, who abhorred violence, kept her objections to herself. Everyone recognized that Sunny Wyler and kung fu were a perfect match.

It was dark by the time Pickles dropped off Sunny, then Salem. "Why don't you eat with us," Pickles said to Eddie. "You can call your parents from my house."

That's what they did.

After dinner, they were talking in Pickles' room.

Pickles said, "You going to put a Love Line in *The Wurple*?"

"Nah. You?"

"Not me."

The Wurple was the Plumstead Middle School newspaper. Its name was a blending of the school colors: white and purple. For its Valentine's Day edition, *The Wurple* was devoting a whole page to "Love Lines," one line per customer, for the students to publish their valentine greetings.

"Aren't you going to do one for Sunny?" said Pickles. Eddie had fallen in love with Sunny on the first day of school.

"Nope," said Eddie. "I gave up on her." He went to the window. "Anyway, I don't even deserve her."

"What do you mean? What's bothering you?"

Eddie turned. "What's bothering me? I'll show you what's bothering me." He strode over to Pickles. He rolled up his sleeve and thrust out his arm. "*This* is what's bothering me."

Pickles inspected the arm. "What's the matter with it?"

Eddie pulled it away and rolled his sleeve down. "It's scrawny, that's what's the matter."

"So?"

Eddie screeched, "*See?* You know it. It *is* scrawny!"

"You're the one who said it."

"You agreed!"

Pickles sighed. He sat down beside Eddie. "What's the problem?"

"The problem," Eddie whined, "is I'm too little. I try and I try to be a regular sixth-grader, 'cause

I'm not in grade school anymore. I tell myself over and over" — he punched the mattress — "you're in middle school now, you're in middle school now, but . . . but . . . I still look like I'm in first grade!" His voice was quivering, his eyes watery.

Pickles laid a hand on Eddie's knee. He chuckled. "Take my word for it, you don't look like first grade."

"Well," Eddie sniffed, "fourth grade." He thrust his face into Pickles'. "And that's no kidding. I know fourth-graders who are bigger than me."

Pickles flapped his hand. "Ah, that's no big deal. I'll bet most of them are girls. A lot of girls are taller than boys at our age."

"It's not just taller." Eddie yanked up his sleeve again, then the other sleeve. Then he pulled his pants up over his knees. He pulled his shirttail to his shoulders. "It's scrawny. I'm the scrawniest, skinniest, shrimpiest, runtiest kid in all of Plumstead Middle School." He jutted his jaw. "And you know it."

The sight before him — his best friend looking like something from a 1920s' bathing beach — sent Pickles into gales of laughter. Each time he tried to stop, he took another look and had to laugh some more. And the dead serious look on Eddie's face didn't help any. Finally, fearing a hernia, Pickles reached out and pulled down Eddie's shirt, pant legs, and sleeves. He then flopped onto his back to recuperate, like a distance runner after a race.

Eddie sat on the bed. "I gotta bulk up."

"Why don't you just wait," said Pickles. "You're only eleven. You have seven more years to grow."

"Seven more years for Tuna Casseroli to hang me upside down. Seven more years of torture from the nickelheads. I'll be dead!"

"Well," said Pickles, "you still can't do it overnight. You could eat ten times a day for a year and not get as big as Tuna's left leg."

Eddie held out pleading hands. "All I want right now is to weigh ninety pounds. That's my dream in life."

Pickles sat up, studied his pal. "Stand up." Eddie stood. "You don't weigh ninety?"

"Not even close."

"You're not the shortest kid in school."

"I *told* you, I'm not talking short, I'm talking scrawny. Bony." He held out his wrist. "Put your hand around there." Pickles curled his fingers around Eddie's wrist. They could have almost gone around twice.

Eddie pulled his wrist away. "See? I take after my mother. I have the world's littlest bones. The only difference between me and a skeleton is skin."

Pickles was in thought. "You say you'd like to weigh ninety?"

"Right now I'd be happy with eighty."

"How about a hundred?"

"Huh?"

"Would you feel good if you looked down at a scale and it said one hundred pounds?"

"It ain't gonna — "

"Just *would* you?"

Eddie shrugged. "Yeah. Sure."

Pickles popped up and dragged Eddie to his closet. He began pulling out clothes and putting them on Eddie. A sweatshirt. A sweater. A winter jacket. Another jacket. Two pair of pants. Boots (after pulling off Eddie's sneakers). And hats, five of them stacked atop one another.

Pickles looked around. "You bring a book bag?"

"No."

Pickles got his, dumped more books into it, and hung it over Eddie's shoulder. He then led Eddie into the bathroom. With the green toe of his sneaker, he pushed the scale out from under the sink. "Okay, climb on."

Eddie got on. The pointer moved past 70 . . . past 80 . . . 90 . . . and stopped at 92.

Pickles ordered, "Don't move," and rushed off. In seconds he was back with a typewriter, an old black Underwood. "My mother's," he said. "Hold out your arms." He placed the typewriter in Eddie's arms. Eddie's knees buckled, but he held on. Pickles crouched like a spotter in a weight room. The pointer shot past 100. Eddie pushed out the typewriter so he could see.

"One hundred and four pounds," Pickles announced. "How's it feel?"

Eddie gave Pickles a disgusted look. He handed back the typewriter and stepped off the scale. "It feels stupid. How dumb do you think I am?"

"Just thought I'd try a little psychology. Guess it didn't work."

Pickles left with the typewriter. When he returned, he said, "We'll start bulking you up tomorrow. In the meantime" — there was a sly grin on his lips, a gleam in his eyes — "are you ready to see something in the basement?"

Eddie was puzzled at first, then his eyes widened. "It's done?"

"Almost."

"You're gonna let me see it?"

"You'll be the first."

Thoughts of pounds vanished as Eddie clapped, "All *right*!" and the two of them raced downstairs.

7

Eddie spun in the middle of the basement. "Where?"

Pickles pointed to a corner in the back. "There." A long, low something was hidden under an olive green tarpaulin.

Eddie approached with the reverence of a kid discovering his first whisker. He stood before the tarp.

"Take it off," said Pickles.

Eddie gave a tug, and the tarp slid to the floor. Eddie gasped. He could not speak.

Pickles came up behind him. "What do you think?"

Eddie wagged his head. "Wow."

"All I have to do is paint on the name."

"What's that?"

"Pickleboggan."

It was unlike anything the world had seen. Part sled, part boat, part bus, part pure Pickles. No fewer than six sleds, modified and wired together, formed the deck. From the deck rose plywood walls two feet high. In the stern was a coxswain's perch and a homemade pennant showing a pickle schussing downhill on skis; in the bow, a tiller for steering and a motorcycle headlight. The runners were painted silver; the rest, of course, was green.

Eddie said, "Did Sunny and Salem see it yet?"

"You're the first."

"The first kid?"

"The first human."

Eddie wanted to weep at the honor of it. "Wait till they see."

"Yeah," said Pickles. "But it's not for seeing, it's for sledding."

Eddie smiled wistfully. "I was just picturing us going down Heller's. The four of us."

"A green flash."

"I'll bet this baby could do fifty."

"Sixty if the snow's got some ice on it."

They stared at the great, green snow cruiser, each conjuring up a picture of Heller's Hill, the best sledding hill in town, maybe in the world. It had the two chief requirements of a Class A hill: It was both steep and long. A mile long, some said. They saw themselves ripping down the roller coaster slope, vaporizing snow, firing ice to diamonds, screaming, screaming, then, at Mach 1, a sudden silence, outracing their own voices, sledding into history. . . .

"You dream of weighing ninety," said Pickles. "I dream of snow."

Eddie nodded sadly. "Is it possible to have a winter without snow?"

There was no answer. And there was no snow on Heller's Hill. This had been the great tragedy of the winter. Here they were, in the beginning of February, and not so much as a single flake had fallen to earth. No snow days off. No snowballs. No sledding.

The tarp crackled like bottled thunder as Pickles shook it out and drew it over the sled. "I'm making a solemn vow right now — until it snows, nobody else will lay eyes on this thing. I swear."

8

Next day was Saturday. In February it had another name: Mallday.

The four friends, flush with allowances and advances, were dumped off by Sunny's mother at the entrance to Kingswood Mall. Before they went inside, Pickles looked up at the sky. He shielded his eyes from the sun. "Not a cloud in sight." He held his jacket open. "Not even cold."

Eddie pointed to the time and temperature display above the entrance. "Look."

The temperature was 56 degrees Fahrenheit.

Eddie grumped, "It's never going to snow."

Sunny said, "Maybe winter's over. That was it."

They went inside.

Salem asked Pickles, "Is your super-duper secret sled ready yet?"

"Almost. Just have to paint the name on."

"What's that?"

"You'll see."

"Will it hold all four of us?"

"Four of us?" blurted Eddie. "It'll hold half the school!"

The two girls stopped walking and stared at Pickles, who glared at Eddie, who winced and went, "Oops."

"He saw it," said Sunny.

"You said nobody could see it till it was finished," said Salem.

"I just gave him a peek," said Pickles. "It was a special case."

"So we're not special?"

Pickles rolled his eyes. "He was feeling bad bad about something, so I just did it to cheer him up."

"I feel bad about something, too," said Sunny. "How about cheering me up?"

Pickles shook his head. "No more peeks. Until it snows. I took a vow. I'm not even going to look at it myself."

Sunny stepped up to Pickles; she poked him in the chest. "Well, I've got news for you, buster. Whenever it does snow, don't come around for me. You couldn't *beg* me to look at that thing. You couldn't force me if you drove up in a tank. I'll sew my eyes shut first. I'll nail a football helmet to my face backwards." She started to pull Salem away. "Come on."

Salem resisted. "Wait a minute. Eddie, why were you feeling bad?"

Salem loved to hear about other people's problems and feelings. As a practicing author, she viewed all of humankind as a great research library from which she would gather material for the novels in her future. She thus felt entitled to know everyone's business, kind of like a psychiatrist or doctor.

Eddie, on his part, found it almost impossible to keep his business to himself. He was a terrible liar and a hopeless denier. His timid resistance was no match for such a stern and relentless interrogator as Salem Brownmiller.

Pickles knew this, of course, and attempted to drag Eddie off.

"Eddie, tell me," said Salem, herself tugged in the opposite direction by Sunny.

Even as he was being dragged away, Eddie's head tilted toward Salem as though she had him lassoed.

"Eddie," she repeated, locking onto his eyes, freezing them.

Eddie spoke as if to a hypnotist. "I'm too scrawny. I gotta bulk up."

Sunny cackled in full voice: "He wants to be a *hunk*!"

All around them mall walkers turned and stared and tittered.

Pickles growled at Eddie, "You satisfied, flush-mouth?" and dragged him away.

9

As they walked off in the opposite direction from the guys, Salem said to Sunny, "So, what are *you* feeling bad about?"

Sunny bristled. "Hey, don't try that stuff here. Maybe it works on the hunk, but not me."

"Who's trying stuff? I'm asking a question, that's all."

"Why?"

"Because I'm interested."

"Interested in writing a book."

"I'm interested in you."

"Sure."

Salem stopped and stomped her foot. "I *am*. You saved my hat." She pulled off her hat and wagged it in Sunny's face. "I *care*."

Sunny resumed walking. Her jaw kept its hard set, but her eyes softened. "I'm not allowed to join the Kung Fu Academy."

"Oh," said Salem, "I'm sorry."

Sunny sneered, "No, you're not." Salem just

stared. "You don't want me to join either, and you know it."

"I didn't say that."

"You're just like my mother. You think everything's violence. You think stabbing a lima bean with a fork is violence. You don't think people should learn to defend themselves. You think if somebody comes up and smacks me, I'm supposed to say" — she fluttered her fingertips and made her voice mincy — " 'Oh thank you, that was nice. Here's my other cheek, do it again. Make it a good one this time.' "

Salem clenched her teeth to keep a straight face. "It's not a laughing matter."

"Who says it is? Do I look like I'm laughing? All I'm saying is" — she poked Salem in the chest — "I don't care what she says. I'm doing it."

"You can't."

"Watch me."

Sunny marched off.

"Where are you going?"

"What do you care?"

Salem groaned and watched her incorrigible friend disappear into Sears. She was about to follow when her eye was caught by a display in Thrift Drug. The entire window to the right of the door was filled with hearts: heart-shaped boxes of valentine candy. They ranged from simple little $3.95 cardboard boxes with four chocolates to a huge lace-and-satin-covered wonder with a fat lavender bow and a $39.95 price tag.

Was there a heart-shaped candy box in her future? Salem wondered. At the moment, she would have been quite happy — thrilled, in fact — with the $3.95 version. Heck, she'd settle for a love line in *The Wurple*'s soon-to-be published Valentine's Day edition. Was some secret admirer even now, pencil in hand, composing his love line to her? Miss O'Malley was *The Wurple*'s faculty adviser. In her classroom sat the red-papered box with a slit in top for depositing love lines. The box had already been filled and emptied once. There was a lot of love out there.

Salem pulled herself away and entered Sears. She found Sunny in, of all places, men's wear, looking through the pajamas.

"Present for your father?" said Salem.

"No."

"Who?"

"Me."

Sunny looked at every pair on the counter. "No white."

"Pajamas don't usually come in white," said Salem. "Especially men's. And why are you looking for men's pajamas anyway?"

Sunny didn't answer. She went back through the small sizes, intensely inspecting each plastic-wrapped package. She pulled out a pair of plain, collarless pajamas the color of tea with milk in it.

The tag said BEIGE. She held it up to Salem. "What do you think?"

"*Think?*" Salem squeaked. "How am I supposed to know *what* to think? I don't even know what you're *doing!*"

"My, my," said Sunny. She touched Salem's nose with her fingertip and jerked it away as if the nose were hot. "Touchy, aren't we?" She walked off.

She led Salem through men's clothing, through women's clothing, and was heading into the dressing room when Salem stopped her. "Where are you going?"

"Where's it look like?"

"You don't try on pajamas in the store."

"That so?"

"And you especially don't try on men's pajamas in the women's dressing room."

"Really?"

Sunny marched down to the last stall on the right, stepped in, and closed the curtain. Salem remained firmly at the entrance. She would not involve herself in this nonsense any further.

After a minute or so, Sunny's voice drifted out: "Salem, come here."

Salem folded her arms. "No."

"*Salem!*"

Salem went. When she opened the curtain, she found Sunny wearing the pajamas; her socks, sneakers, and jeans were piled on the floor. Sunny assumed what she believed to be a martial-arts stance: torso turned over widely spread legs, elbows high and crooked, hands flat, scissorlike. "What do you think?"

"I think they're too big."

"They're supposed to be big. Roomy. So you're free to move — like lightning." Sunny flashed her scissory hands.

"If you're not allowed to join the academy," Salem said, "what's the point?"

"The point is, I'll be my own academy. I'll teach myself." Over Salem's objections, she untied Salem's black writing scarf and tied it around her waist. "See? I'm a black belt already." She assumed a chopping stance over an imaginary board; she reared back; she drove the edge of her hand down mightily: "Hai-YAH!" The imaginary board fell to the floor in two imaginary pieces.

That's when they heard the giggle.

10

They looked at the curtain. Nothing. Then they looked under the curtain, in the twelve inches of space between its bottom edge and the floor. The sideways face of a little boy grinned up at them. Also showing beneath the curtain was a hand, clutching a braided, half-eaten licorice stick; his grinning teeth were black from it.

All of this registered in the girls' minds in a second or two. In less time than that, like a lizard, the black-toothed grinner darted under the curtain on his belly, snatched Sunny's jeans with his own "Hai-YAH!," and took off.

Sunny lit out after him. "You're in pajamas!" Salem called, as if anyone ever listened to her. By the time she emerged from the dressing room, the boy was racing through lingerie and underwear, display trees of bikinis wobbling and wiggling in his wake. Alarmed shoppers were swinging their heads to his shouts of "Hai-YAH! . . . Hai-YAH!" Those who continued to stare saw a black-haired

40

girl in hot pursuit and men's pajamas, yelling, "You're dead! . . . You're horsemeat!"

Salem wanted to race after them, but her dignity forbade it. She set off at a fast walk, following their shrieking voices and the shoppers' turning heads. She made a point of looking at the merchandise as she passed, lest anyone think she was associated with the two stampeding delinquents. When she heard the volume of their voices abruptly bloom, she knew they had burst from Sears into the open mall.

Sunny chased the thief past Fluf 'N Stuf, Woolworth, Foot Locker, store after store, hips slamming from side to side to avoid the oncoming shoppers. The kid was small as a squirrel and just as shifty, quick as a fly. She thought she had him at Hickory Farms, where the little fleabrain slowed down to snatch a free sample of bratwurst (how appropriate!); but when she reached out for him, all she came away with was a fistful of sticky black licorice.

On through the food court — Mexican Delite, Pita Pockets, La Roma Pizza — sodas spilling, trays clattering, the kid yelling, "Hai-YAH!," the voice of the mall intercom intoning over the tumult: "Code Ten food court . . . Code Ten food court."

Out of the food court, around the soft pretzel kiosk, up the down escalator, down the up escalator, Shirts Plus, Shazzam Comics, Gold Medal

41

Sporting Goods, on toward the other end of the mall, where the pool in front of Penney's geysered skyward in the middle like a water fountain for a giant. The kid never hesitated, never flinched for an instant, but dashed straight into the pool. (Something far below Sunny's thoughts took notice and registered a kindred approval.)

As Sunny slowly circled the pool, like a stalking lion, the kid kept the geyser between himself and her. He held her jeans above his head and so far had not allowed them to get wet. His antic mischief had given way to a casual smugness, the confidence that comes to a little kid who has gone where anyone older or bigger dare not follow. He did not know Sunny Wyler.

Seeing that the kid was not about to come out on his own, Sunny waded in after him. The kid seemed both terrified and delighted at once. He screamed. He reared back and flung her jeans high; they landed upon the roiling peak of the geyser and, for a good five seconds, as the gathering audience whistled and clapped, the pants did a funky, disembodied dance before joining the rain in its fall to the pool.

Sunny and the kid circled the geyser, and suddenly there were two new boys splashing into the pool, yelling and laughing and smacking small floods of water at her and the first kid and each other. The crowd was going wild, pennies were copperraining into the water, the mall intercom was repeating: "Code Ten Penney's fountain . . . Code Ten Penney's fountain." And outlouding everything was a booming voice, a familiar voice: "Get outta there, you nosepickers! You got five seconds!"

Salem arrived in time to join Pickles and Eddie in the applauding, pennypitching crowd. "You hear that?" she said. The three of them turned to see first a stomach, then a man with hairy ears emerge from the crowd and step to the edge of the pool. He spiked a stiff finger to the floor. "Now!"

Eddie gasped, "Bobo!"

"The three mouths to feed," said Salem.

Pickles chuckled in wonder. "They *are* monkeys."

11

It had been a day of adventure for Salem, a day to nourish a young writer. New vistas of human behavior had been revealed to her. It amazed her that Sunny could be her best friend and yet repeatedly surprise her.

The security people had shown up while the three monkeys, ignoring their father's blustering orders, filled their pockets with pool pennies. They, along with Sunny, were herded off to security headquarters by four semi-police-looking guys.

Bobo kept ranting at his kids, saying he was going to let them rot in jail. Salem, Pickles, and Eddie followed in their wet tracks. For a joke, Pickles suggested to one of the guards that he'd better handcuff Sunny. Eddie just gawked in wonder. This was the closest he had ever been to crime.

Bobo was allowed to follow into the security office. Friends of the perpetrators had to wait outside. The door was shut. Noting that the Book Bin was across the way, Salem went over to browse, and who did she meet but Miss Billups.

"Well, well," said the teacher, "I was just thinking of you. I just picked this up." It was a paperback titled *Valley Forge: A Soldier's Diary*. She held it out. "Would you like it?"

Salem gasped, "For me?"

"It's too seldom I get a student as interested in history as you are." She clawed Salem's shoulder playfully. "I want to keep you in my clutches. Besides" — she lowered her voice to a whisper — "I got it off the dollar ninety-five table."

Salem was overcome. She hugged her teacher.

Miss Billups was carrying a handled shopping bag. Salem could not help noticing one of the items inside: a heart-shaped candy box. "Sending that to your secret valentine?" she said kiddingly.

Miss Billups did not react at first, then she laughed. "Yes, my little nephew. He's my cutie."

"To tell you the truth," said Salem, "I think I'd even settle for a valentine from a relative." Then she remembered the dinky little scrap she received in second grade from her cousin Harold. It showed a cowboy lassoing a horsy-looking heart. She found out later that Aunt Helen had made Harold do it. "Wait a minute," she said, "I take that back." She and Miss Billups shared a big laugh.

Then Sunny and the guys had shown up. The

mall people had lent Sunny a gray sweatsuit, which she had to return. The four of them went back to Sears to fetch Sunny's shoes and socks, Salem took back her writing scarf, Sunny's mother came to get them, and at last it was over.

And now, well into Saturday night, a new adventure occupied Salem. As she lay on her bed reading *A Soldier's Diary*, she was transported back to the terrible winter of 1777–78 and the life of a nineteen-year-old private named Patrick Wister. She shivered with him in the merciless cold. She hungered with him as he boiled bone and scraps for soup. She suffered with him through the fever and celebrated with him when General Washington rationed a few ounces of grog to the troops for Christmas.

But most of all she shared Patrick's longing as he wrote loving letters to his fiancé Abigail Norton in Portsmouth, Virginia. She feared his fears and wondered his wonderings. From the *Diary*'s first page to the last, Patrick received not one letter in return from Abigail. Why? Had his letters not reached her? Was she angry? Ill? Wounded? Worse? Did she still love him? "A hundred times a day," he wrote, "I cry out in silence to the gray sky above, Do you yet wait for me?"

And each time she read it, Salem cried out (not so silently), "Yes, Patrick, I am here! I will wait for you forever!" She read, wept, cried out, read, wept, cried out. She composed a letter, with her

46

father's fountain pen, pledging her love and reassuring him and begging him to return home safely to her.

She felt the cruel emptiness of uncompleted history, as the afterword informed her that the diary was the sole trace on earth left by Patrick Wister; nothing was known of either him or Abigail Norton from that winter onward.

Well after midnight Salem lay down to sleep on the floor. Thinking of Patrick on his hard planked bunk, how could she do any less?

As often happened when the lights went out, Salem's imagination came on. She imagined a ghost story. It was the day *The Wurple*'s Valentine's Day edition came out. As Salem read the "Love Lines" page, she saw something that at first stopped her heart, then sent it wildly pounding:

"SB. I'll love you forever. PW."

12

The picklebus was in the basement for repairs Monday morning, so the picklekids caught the school bus at Eddie's corner. It had been over a month since they had taken the yellow one, and they were surprised to discover a new driver.

"Bobo!" declared Pickles as he climbed aboard. "This isn't your route, is it?"

"No," growled Bobo through his mutilated cigar butt, "it's my grandmother's."

"Eddie and I have to raise the flag, you know. We can't be late."

"I'll write ya a note," snarled Bobo. "Sit down." The kids sat down.

"So," said Salem perkily, "who wants to camp out with me?"

She got stares but no takers.

"What's this?" said Pickles. "You're not exactly the camp-out type."

"Yeah," snickered Sunny, "if you'll remember."

On a weekend in October, Sunny's family had

48

taken Salem along to a campground. Salem was so jumpy at night that she wouldn't calm down until she was allowed to squeeze into Sunny's sleeping bag. Even then, she kept flinching at every little noise and imagined that assorted nocturnal rodents were keeping company in the bag with them. "Never again," a sleepless Sunny had vowed when they got home.

Salem flicked her hand. "Oh, that was different. I wasn't motivated. This is history. We'll do it just like Valley Forge."

"You going to build a hut?" said Eddie. He popped several peanuts into his mouth.

"Well, no, not exactly. But we can have a tent. Sunny has tents. And we'll make a fire and bone soup and write diaries and do all the things they did."

"Like freeze," said Pickles.

"Not if it stays like this. We're having a heat wave."

Pickles moaned, "You got that right."

"My mother said the temperature's going over sixty today," Eddie reported, popping more peanuts.

Pickles shook his head forlornly. "George Washington got the winter we wanted."

They looked out the bus windows. All four longed for snow. Only three wanted it for sledding.

"We won't do it till it turns cold again," said

Salem. "We want it as much like the winter of 1778 as possible. We have to suffer at least a little."

Sunny scowled. "You suffer in the tent, I'll suffer in my bed at home."

Eddie yelped, "Hey!" and pointed out the window. "It's Raymond Hall!"

The four of them scooted to the back window. Raymond Hall, a sixth-grade classmate, was racing after the bus, cheeks puffing, book bag flying. He was falling farther behind with every step.

Pickles called up the aisle, "Bobo, you didn't stop for Raymond Hall."

"Wasn't nobody there," growled Bobo. "You ain't there, the bus don't stop. This ain't a taxi."

Fortunately, the next corner was a route stop, with five kids waiting. By the time the last one got on, Raymond Hall had caught up. He staggered aboard and collapsed on the front seat.

Sunny held out her hand to Eddie. "Gimme some peanuts."

Eddie gave her one.

Sunny's eyes widened. "Wow, can you spare it?"

"It's bulk-up food," said Pickles. "We designed a diet for him."

"Peanuts for a peanut, huh?"

A laugh escaped from Salem before she caught herself.

"Well," drawled Sunny, "I got news for ya. He's never gonna be big enough to do this." She placed the peanut on the seat back in front of her. She stood. She flattened her hand. Three times she swung the edge of her hand down to within a hair's width of the peanut, each time drawing in a long, whistling breath. Then, suddenly, a mighty chop and a "Hai-YAH!" The peanut was dust.

The bus stopped. Several sixth-graders got on, then a big kid. A *real* big kid. Only it wasn't a kid.

"Miss Billups!" cried Salem.

The teacher came down the aisle and took a seat in front of them. "What are you doing here?" said Salem.

"Did your car break?" said Eddie.

"Break *down*, halfahunk," said Sunny.

The teacher turned in her seat to face them. "No, my car's fine." She glanced toward the front of the bus; she spoke in a whisper. "I'm doing undercover work. The principal has asked me to ride the bus for a week to monitor the bus driver and report back to him. That man is a menace to the school and the community, and he would have been fired a long time ago, except we don't have enough bus drivers as it is. And then he's got those three little mouths to feed."

"Hah!" exclaimed Sunny. "Somebody ought to feed *them* to the boa constrictor in the pet store."

Suddenly horns were blaring all around, brakes were screeching. The kids looked out. Pickles called: "Hey, Bobo, this is a one-way street!"

Someone screamed: "We're all gonna die!"

Half the bus screamed. Bobo yelled, "Shaddap, nosepickers, or I'll dump ya all off here!" The bus careened through a right turn, jumped a curb, sent thirty-nine students and one teacher bouncing off their seats, and went roaring down the narrowest street the passengers had ever seen.

Pickles called: "Yo, Bobo, this is an *alley*!"

"Shortcut," answered Bobo.

Garages and backyards went by. The right bumper caught a carelessly placed metal trash can and sent it flying with a racket like New Year's Eve.

Miss Billups had taken out a spiral notebook and was writing it all down. She kept muttering, "A menace . . . a menace . . ."

Another jumped curb and the bus was back on a street.

"Yo, Bobo," called Pickles, "this isn't our route. You're going the wrong way. You're missing people."

No reply came from the driver's seat. The bus went up one street, down another. It zoomed past students frantically waving on corners. At one point it looped through another township. Other school buses passed. They were empty.

"We're late!" someone screamed.

Sixth-graders began to groan and cry; eighth-graders pounded the walls and shouted, "All *riiiight!*"

By the time the bus pulled into the school driveway, Mr. Brimlow, the principal, was waiting. He placed himself at the bus door as it opened and announced, "Sir" — a busful of ears perked up at the absurdity of calling Bobo sir — "you shall report to Late Room at two thirty-five. The rest of you are excused to first class."

The bus emptied in seconds to a chorus of cheers. Left outside were one principal sternly staring, one teacher closing a notebook, and one bus driver chewing slyly on a cigar stump and closing the door.

13

Eddie burped.
Twice in math. Four times in social studies. A record seven times in music. In English, only once, but that one outdid the other thirteen combined.

It happened while he was standing and reciting lines from "The Raven" by Edgar Allan Poe, as directed by Miss O'Malley. When he came to the line, "Quoth the Raven, 'Nevermore,' " it came out:

"Quoth the Raven, *Brrraaaaawwgh!*"

It took Miss O'Malley ten minutes to settle down the class. It took her two seconds to say, "Detention Room after school, Edward Mott."

Salem heard none of this. *The Wurple* had just been distributed, and she could not help losing herself in the "Love Lines" section while sitting in class. So many students had submitted valen-

54

tines that "Love Lines" had been expanded to two full pages.

There were dozens and dozens of messages from sixth-, seventh-, and eighth-graders. Some carried full names, some initials, some code names:

"Steph, I love you. Ron."

"RT, I am yours. JY."

"Bumble, Bee my honey. Daisy."

As the bell rang to end the period, a particular item caught Salem's eye. It was toward the bottom of the second page. It read:

SB. Be my valentine? AK.

The kids all thought Eddie was burping on purpose. He wasn't. Since he had begun his new bulk-up diet, his whole system had gone flooey. After the peanuts, he had nibbled his way through bags of bagel bits, banana chips, and raisins. The plan, designed by Pickles, was to eat constantly, every waking minute. The burps were his body's protest.

Though Eddie had always admired the great burpmasters of his generation, he had never been much of a burper himself. It was hard for him to tell when one was coming on. It usually took him by surprise and was out of his mouth long before he could stifle it.

Pickles greeted him on the way to lunch. "Hey, it's the burpster. Burpman. Burpalator."

"I never counted on this," said Eddie. "Is there something that can make me stop?"

"I'll work on it."

"I never had a detention in my life."

"Just the price you're paying for bulking up. It'll be worth it."

"What if my parents find out? Will it go on my report card, the detention?"

Pickles winked at Sunny and Salem, who had joined them. "It'll go on your report card — and your school record."

"And a copy of it goes to the police department," added Sunny. "It follows you the rest of your life."

Pickles' and Sunny's straight faces collapsed at the sight of Eddie's wide, gullible eyes. "Just kidding." Pickles laughed and clamped Eddie in a headlock that served, among sixth-grade boys, as a hug.

"Where's Salem?" said Sunny.

Pickles looked around. "Don't know. Let's eat. She'll find us."

Salem, as it happened, was in the Music Room instrument closet, trying to catch her breath. Her heart was thumping like a bass drum.

This was no midnight phantom fantasy. *The Wurple* clutched in her fist was real. The print on the page, the words — all thrillingly real. "SB . . . SB . . . SB . . ." she kept whispering to the clarinet cases. SB. Salem Brownmiller.

Who else could it be? She knew of at least one other SB in school, a Sarah Berkheimer, also in sixth grade. Was SB Sarah Berkheimer? Salem pictured Sarah in her mind's eye. Did Sarah look like someone to whom something this momentously romantic would happen? In a word — no.

How many other SB's were there? Salem thought of going to the office and asking to see the enrollment roster. Narrow it down to the B's, eliminate the boy B's, eliminate all but the girl SB's, eliminate Sarah Berkheimer. Would that leave anyone but herself?

It began to dawn on Salem that it didn't matter. There could be twenty other SB's, but all her instincts told her that this was no matter for enrollment rosters. This was destiny. This was romance. She had been chosen. She was Cupid's bull's-eye. She felt it. She knew it. SB had to be — could only be — herself.

Now . . . *who was AK?*

At the lunch line, Eddie held back. "I don't know," he said. "I'm not very hungry."

"That's why you're so tiny," said Sunny. "You eat like a bird."

Eddie snapped, "I've been eating all day, that's why I'm not hungry. And I'm not tiny."

"You're teeny."

"I'm not!"

"You're weeny."

Pickles sealed Sunny's mouth with the palm of his hand. "She's raggin' you. Just keep thinking of the day when you'll be big enough to beat her up."

Sunny laughed, but with her mouth sealed shut, the laugh burst from her nose, leaving nostril juice on Pickles' hand. Pickles jerked his hand away, screeched, "Eeeeww!" and wiped it on Sunny's DEATH TO MUSHROOMS T-shirt. Sunny slugged Pickles in the arm. Eddie laughed.

In the lunch line Pickles picked out milk and a dessert for Eddie, who had brought the rest from home. At the table, while the others tore into their tacos, Eddie pulled two sandwiches from his book bag.

Sunny exclaimed, "Chocolate bread?"

"Pumpernickel," said Pickles. "It's better for you."

The others had finished their first tacos, and Eddie still hadn't taken a bite. "Well," said Sunny, "aren't you going to eat?"

Pickles reached over and unwrapped the sandwiches. He handed half of one to Eddie. Eddie held it as though it were a live hand grenade. Sunny grabbed the other half and opened it. She screamed and slammed it shut. "What is it?"

Pickles said matter-of-factly, "Peanut butter and mayonnaise. A protein bomb." He lifted Eddie's hand to his mouth. "Eat."

Sunny steered her eyes elsewhere. "I'm afraid to ask. What's in the other one?"

"Parsley," said Pickles.

"Parsley? That's all? A parsley sandwich?"

"Iron," said Pickles. "There's more iron in a sprig of parsley than in a porterhouse steak." He opened the sandwich for display. "That's worth about what . . . ten steaks there."

Sunny snorted, "Ironman Mott."

Eddie forced down the last bite just as lunch ended. On the way out, Pickles said, "Feel yourself getting any bigger?"

Eddie burped. "Yeah, my stomach."

Pickles slapped Eddie on the back, prompting another burp.

Sunny said, "Where the heck is Salem?"

At that moment Salem was walking out of the main office. Posing as a reporter for *The Wurple*, she had persuaded the secretary, Mrs. Wilburham, to let her see a list of students whose last names began with K.

There were eight K's in Plumstead. Five of them were boys; of those, two were AK's: Avery Kribble and Alan Kent. Avery Kribble was an obnoxious lunkhead sixth-grader. He never took a bath. The only thing dirtier than his body was his mouth. He was always in trouble, and the only people who liked him were nickelheads. He was totally incapable of writing — or feeling — a Love Line.

In a daze, too stunned to feel anything, Salem left the office with one name on her lips. "Alan Kent." She sipped it, as she would a new, exotic tropical juice. "Alan Kent." She nibbled it, as she would an unidentified piece of candy from a heart-shaped box of chocolates. "Alan Kent." She had never heard the name, and suddenly it was as though she had never heard any other. She knew nothing of him. Except one thing.

Whoever Alan Kent was, he loved her.

For Eddie, last period of the day was Study Hall. With ten minutes left in the period, he asked to go to the bathroom and was excused. He prayed that the teacher would not ask why he was taking his book bag along. She didn't.

He hadn't really wanted to use the bathroom, but it was the only place that offered both water and privacy. Well, water for sure; privacy maybe, if no big kids came in to terrorize him, which was why he hadn't been crazy about using the bathroom in the first place.

He set his book bag on the sink and pulled out the can of Moocho Malt. He and Pickles had bought it at the mall on Saturday. Moocho Malt was a powdered concoction that you mixed with water to make a shake "Packed," the can said, "With the Stuff to Make You MASSIVE!" Eddie got the shivers just thinking of that word — MAS-SIVE — applied to himself. He had always been identified with words like "little" and "skinny" and "small." "Massive," on the other hand, brought to mind Arnold Schwarzenegger, King Kong, mountains, and the planet Jupiter. Eddie Mott . . . massive? It seemed all wrong, misplaced, scary.

But thrilling, too. Massive Eddie Mott. In the boys' room mirror he imagined himself growing, swelling hugely, Moocho Malted mass bursting against cord and vein, his bare chest invading the next mirror, his nipples the size of pancakes . . .

He opened the can. He took the plastic glass from his bag. A hand clamped around his wrist. A voice said, "Waddaya got there, runt?"

14

Eddie did not bother to turn. In the mirror he saw two grinning nickelheads. One was Baloney, the other was Salami. Nickelheads had weird names. They insisted the names were on their birth certificates, but Eddie doubted that. Eighth-graders found nickelhead names funny; sixth-graders found them frightening.

The hand released Eddie's wrist and picked up the can. "Hey, Salami, look at this."

"What is it?"

Baloney studied the can. "Moocho Malt."

Salami was swinging from a stall door. "Mooocho? What's that? Cow food?" He cackled at his own joke.

Baloney studied the can some more. "Says it makes you mass . . . mass . . . ive. What's that mean?"

"It means big, peanut brain. Like bodybuilders."

Baloney's grin got wider and crookeder. He

crowed to the world, "He wants to be big! He wants muscles!" He read the can some more. "Like a chocolate shake . . . just add water."

Baloney grabbed the plastic glass out of Eddie's hand. He opened the can, pulled the dispenser from the chocolaty powder, dumped three heaping scoopfuls into the glass, added water, stirred with one of Eddie's pencils, and said, "Okay, muscles, drink up."

Eddie drank up. What the heck, he was going to anyway.

Then Baloney made him another shake.

"Only supposed to drink one," said Eddie.

Baloney scowled: "Drink."

"I can't. I'm full. I'm stuffed." He burped.

Baloney pressed the glass against Eddie's nose: "Drink."

Eddie took a deep breath, closed his eyes, drank.

Baloney made him another: "Drink."

Eddie burped. He flatly protested: "No."

Suddenly Salami was with Baloney — a cold cut sandwich — both of them inches from his face. They pronounced together: "Drink."

Eddie imagined himself to be a balloon one puff from bursting. But he had no choice. Trembling under the nickelheads' cold gaze, swallow by swallow he drained the glass. He could see the headlines:

STUDENT FOUND DEAD FROM
OVERDOSE OF MOOCHO MALT

At that moment things began to happen very quickly.

The bell rang. Baloney said, "Quick, one more." They made another shake. As they tried to give it to Eddie, they saw his face: It was the school colors, purple and white. His eyes were popping like a frog's. His chest was heaving, burps were coming like a slow-motion machine gun. "Uh-oh," said Salami, "he's gonna do it. Let's get outta here!" They flung the glass into the sink and took off. At the door they met fellow nickelhead Tuna Casseroli coming in. Tuna, spotting one of his favorite victims, exclaimed, "Mini Mott!" He strode over to Eddie and without warning snatched him by the ankles and hoisted him upside down. "You heard of the bench press?" he called to Baloney and Salami. "Well, this is the Mott lift." He began raising and lowering Eddie and counting: "One . . . two . . . three . . ." The nickelheads screamed, "Tuna, DON'T!"

It was too late. Eddie began barfing at the high point of the lift, when his upside-down mouth was opposite Tuna's thighs. As Tuna, unaware of what was happening, lowered him, he spray-barfed Tuna's jeans from thigh to ankle, then slathered his sneakers.

Not wanting to be accomplices to murder, Baloney and Salami fled. Tuna stood frozen, beginning now to feel the warmth seeping through the denim. He held Eddie farther out from himself, as if the damage were not already done. When he finally gathered his courage to look down, he saw his victim's upside-down face, featuring the tiny twin pipes of his nostrils, and his own feet — or at least he assumed his feet were there, for nothing of his sneakers showed above the barf but two plastic lace tips. For some reason Eddie thought of a promotion Little Caesar's Pizza was running: "Extra Topping No Extra Charge."

To Eddie's amazement, the next voice was not Tuna's but someone else's, a man's deep voice booming: "Let him down easy, nosepicker."

15

Eddie swung his upside-down head past Tuna's pant leg. It was Bobo! Holding the cigar butt in his hand and advancing. "You got to the count of one, nosepicker."

Tuna let Eddie down, Bobo helped Eddie gather up his stuff, and they left. The last thing Eddie heard was the *squush-squush* of Tuna trying to walk.

In the hallway Bobo cupped Eddie's chin in one meaty paw. "You look sick. What was going on in there?"

"I'm okay now," said Eddie, "just weak. I think I lost about ten pounds of mass back there."

Cries of "Yo, Bobo!" erupted from students rushing for homeroom.

Eddie felt a sob coming on. The ordeal, the rescue, had left him drained of everything but an urge to hug the bus driver walking beside him and tear out into that big belly. He heard Bobo's gravelly voice say, "You better get goin' where you're supposed to go."

The hall was empty. Quickly, Eddie pressed his forehead into the belly (now, *that* was massive), whispered "Thanks," and ran off. Two rooms down he stopped, turned. "Hey, Bobo, what are you doing here, anyway?"

The cigar butt shifted in Bobo's mouth. "Late Room."

Eddie laughed at the joke and ran on.

As Eddie soon found out, it was no joke. Detention Room was in the same place as Late Room, and when he reported for his detention, sure enough, there was Bobo sitting in the front row.

"I thought you were kidding," said Eddie.

"I don't kid, kid," growled the bus driver.

Late- and Detention-Room monitors changed every week. This week it happened to be Miss Billups. "Eddie Mott?" she said. "Mr. Brimlow said the students on the bus did not have to come to Late Room. Only the driver."

Eddie cleared his throat and swallowed a few times. "I'm not here for Late Room."

Surprise showed on the teacher's face. Eddie Mott was not known as a troublemaker. "You're not? Are you on the detention list? I haven't even looked." She rummaged around the desk till she found the list. She looked from the paper to him.

"You are." She still didn't sound convinced. "May I ask what brings you here?"

Before Eddie could form an answer, Pickles, Salem, and Sunny entered the room. Miss Billups looked back at the detention sheet. "Now, you three definitely are not on the list."

"No, we're not," said Salem. "We're just here to give moral support to Eddie. It's his first-ever detention, and we thought maybe we could help him get through it."

"There's no rule against volunteering for detention, is there?" said Pickles.

Miss Billups chuckled. "No, I guess not. But I'd still like to find out why Mr. Mott's name is on this." She waved the sheet at them.

Sunny answered without hesitation. "He burped."

The teacher blinked. "He burped?"

"Big time."

"Big time?"

"He burped all over school, all day. He was grossing out teachers left and right. The last straw was in English class. He said, "Quoth the Raven . . . *Brrraawwwpp!*' Miss O'Malley told him, 'Edward Mott, you are the most disgusting, revolting, sickening student I have ever had in my life. You are grosser than — ' "

Eddie yelped, "She didn't say that!"

Miss Billups nodded with a faint smile. "I know. Why don't you just write 'I will mind my manners

68

in class' fifty times on the blackboard, and then you may go."

Pickles turned to Bobo. "Shouldn't you be out in your bus?"

Bobo turned his seat sideways and put his feet up on another desk. "I got late bus today."

"I don't believe you're really here."

"What do I look like, a mirage?"

"I don't believe you're really listening to Mr. Brimlow."

"That's life, kid. Some people you listen to, the rest you kick in the shins."

"The rest *you* kick in the shins," amended Miss Billups.

"You really think they would fire you?" said Sunny.

"Sure," said Bobo. "If they had more people wanted to be drivers, I'da been gone long ago." He flapped his hand. "*Sayonara.*"

"What's that mean?" said Eddie.

"It means good-bye in Japanese," said Salem.

Eddie's eyes bulged. "You speak Japanese?"

"Mr. Mott," said Miss Billups, "if you don't get up to the blackboard this minute, your penance will be doubled."

"What does penance mean?"

"Mr. Mott!"

Eddie went to the blackboard and began writing his fifty sentences — and so did Pickles, Sunny, and Salem.

For a minute Miss Billups just gaped at them: four students, backs to the classroom, all writing the same sentence over and over. "What," she said at last, "are you doing?"

"We're just supporting Eddie," said Pickles, continuing to write.

"Even though he's a criminal," said Sunny, whose sentences were the sloppiest.

Miss Billups just stared at them. Something good is happening here, she thought, something we don't teach them in school. The only sounds were the scrapes and squeaks of four pieces of chalk.

16

"Was I dreaming back there?" said Pickles.

"He didn't really say that, did he?" said Sunny.

"Yeah, he did," said Eddie.

Since the picklebus had been left home this day, the pickle posse was walking. After completing their sentences — all 200 of them — they had cleaned the blackboards and were bidding good-bye to Miss Billups when Bobo spoke up: "How'd you like a baby-sitting job?"

The four of them had simply stopped at the doorway and gawked. He went on to explain that he could never go anywhere because he could not find anyone to baby-sit for his three little ones. (*No kidding*, Sunny had thought.) Now he was thinking that the four of them together could do it. Pickles had said they would have to think about it.

At the end of the school driveway, they turned for home. "Do you believe him?" said Pickles.

"I don't," said Sunny.

"Neither do I," said Salem.

"I do," said Eddie.

"It's not like him," said Salem.

"Why should he give us a job?" said Sunny. "He hates kids."

"He doesn't hate kids," said Eddie. "And he said he would probably pay us good."

"Maybe it's a trick," said Pickles.

"Yeah," said Sunny. "He's trying to lure us into his house so he can murder us."

"No, he's not," said Eddie firmly. "He likes us."

Sunny finger-flicked the back of Eddie's head. "Who made you the big Bobo expert all of a sudden?"

"I did," said Eddie primly, and he told them the whole story of his adventures in the boys' room.

"Gosh," was all Salem could say.

"He saved your life," said Pickles.

Sunny said nothing.

They walked on.

Salem cleared her throat and said, as casually as possible, "Anybody ever hear of an Alan Kent?"

"Not me," said Pickles.

"He go to our school?" said Eddie.

"I really don't know," Salem nonchalantly lied.

Sunny plucked off Salem's black, floppy hat and plunked it on her own head. "What's this, you got the hots for this kid or something?" She scrutinized Salem, mischief in her eyes. "Is *that* why you weren't around for lunch today?"

Salem felt her cheeks burning. She snatched back her hat, and laughed. "Right. Do I look like a *hots* type of person?"

Before she sank any deeper, Pickles unwittingly saved her. He suddenly darted into the middle of the street. "Where's the snow?" he barked. He lifted his face to the sky and threw out his arms. "I . . . WANT . . . SNOW!'

The others were stunned. Normally Pickles was the coolest of them all.

"He's bumped his pumpkin," said Sunny.

Eddie jumped from the curb. "Hey, I have an idea. I got it from Pickles there, the way he's standing. You heard of a rain dance? Let's have — "

Salem finished it: "A *snow* dance!"

A car beeped; Pickles came back nodding. "Yeah . . . why not?"

"Let's go to the library," said Salem.

"And look up rain dancing," said Eddie.

"And change it to snow dancing!" said Pickles.

They started off walking; soon they were running.

The library had plenty of material on rain, but not much on rain dancing. Most helpful were pictures from the vertical file. They generally showed natives wearing skimpy costumes and masks, dancing under cloudless skies in various desert areas of the globe.

"You can't tell what the dance is like," said Pickles.

"All you can see is one step."

"We need movies," said Eddie.

They checked the video section, especially the *National Geographic* tapes. Nothing.

"We'll make our own dance," said Salem.

"Good idea," said Sunny. She did some swooping turns and elaborate arm movements.

"Snow does not listen to kung fu," said Salem.

"That's for the snow to decide," said Sunny and went off to section 796.815: Martial Arts.

Pickles continued to look through such subjects as Rain and Dance and Snow and Weather. Eddie looked into Bulk Up and Weight and Muscles and, when he was sure no one was looking, Hunk.

Salem headed for a special section in Reference. In this section the public library kept the yearbooks of each school in town. Since Plumstead was a brand-new middle school this year, it had no yearbook yet. The other middle school was Cedar Grove. When Plumstead opened, many Cedar Grove students were transferred there. Salem pulled last year's Cedar Grove yearbook off the shelf.

And hit paydirt.

There, among the seventh-grade class, was a

boy identified as Alan Kent. That made him an eighth-grader now. He had light-brown hair, a friendly smile. Could that face have written the love line question: "Be my valentine?"? Yes, she decided, he most certainly could have.

She went through the whole yearbook, searching for more of Alan Kent. He was in the school chorus and was a member of the Students for Earth Day committee. Even the grade schools had modest yearbooks. She found him in Drumore Elementary, Sunny's old school.

She dropped a dime in the copier and made a copy of his Cedar Grove picture. Best ten cents she'd ever spent. She put the picture in her book bag, then took it out. She couldn't stop looking at it.

She wandered among the stacks, trying to digest it all. An *eighth-grader*! Most eighth-grade boys didn't know sixth-grade girls existed. But of course, Alan Kent was no ordinary eighth-grade boy. Salem could see that already. He must be a strong and confident person, she thought, comfortable with himself and not afraid of his classmates ribbing him for "robbing the cradle." He's the type of person who sets a course and never strays from it, regardless of public pressure.

And that, Salem happily realized, was a description of herself as well. No wonder, when he cast his eyes over the student body, that he singled out the elegant girl with the long, brown hair,

Salem Brownmiller, whose maturity belied her age. Already she could feel herself bonding with this extraordinary young man.

Be my valentine?

"Yes," Salem whispered, pressing her lips to the ink-scented copy of his picture. "Yes, Alan, yes — "

At that moment — *POW!* — something walloped her in the forehead and sent her staggering back into Biography. As her senses cleared, she saw Sunny rushing, alarm in her eyes and a giggle in her voice. "Salem, I'm sorry. I was practicing my high kick." Sunny stood before her in stocking feet, an open book in one hand, the other reaching, touching her forehead. "Are you okay?"

Salem blew hair from her eyes. She glared. "Sure. Feel free to kick me any time."

Truth be told, Salem was barely annoyed. She had felt no pain from the kick, only force, and that was piddling. After all, what was a kick in the head compared to Cupid's arrow in the heart?

17

Salem was in the middle of math homework that night when the phone rang. It was Sunny. "He's in eighth grade, he's on Hi-Q, and he's in Homeroom 221."

Salem pretended ignorance. "What are you talking about? Who?"

"Okay, play dumb. AK. Ring a bell?"

AK. She knew. She saw the Love Line.

Salem's heart was racing. She could not speak. She heard Sunny's voice saying, "I felt bad about kicking you today, even if it *was* an accident, so I thought I'd do you a favor and find out more about AK. So I made a couple of phone calls. He's supposed to be shy, too."

Shy. Yes, that seemed right. Shyness could be so adorable in a boy. And Hi-Q, meaning he represented Plumstead in *Jeopardy*-like competitions with other schools. Meaning he was smart. It figured. Smart people seek each other out. Salem had intended to try out for the Hi-Q team next year.

"You're not talking," said Sunny.

"I know."

Sunny snickered, "It *could* be Avery Kribble, you know."

"God forbid!" yelped Salem, and all her pent-up emotions burst forth in loud, almost hysterical laughter. Sunny joined in.

"Mrs. Salem Kribble!" Sunny shrieked, and they howled some more.

The laughter lapsed into more silence, which became increasingly awkward. Finally Salem braced herself and said, "You won't go around saying anything, will you?"

"No," came the simple, prompt reply.

"Not even to Pickles and Eddie."

"Don't worry."

More silence. Then: "Sal?"

Salem winced. Rarely did Sunny call her Sal. When she did, it was usually because Salem was vulnerable. And suddenly Salem knew: Sunny was considering whether or not to point out that there were other SB's in school. Salem replied, "Yes?" as she silently prayed: *Don't say it, Sunny. Please don't.*

She didn't. "Nothing," she said. "Gotta go. Good luck. 'Bye." She hung up.

Salem laid down the receiver, but she kept her hand on it for a long time.

18

Homeroom 221 was at the far end of the second floor. After telling Pickles not to pick her up next morning, Salem arrived at 221 with exactly thirteen minutes before last bell.

On one side of 221 was the stairway to the first floor. On the other side was a water fountain. Salem spent a good two thirds of forever trying to appear inconspicuous as she strolled back and forth between stairway and fountain.

He wasn't there, and he wasn't there, and suddenly he was, seconds before last bell, racing up the stairs two — no, three — at a time, so fast that he was past her before she recognized him. He was bigger-looking than his seventh-grade picture and with longer hair and so much more real than copy toner and paper. His mad dash up the stairs identified him as a last-minute arriver and a real go-getter. Salem was liking him more and more. He flew into 221 as she ran to her own homeroom, more from excitement than fear of being late, which she was.

She watched for him in the hallways between classes. It wasn't until after fourth period that she spotted him, heading her way, talking to another boy, part of the mob. She wondered how many times he had spotted her in the hallways, followed her with his eyes, felt the feeling that became the thought that became the question in Love Lines.

Another two inches and they would have brushed shoulders. He breezed on by, talking to his friend. Did he see her? His eyes seemed to sweep over her, as they swept over the hallway, the mob — but did he *see* her? Did his eyes, for an atomized instant, land on her? Yes, she thought. No, she thought.

"He's supposed to be shy," Sunny had said.

Salem was useless the rest of the day.

At dismissal she raced upstairs, three at a time as he had. He was at his locker, shuffling books, fooling around, taking forever. Fast before school, slow after. She liked that. She lingered at a distance. At last he closed the locker and headed down the stairs. She followed. She hoped he was going home. She was about to find out where Alan Kent lived.

One foot each on the picklebus, Pickles and Eddie waited for the girls after school. They were at the side door by the parking lot, the picklebus terminal.

"What's keeping them?" said Eddie.

"Beats me," said Pickles. "They say anything about being late?"

"Nope, not to me."

They waited.

Pickles pointed to a nearby tree. "Look."

Eddie looked. "What?"

"The tree."

"What about it?"

"The branches. The limbs."

"I'm *looking*."

"Buds."

Eddie squinted. "Those little nubbers?"

"Those little nubbers."

Eddie nodded. "Okay." He shrugged. "So?"

"So, buds are supposed to come in the spring. This is February. That shows you how warm it's been. The weather's all screwed up. It's even messing up the trees." He gazed upward. "Must be the ozone hole."

"What's that?"

"A hole in the atmosphere."

Eddie squinted into a sky that was brightly overcast, a high silken blanket. "I don't see a hole."

"You can't see it. Anyway, it's over the South Pole. But it's letting too much sun in, warming everything up."

"I like warm," said Eddie. "I don't like cold weather."

"It doesn't snow in warm weather."

"I know, but that's the *only* thing I like about cold weather — snow. I wish it could snow in the summer. That's what I'd like. Is there any place like that? I'd move there."

"Maybe Mars." Pickles scanned the students swarming out of school. "Still don't see them." He turned back to Eddie, grinned and whispered, "Moocho Malt."

Eddie shrieked and covered his ears. Since the three-glass, upside-down Tuna shake in the boys' room, he could not bear the sound or thought of those two words. He didn't do so well with "mayonnaise," "peanut butter," or "parsley" either.

Pickles laughed and pulled Eddie's hands away. "You can come out now. I won't do it anymore." He put his arm around Eddie. "You know, since you can't drink you-know-what anymore, we're going to have to bulk you up some other way."

Eddie nodded. "Yeah, like what?"

Pickles pointed to his head. "Your mind. I'm going to start reading up on hypnotism. I'll put you under" — he wiggled his fingers before Eddie's eyes — "and make you believe that skinny is beautiful."

Eddie was trying to figure out if his leg was being pulled when Pickles said, "There's Salem. Going out the front door. Let's go."

19

Oh no! Salem groaned when she saw them coming.

Eddie called, "Salem!"

Salem pretended not to hear and kept walking. Alan Kent was ten feet ahead of her, heading down the driveway in the midst of the raucous, horseplaying, homebound mob.

The picklebus pulled alongside her. "Come on, Salem," said Eddie, sliding back on the green surfboard to give her room in the middle, "hop on."

She wished Eddie would keep his voice down. "I think I'll walk today," she practically whispered. "I could use the exercise."

Eddie and Pickles yapped together: *"Exercise?"* Salem was widely known to be allergic to exercise. "Well, we'll just cruise close by then," said Pickles, "so we can pick you up and take you to the hospital when you collapse."

Salem wanted to kill them. "Don't bother," she gritted.

"No bother," Pickles said cheerily.

"Picklepeople forever," chimed Eddie.

They weren't going to vanish. Every passing second increased the risk that Alan Kent would overhear or turn and get the impression that she liked these two bozos. He was turning left at the end of the driveway, in the direction the picklebus would normally go.

She gave Alan Kent a departing look and snarled, "O-*kay* — but I want to go this way today." She pointed to the right. "I need a change of scenery."

"No problem," said Pickles. "Alllll aboard!"

She hopped on before he got any louder, and they pushed off.

"Where's Sunny?" Salem asked as they left the school behind.

Pickles shrugged. "That girl? Who knows what she's up to?"

Before long, they would all know.

The picklebus dropped Salem off at her house. At Pickles' house, his mother met them in the living room. "Sunny said to tell you she couldn't wait any longer. She'll see you tomorrow."

Pickles stared at her. "She was here?"

"In the basement. She said she was supposed to meet you there. You had something to show — "

Pickles was flying down the stairs, Eddie at his

heels. The basement light was still on. In the back corner the olive green tarp was on the floor. The pickleboggan was naked. As they approached, they saw a note taped to the green-painted side. It said, in Sunny Wyler's bold handwriting:

DON'T EVER TRY
TO KEEP A SECRET
FROM ME AGAIN!!!!!!
(ha-ha)

That evening, shortly after finishing dinner, Salem received a phone call. A strange, raspy voice croaked cryptically, "The main entrance to the school. Who will get there first? You . . . or the TV stations?" *Click.*

Salem was not good at mysteries. For several minutes the weird phone call meant absolutely nothing to her. Then, somehow, it did. What came to her at first was not knowledge, but a queasy, chilling, unarticulated feeling that she'd better get on over to that school — *pronto!*

She was not allowed out alone after dark, but there was no way she would ask her father to drive. It was only six o'clock. Running, she could make it in five minutes. She threw on a jacket and sneaked out the back door.

She knew by now that the voice had been Sunny's, disguised. As she ran, she kept hearing her own plea: "You won't go around saying anything, will you . . . will you . . . will you . . .?"

She ran faster.

The banner was visible from the sidewalk. She dragged herself and the sharp stitch in her side up the driveway. The banner was made of sheets of paper stapled together. It stretched across all four front doors, about fifteen feet. It said, in huge red letters:

SALEM BROWNMILLER LOVES
ALAN KENT

Gasping, she took it down. She slumped back down the driveway, dragging the banner behind. She stopped to gather it up. She folded it, pleating it neatly sheet by sheet. She would save it forever. She was almost — *almost* — glad that Sunny did it.

20

Sunny finished cutting the eyeholes and laid down the scissors. "Why am I doing this?"

"You're doing it to bring snow," said Salem.

"Get serious."

"You're doing it because you want to make up for the rotten trick you played on your best friend last night."

"Who's my best friend?"

"Don't be funny."

Sunny scoffed, "Rotten? You're not even close. I did it on Friday night, when nobody would be there for two days, didn't I? I called you, didn't I?"

"You promised you wouldn't say anything."

"I didn't. I wrote it. Try again."

Salem sighed mightily. "You're doing it because Pickles is desperate for snow, and you love him so you'll do anything to help him out. That's my last reason. If you don't like it, go home."

Sunny stood before Salem's mirror and held the

sheet in front of her, as though appraising a dress. "I don't love Pickles."

"Of course you do. Like you love Eddie and yours truly."

"Who's yours truly?"

"Me."

"I love kung fu, that's who I love." She did a left-leg side-high kick. "Hai-YAH!"

Salem flinched. "You know, Miss Wyler, you have a problem."

"That so?"

"Yes. You don't come to terms with your feelings. You — "

"Ah!" Sunny raised her finger. "But I do come to terms with *your* feelings."

"While you're giving me a heart attack. As I was saying, you can get away with it now, because you're a youngster. Plus, we understand you, we know that's how you are, we know you're not as heartless as you talk." She glared at Sunny. "Or *act*. But someday . . . someday you're going to meet somebody you like, but nothing will come of it because you don't know how to admit it."

Arms folded, Sunny waited for Salem to finish. Then she replied, in wincing disbelief, "*Youngster?* I never heard anybody under ninety use that word." She pronounced it again: "*Youngster.*"

Salem sniffed, "I beg your pardon. I keep forgetting how *minuscule* your vocabulary is."

Sunny simpered, "Boo-hoo." She pulled the

sheet over herself, working the eyeholes into position. "I'm still waiting for some answer that makes sense. Why are you and I standing here in your bedroom with sheets over our heads?"

Salem sighed. "Okay, how about this? We don't really believe it's going to bring snow, or at least we're not sure. But mostly we're doing it because we're kids and it's Saturday and we're bored and it's something to do."

Sunny pointed, making her sheet tepee toward Salem. "Bingo."

The doorbell rang. "That's the guys," said Salem. "Let's go."

The two-eyed sheets floated down the stairway like a pair of parachutes.

Five minutes later Salem's backyard looked like a convention of ghosts. Pickles was the most elaborately done up, adding a mask to his plain white sheet. Made of papier-mâché, the mask resembled a pumpkin — a white pumpkin — with a grotesque slash for a mouth and monsterish eyes. Erupting from the top was a twelve-inch stack of bristles from a household broom, also painted white.

Sunny rapped on the mask. "Knock-knock."

Pickles' voice sounded slightly hollow. "Who's there?"

"Atch."

"Atch who?"

"*Gesundheit*. Knock-knock."

"Who's there?"

"Sunny."

"Sunny who?"

"Sunny and warm the rest of the winter. Not a flake of snow."

"Sunny," snapped Salem, "try to be a little serious for once in your life, will you?"

Sunny howled. "Serious? How can I be serious looking at him. He looks like Snow Broom Butt from Outer Space." She lurched about the yard, hooting ghostily, "Boooo . . . booooo." Then she sneaked up behind Eddie and lifted his sheet.

"Hey!" he yelped.

"Just wanted to see if you were wearing your Superman undies." She lurched away. "Boooo . . . boooo."

"She's outta control," said Eddie.

"Pickles," said Salem, "she didn't want to do this in the first place. Maybe it's better without her. She's only going to mess it up."

Silence within the white pumpkinoid. Then, in a voice with a gangsterish twang: "She's in the pickle posse, she stays in the pickle posse. The only way anybody leaves this gang is in a coffin."

Sunny raced to Pickles, fell at his feet. "Oh thank you, Great White Broom Butt. Thank you for keeping me. I'll make you proud." She skipped about the yard, squeaking like a tot, "I'm in the gang! I'm in the gang! I'm a little baby snowflake.

Now I melted and went to snowflake heaven. Now I'm a leeee-tle baby snowflake ghost. I don't say boo anymore, I say goo . . . goooo . . . goooo . . ."

There was no use fighting it. The other three sheets cracked up.

When they finally laughed themselves out over Sunny's antics, Pickles said, "Okay, can we get down to business now?"

As Pickles was saying this, Sunny circled around behind him. Salem and Eddie saw her remove her shoe, they saw her lift her sheet to her waist, they saw her take aim — and still they did not believe that she would do it.

She did.

With a ringing "Hai-YAH!" she snapped her right leg high; the heel of her foot caught Pickles' papier-mâché mask dead center. The mask split vertically in two from back to front. The eyes parted, the nose disappeared, the horrible mouth became two. All that held the mask together was the broom top, and when Sunny neatly plucked it out, the two halves fell to the ground like a cracked nutshell. The nut itself stood there for a full minute, shook his head in disgust, said, "I give up," yanked off his sheet, and stomped away.

"Party pooper Pickles," Sunny called.

Salem chuckled, "Hey, try saying that five times fast."

For the next minute Salem's backyard resounded to sounds most curious: "Party pooper pickles. Party pooper pickles. Party pipper pickles. Party pooper pickers. Perty popple pickles. Pookle perpy pittles. Picky packer pooples. Pocker pooker picker . . ."

Pickles, who had stopped at the driveway, turned slowly, hands on hips. "I hope you all have sleds of your own — "

"Pickle packle peekle," said Sunny.

"Pooter poopy doopy," said Eddie.

" — because when it snows I'll be going up to Heller's Hill by myself."

"Poofles," said Sunny.

"Poo," said Eddie.

Pickles sagged. He slumped to a seat in the driveway. He looked at himself — the sheet slung over his shoulder, half a snow dance mask in each hand. He wanted to cry, he really did.

21

Salem knew Miss Billups was talking to the class, and she knew she ought to be paying attention, but how could she, with Alan Kent somewhere in the same building — the same town — the same planet? Salem had written of love in a few of her stories, but she'd had no idea it could be this powerful, this all-consuming.

And frustrating.

She was beginning to understand how well earned was Alan's reputation for shyness. Again this morning, she had passed him in the hall, and again he had failed to acknowledge her. Which was not to say he did not see her. She felt certain this time that he had. For a good three or four seconds, he was unmistakably looking her way. Apparently, not even his shyness could prevent a deeper, primal urge to feast his eyes upon her. But then he looked away and, as before, went on walking and talking by. No smile, no nod, nothing.

Maybe it wasn't shyness, maybe it was self-discipline. Maybe, while his heart was saying, "Go get her," his head was saying, "You're not ready for women yet." Or maybe he was unsure of her. Maybe he was afraid that she, a mere sixth-grader, would simply laugh or blubber if he made his move.

Maybe, maybe.

Salem was getting fed up with maybes. There was no maybe about her answer to Alan's big question. The answer was yes. Yes, Alan, I *will* be your valentine. She wanted to shout it in his face, shout it over the PA system, shout it from the top of the bleachers on the football field. YES!

And Valentine's Day itself, February 14, was Thursday, only three days away. Valentine's Day was not a day for maybes, for questions, for suspense. It was a day when matters became settled, a day for answers, for yesses. A day for — she shivered at the very thought of the word — *couples*. Would Thursday dawn to find Salem Brownmiller and Alan Kent a couple? To think so made her want to giggle and squeal like a second-grader.

What a crime, what a stupid and senseless crime it would be if Valentine's Day came and went and still nothing was settled. Well, that wasn't going to happen, not if Salem could help it. She had to break through this barrier between them. She did not care to give her answer to someone who was afraid to say hello to her. She was a female. She was supposed to have feminine wiles. What was she waiting for? Use them! If he was having a hard time approaching her, she would make it easier. She would make herself impossible to miss.

"Well, it looks like you got your wish," Sunny said to her as they walked out of class.

Salem blinked, stared at Sunny. "Huh? What wish?"

"The big George Washington camp-out," said Pickles.

Eddie snapped his fingers in front of her face. "Hey, are you here?"

Salem stared at them all. She smiled weakly. "Now I am. I guess I wasn't listening in class. I was doing my, uh, math homework."

"Yeah," snickered Sunny, "one plus one equals two."

Salem shot her a look.

"Everybody has to do a project," said Pickles. "You're allowed to go together, up to four to a team."

"It can be almost anything," said Eddie, "as long as it has to do with that winter at Valley Forge."

"So we figured we might as well do your bone

soup thing," said Pickles. "How about this Saturday night? My backyard."

"I'll bring the tent," said Sunny.

"I'll bring firewood," said Eddie.

"I'll bring the pot," said Pickles.

Everyone turned grinning to Salem. She rolled her eyes. "O-*kay*. I'll bring the bone."

That night, while plotting her strategy, Salem received a phone call.

"Hello," said a deep voice, "this is Alan Kent. I just want you to know that you are the most beautiful girl I ever saw and I hope some day you will become my wife."

"Hello, Sunny," said Salem.

"Eddie just called," said Sunny.

"So?"

"Pickles just called him."

"So?"

"Bobo just called him."

"Bobo? The bus driver?"

"Yeah."

"Why?"

"Remember he asked us that day if we would baby-sit for him?"

"Yeah."

"He's asking."

"What did Pickles tell him?"

"He told him no."

"Why?"

"It's for Saturday night."
"And that's the night we're camping out."
"Right."
"Okay."
"Okay. 'Bye."
" 'Bye."

22

In the old days, or at least in the old stories and movies, when a lady wished to attract the attention of a gentleman, she would drop an embroidered hanky as she was strolling through the park, preferably with a parasol. Whereupon the gentleman would gallantly retrieve the hanky from the ground and call, "Ma'am!" The lady would stop, the parasol would swing, she would turn just enough and say sweetly, innocently, "Yes?" He would not say it then; first he would walk briskly to her, and then he would say it: "You dropped something." And she would say, eyes all wide and innocent, "Well my, my, so I did," or simply, "Why, thank you." And then he would return the hanky to her, preferably passing it under his nose, for the hanky would be perfumed, and their fingers would touch for a moment, and their eyes would more than touch, and he would smile and nod and say "Charmed," and she would smile and the parasol would begin to slowly spin and they would live happily ever after.

Back then, every day was Valentine's Day.

Well, there was no park and no parasol, but also no reason why the old wile couldn't work. And so Salem had stationed herself on the stairway landing outside Room 221 just after the doors opened on Tuesday morning. All the ingredients were here, just brought up to date. Instead of a park, there was Plumstead Middle School. Instead of an embroidered hanky, a black, floppy felt hat.

The minutes and the students went by; the gabble and rush of opening bell. She waited, hat in hand, growing increasingly nervous as the time neared 7:48 and the student flood became a trickle. She half expected him to be late, as before, and he was. The stairwell was an echoing hollow below her when a loud thump signaled that the first floor's swinging door had been slammed open. Foot sounds followed, at intervals indicating at least three steps at a time — and there he was, book bag flapping wildly, careening through the turn at the mid-stair landing, heading straight for her now, head down, pounding the steps, panting . . .

She dropped her hat. She dropped it on the top step, in the middle, directly in his path. He couldn't possibly miss it. And he didn't. He ran right over it, planted his right foot smack on top of it, kept on going, burst through the door, and was into his homeroom.

Salem stared at her hat, or was that her heart lying there? She picked it up. A dusting of light brown showed where his foot had landed. She was about to brush it off when she remembered whose sneaker the dust had come from. She slipped the hat into her book bag. The bell rang. This time she did not run.

23

By the end of first period, she had it figured out. He didn't mean to step on her hat. He was going so fast, he didn't even see it. Or if he did, it was just a black blur on the step as he flew by. In any case, he certainly did not know he was stepping on his Love Line person's hat.

She felt better. And ready for another try.

They were scheduled to make their daily hallway pass-by after fourth period. This time she would drop the passive, little lady role. Since he was afraid to make a move, she would make it for him. She would speak. She would say "Hi" to him. Maybe "Hi, Alan." With a big smile. And with a look in her eyes that would answer his question, that would say, *Yes, I will be your valentine.*

When the bell ended fourth period, she was first out the door. She was racing to the spot where they usually passed, in front of the Science Lab, when she realized that if she outraced her usual pace, she might miss him. So she slowed down.

She kept to the middle of the hall, so she could move to either side to pass closely by him.

And here he came, gabbing away as usual with his after-fourth-period friend. She took a deep breath, she put on her best smile, she put the *Yes* in her eyes, the valentine in her voice: "Hi, Alan."

He stopped talking. His eyes darted about the mob. His head swung to one side, then the other. He smiled — the first time she had ever seen him smile in person, the most wonderful smile — and said, "Hi" — to the girl walking behind her.

By afternoon she had it figured. The hall was just too crowded. He hadn't seen her coming. All he heard was a voice in the mob. How was he to know which of those dozens of girls' faces passing by was the one who spoke his name? He just happened to pick out the wrong one, that's all.

It was time for a new approach. She would have to isolate him, one on one. At his locker after school. When there would be no rush, no confounding mob. No more messing around, no wiles, no excuses, no shyness. Just him and her and the answer to a question.

After school she waited by the water fountain outside Room 221. She watched the students come out, visit their lockers, drift, or dash away. He didn't come out. The hallway was deserted. The teacher came out and walked past her down the blue-carpeted avenue.

Salem peeked inside the room. Empty. On the way out, she stopped by the office to check the bulletin board. There was a Hi-Q meet today, at Tarrytown Middle School. The team bus had left after sixth period. He hadn't been in school for over an hour.

Sunny called that night.
"Where you been?"
Salem did not reply.
"I said — "
"I heard what you said."
"So answer the question."
"There you go again."
"There I go what?"
"That tone of voice."
"Huh?"
"I do not respond to questions that are growled at me like commands."
Sunny paused. "What are you so touchy about all of a sudden?" There was no answer. "As if I didn't know."
"What's that supposed to mean?"
"AK. That's what it means. It means you're all wrapped up in this stupid eighth-grader like you're twenty-one years old or something and you don't ride home on the picklebus anymore and you don't have time for your friends anymore because you're being a lovesick jerk, that's what — "
Click. Salem hung up.

Five seconds later the phone rang again. Salem picked it up.

" — it means. And anyway that's not even why I called, which I half wish I hadn't now, but I'm supposed to tell you. Bobo wants us to baby-sit so bad that he said we can do the camp-out in his yard Saturday night and watch the three monsters at the same time. So Pickles told him okay. So you still bring the bone. Oh, excuse me, there I go growling at you again. How's this? If you please, Miss Brownmiller, you are requested to be in the company of a bone when you attend the activities Saturday night. A bone from your own body will do nicely." *Click.*

24

First thing Wednesday morning Salem headed for Room 221, but this time she wasn't going to hang around. No waiting by the water fountain or lingering on the landing. What she had to do would take only a second.

The night before, she had hatched a new plan. She would cut right to the heart of the matter. She would answer his Love Line question, not with her eyes, but directly, unmistakably. In writing. She could have kicked herself for not thinking of it before. She was a writer, and here was the perfect chance to show her stuff.

She started composing at eight o'clock. By the time she finished polishing the final draft, it was almost eleven. It wasn't long, but it was perfect.

> *Dear Alan,*
> *Your question still echoes in my heart: "Be my valentine?"*

*When I think of the shyness you
had to overcome in order to write
that, I perceive the depths of your
feeling.*

*When I think of your courage to face
the mocking mobs who would laugh
and say, "She's too young!" I feel the
presence of true love.*

*Be shy no more, dearest Alan. Fear
not, for the answer is a resounding
YES! YES! YES!*

Your valentine,
Salem
(SB)

She had sprayed two puffs of her mother's perfume on the note, put it in a small envelope, sealed it, and placed it under her pillow and slept on it. And now as she approached his locker, she drew it from her pocket. A girl went to a nearby locker. Salem detoured to the water fountain. When the girl left, she glanced around, saw the coast was clear, rushed to his locker, and slipped the envelope into the crack at the bottom of the locker door. It wouldn't go through. Too thick. Loud voices echoed in the stairwell — kids were coming. She emitted a strangled screech. She tore off the envelope, she unfolded the note. It couldn't get any thinner. Footsteps pounded the stairs. Shouts, laughter. *Fit*, she prayed, *please fit*. She slipped it in. It went. The door thumped open. She ran.

The next day and a half were the longest in Salem's life. She learned what they meant in novels about the pain of waiting. She could not eat, she could not sleep, she could not concentrate. She could only wait, a helpless hostage of time. She had never wanted to understand Patrick Wister this well.

When she passed Alan in the hall after fourth period that day, she made no attempt to attract his attention. She did, however, study him closely as he passed. If a boy received a note in his locker, could you tell just by looking at him later in the hall? She imagined it might show in his eyes. They might be wandering over the crowd, anxiously, even desperately, scanning the faces, seeking that special one. But he was looking only at his hallway buddy, gabbing away with him as usual.

Maybe, she thought, considering how rushed he was each morning, he hadn't even seen it yet.

After school, she stayed away from 221. She lingered just inside the main door, where he would pass on his way home. Maybe he was just now visiting his locker for the first time today. Maybe he was just now noticing the note. She tried to picture it: He unlocks the lock, opens the door. He's reaching for books or whatever when, suddenly, he sees it. Maybe he doesn't even realize what it is at first, maybe he assumes it's just a loose sheet of his own paper. He's about to close the locker when — *ah!* — he gets a whiff of the perfume. Now where could that enchanting scent be coming from? That piece of paper? He picks it up, sniffs it. His senses drown in a confusion of ecstasy. (Thank you, Mother.) At last he opens his eyes and — yes, *now* — he reads the note.

Just thinking about it in the doorway, Salem began to tremble and sweat. Oh great, she thought, he finally comes to me and I'm a shaking, soggy, smelly mess. She brought herself under control. She thought of other, calmer things.

It was critical that she make herself available to him now at every possible moment. The worst thing that could happen would be for him to read the note and to come looking for her and — she shuddered at the thought — *not* be able to find her.

And so she waited and waited in the doorway. She knew her picklepals would once again be waiting for her in vain, and she did feel bad about that. They simply would not understand that matters of the heart override all else. She would make it up to them Saturday night.

It was as if her heart saw him first, for it seemed to quicken a split second before her eyes found him in the crowd passing the glass tank that housed Humphrey the hamster, the school mascot. He was passing the office now, now the student art display, in the midst of the departing mob, chatting with a girl . . . a brown-haired girl . . . chatting and laughing, passing by now, right in front of her — how could he not see her? — and through the doorway and out into the sunshine, still laughing as they buttoned up their jackets because the weather had finally turned cold. The girl was much taller than Salem, obviously an eighth-grader. Her eyelashes, as they had passed, seemed a foot long. They did not part outside the building. They did not go to separate buses. Salem stepped outside and watched them walk down the long driveway, bobbing into and out of view among the surging students. They did not separate at the end of the driveway, but both turned to the left and walked up the sidewalk.

Together.

The rest of that day and night was a nightmare from which Salem could not awaken.

Was the girl a friend — or *girl*friend? How could it be that Salem presented herself to Alan over three days, and not once did he speak to her, or nod, or smile? Just how shy could a shy person possibly be? Or how wrong? Had there been a horrible mistake? Was someone else AK? Avery Kribble? No. That was as laughable, as unthinkable as ever. AK *had* to be Alan Kent. So then:

SB. Did SB *have* to be Salem Brownmiller? Maybe the girl with short brown hair and foot-long eyelashes was an SB. Or maybe she was just a friend. He was allowed to have friends who happened to be girls, wasn't he?

Wasn't he?

25

February 14.

Salem stood at her bedroom window, one sock on, one in hand. The sun humped reddish over the horizon like one lobe of a heavenly valentine. Her plan had been to wait as long as necessary for a response to her note. That was no longer possible. Suspense was blowing her up like a balloon. If she didn't do something quick, she would pop.

Forty minutes later she stood by the stairway leading to Room 221 — not at the top, but at the bottom. She did not walk back and forth, she did not pretend she was doing something else. She simply planted herself in front of the bottom step and waited. Whatever happened, one thing was certain: He was not going to miss her this time.

She had rehearsed her part a hundred times, but now she could remember nothing but the first two words, which bolted on their own from her mouth as he came suddenly bursting through the door: "Alan, stop!" She scrunched her shoulders and shut her eyes, waiting for him to bowl her over. When she dared to peek, she was staring into his neck. Had he seemed this much taller than her before? The abrupt halting of his momentum had left him tilted forward, looming almost directly above her head. She could smell the banana he had had for breakfast, probably during his mad dash to school.

In her romantic ruminations, she had never considered being this physically close to a boy. It was a little scary. She tried to back up, but her heel bonked into the bottom step. She ran her heel up the vertical to the lip, then lifted herself onto the step. She was now looking directly into his eyes. They were blue. They were glaring at her. She turned away from them.

"What?" he said, not very pleasantly.

She could not think.

He spoke again, his irritation plainly showing. "Wha'd you stop me for?" He looked up the stairs. "The bell's gonna ring."

She took a deep breath. "Did you get my note?"

He looked baffled. "Huh?"

"The *note*. In your locker yesterday."

His expression went through a series of changes that she could not identify. He stepped back. For the moment he had forgotten the time. "Yeah?" He said it like a question.

"Well?"

112

"Well what?"

She wished he would leave the questions to her. "Well . . . what do you think?"

"About what?"

"The *note*." This was not how she had imagined the conversation going.

He took another step back. He cocked his head to one side. He squinted at her. "Did *you* write that?"

And suddenly, with chilling finality, from the way he said "you" and from the look on his face, she knew the truth. She knew she would never get to say the words.

The bell rang.

He jumped onto the step beside her. He looked down on her, down from a height of twenty feet, it seemed. He said, not unkindly, "What grade are you in?" He waited only a second, then dashed away.

She whispered to the empty stairway: "Sixth."

26

Everyone met at Bobo's house Saturday at five o'clock. Eddie brought the firewood, Sunny the tent, Salem the bone, and Pickles the pot. Everyone but Pickles was taxied to the house by a parent. Pickles came on the long, green, six-wheeled bus. The pot hung from the handlebars; a patchwork quilt was tied to the floor.

Besides the firewood, Eddie arrived with five blankets, a sleeping bag, a pillow, a candy-striped ski cap, a ski mask, a first-aid kit, a flashlight, a Monopoly game, a twenty-six-inch Samsonite suitcase, and a whistle around his neck.

"Where do you think you're going?" Sunny squawked when she saw it all piled on Bobo's back porch. "Siberia?"

"It pays to be prepared," Eddie replied.

She tugged on the whistle. "What's this for?"

"In case we need to call for help."

Sunny wagged her head. Before Eddie could stop her, she unzipped the suitcase. "Oh no!" she cried and pulled out a roll of toilet paper. Just then Bobo came onto the porch. Sunny waved the roll in his face. "It looks like Eddie Mott has plans for your backyard."

Bobo pointed to Eddie, who snatched the roll back. "You take a poop in my backyard," he growled, "and it's the last poop you'll ever take."

Bobo nodded at the tent. "You better put that thing up before it gets dark. I'll keep the monsters inside till I go."

"Can't you take them with you?" Sunny pleaded.

"Then who are you gonna baby-sit?" said Bobo.

"Eddie!" Sunny yipped. Eddie bounced the toilet paper off Sunny's head, everyone laughed, and Pickles dragged the tent into the yard.

The tent was raised and staked by nightfall, thanks mainly to Pickles. As he worked and directed the others, he kept saying, "Feels like snow . . . feels like snow."

Indeed, the temperature had been February-cold for several days, and overcast since Friday. There was no moonlight, and the night air was dense and still and utterly silent, as if waiting.

Pickles never stopped moving, now hammering a stake, now laying the canvas floor of the tent, now starting up a fire in the spot Bobo had designated. Repeating, almost singing, "Feels like snow," he bounced from chore to chore, as if by sheer activity he might persuade snow to fall.

In the meantime, Sunny kept herself and everyone else amused. For the most part she picked on Eddie. He constantly had to chase her from his belongings, as she insisted that if she were allowed a full search, sooner or later she would uncover a teddy bear.

Salem, by way of her mother's friendship with a butcher, had brought a huge shank bone from, it seemed, an apatosaurus. In Sunny's hands it became everything from a Continental soldier's drill musket to a twirler's baton to a flailing, whipsawing, martial-arts weapon.

Salem tried. She really tried to hang onto the devastation that had overwhelmed her at the foot of the stairwell Thursday morning. It seemed as if she had passed through the whole history of love in one week, and all she had to show for it was a flat, clobbered feeling. But at least it was a reminder of romance, and in a perverse sort of way she wanted to hang onto it.

But Sunny was making it awfully hard. Sunny kept poking her in the ribs with the bone. In time Salem began to suspect that Sunny guessed what had happened and was determined not to let her best friend feel sorry for herself. By the time "Michael Jordan" dunked the bone into the pot of boiling water and went into her cackling witch routine, Salem was laughing loudest of all.

Shortly before seven, with earsplitting shrieks, the three little monsters were let loose into the backyard. Bobo called from the porch: "I'll be back around eleven. Have a nice time!" He laughed and was gone.

From the start, the Bobo kids drove the baby-sitters batty. As soon as they discovered the sleeping bags, all three squeezed into one and went rolling about the yard like a giant worm. Then each climbed into a bag of his own, and they played bedroll demolition derby.

They found the toilet paper. Five minutes later a mummy stood where Eddie had been.

When they discovered the name of the baby-sitter with the green sneakers, they brought a jar of finger pickles from the refrigerator and had a finger pickle fight.

They kept trying to take the bone from the boiling water, but it was too hot. So they made the fire even hotter by feeding it the paper money from Eddie's Monopoly game.

And of course, when they discovered the picklebus, the Bobo kids, whose names were Wayne, Mookie, and Bert, went totally gonzo. Sunny, Salem, and Eddie had to forcibly wrench them away as Pickles parked the bus around the front of the house.

At that point the baby-sitters figured they'd better start saying no.

"Wanna see my boogie collection?"

"No."

"Can I cut a window in the tent?"

117

"No."

"Can I put Mookie's gerbil in the blender?"

"No!"

It was an avalanche of no's. So when Wayne had his next idea, he didn't even bother to ask. He just sneaked into the house and did it. When Sunny went looking, she found him dragging his mattress down the stairway.

"What are you doing!" she screeched.

"We're camping out, ain't we?" he said. "I'm bringing my bed."

Sunny yelled for Pickles, and together they lugged the mattress back upstairs. As they lifted it onto the box spring, they heard a whirring noise below. They stared at each other. *"Blender!"*

In the kitchen they found Wayne standing on a chair, a devilish grin on his face and a small, brown animal, presumably Mookie's gerbil, in his hand. He was dangling it over the buzzing blender.

At that moment Eddie came in the back door, saw what was happening and yelled, "Drop it!"

"No!" roared Pickles. *"Don't* drop it!" and he jerked the blender cord from its socket. The whirring blur became silvery blades, spinning, slowing, stopped.

"I'm calling your father," said Sunny.

"You're no fun," grumbled Wayne as Pickles confiscated the gerbil. "You don't let us do nothin'. I want Sally back."

"Sally?" said Sunny. "Who's that?"

"Our reg'lar baby-sitter, that's who. And I'm telling her on you!"

"Fine," said Sunny. "I'll tell your father to send her over. I'm resigning. Pick, give me that paper."

Pickles pulled a scrap of paper from his pocket and handed it over. Bobo had told them he was going to the Moose Lodge to play bingo. He had written the phone number on the paper.

Sunny called from the dining room. The phone rang a long time before some man — or moose — answered. While he went off to get Bobo, Sunny heard music in the background. Didn't sound like bingo.

At last Bobo came on the line. "They burn the house down yet?"

"Everything but," said Sunny. "Wayne tried to blender the gerbil."

The phone in her hand laughed for a full minute. "He just does that to get a rise outta ya. He wouldn't really do it. He loves that varmint. He played that once on me, too."

"Did he do it to Sally?"

Silence. "Who?"

"Sally? The regular baby-sitter?"

"Oh, Sally. Uh, sure, yeah, her, too. So that's all, huh? Gotta get back to bingo. Have a nice night."

He hung up before Sunny could resign.

"What did he say?" said Pickles.

"Have a nice night." She put up the receiver. "He didn't sound like himself."

"What do you mean?"

Sunny shrugged. "I don't know. He was laughing. He sounded, like, in a good mood."

Pickles frowned. "You sure it was Bobo?"

Outside again, Wayne broke open a stick of bubblegum, then tossed the wrapper into the soup. He stared at the baby-sitters, daring them to object. "Let him go," Pickles told the others. "We're not going to eat it anyway."

That was all Wayne, Mookie, and Bert had to hear. In short order, the bone and bubblegum wrapper were joined by a clump of grass, a brick, a cicada shell, a rusty screwdriver, a Dr Pepper can, a handful of stones, and a stiff, shriveled, long-dead earthworm. All of this was accompanied by loud and rising merriment, at the height of which Mookie fell onto his back, pulled off his shoes and socks, and flipped the socks into the pot.

"Sock soup!" shrieked Wayne, and even the baby-sitters had to laugh.

Salem took pictures then, to go along with the written report they had to submit for the project, or what was left of it. Naturally, the little ones wanted their pictures taken, so Salem did them first. Then she shooed them off and snapped another dozen photos of the tent, the pot and fire, her fellow "soldiers."

It was several minutes after the photo session when Eddie said, "Hey, it's quiet."

They glanced around.

"Must be in the tent," said Sunny. She looked. "Nope."

Already Pickles was heading toward the back porch. He disappeared into the shadows beside the house. Several seconds later they heard his cry from the front: "The picklebus is gone!"

27

They clustered out front under the cold, dim glow of the streetlight. Pickles put his finger to his lips. "Listen."

Sunny went off by herself. She dropped into a crouch as if she were guarding a basketball player. She closed her eyes. Suddenly she called: "Yes!"

Then they all heard: A distant hum of wheel on concrete, followed then by tiny, high-pitched voices:

"Wheeeee!"

"Yahoooo!"

"Fasterrrr!"

Eddie took a deep breath and pierced the night with his silver whistle. Houselights went on along the block; front doors opened. Sunny snatched the whistle from Eddie's neck. "Will you shut up!"

"Okay," whispered Pickles, still listening, "now where?"

They listened some more. Sunny pointed across the street. "Over there somewhere. Definitely."

Pickles was trotting. "Let's go."

Not wanting to go through strange backyards, they ran down to the end of the block, turned left, another block, another left. They halted.

"This is where they were," said Sunny.

"Yeah," huffed Eddie, *"were."*

"Fasterrrrr!"

Sunny pointed. "That way!"

Ooguh! Ooguh!

"They found the horn!" Pickles cried. "Come on!"

The chase zipped and dashed in fractured rectangles along the dark streets of Cedar Grove until at last the baby-sitters had the hijackers in sight. They were on the edge of downtown now. There were more lights. They passed Evergreen Bank, Little Flower Shoppe, Hans's Bakery. The hijackers were a block ahead.

Sunny shoved the whistle back at Eddie. "Now!"

Eddie blew. They yelled together, "Stop!"

The hijackers looked back to see their pursuers a half block behind and closing fast. They screamed and leapt from the picklebus, which went on rolling driverless till it coasted off-line and bumped to a stop against the steps of Coletto's Drugstore.

Pickles jumped aboard, and they continued the chase for another half-block, whereupon the hijackers abruptly veered right, bounded up the steps of a building, and burst through the door.

The pursuers paused on the steps. Eddie looked up. "What's that?"

Mounted above the door was the large wooden head of a long-faced, antlered animal.

"That," said Pickles, "is a moose."

"This is where Bobo came," said Salem.

Behind the door music was playing. They went in.

28

"W here's the bingo?" said Sunny.

There was dim lighting, and there was a small band playing slow, old-fashioned music, and there were people dancing in a slow, old-fashioned way, and there were round tables with red table-cloths and huge red hearts swooping from the ceiling on braided red-and-white crepe paper streamers — but there was no bingo.

As they stood inside the doorway, Sunny pointed, "There!"

It was Wayne, leading his brothers through the shadowy figures on the dance floor. Suddenly he called out, "Sally!" and ran up to a dancing couple.

The baby-sitters approached. Even in the shadowy light, the profile of the man proclaimed his identity. "It's Bobo," said Sunny. "Check the gut." The couple had stopped dancing to listen as Wayne chattered up at them. Then they turned to face the baby-sitters, all four of whom stopped in their tracks. Salem gasped: *"Miss Billups!"*

They came closer, not believing their eyes. "Is it you?" said Salem.

"Sal-*leee*," Wayne whined, "come home with us. We don't like them."

"You're Sally?" said Sunny.

Bobo swept Wayne onto his shoulders. He laughed. "Confession time."

The teacher wore a white dress as satiny as the cover on a heart-shaped candy box. Mookie and Bert clung to her hands. She gave an exaggerated shrug of surrender. "You caught me." She smiled. "Let's get away from the traffic." She led everyone to a corner by the buffet table. "Yes," she said, "I'm Sally."

"And you baby-sit for them?"

"Guilty."

"And you came to the dance," said Sunny, "with *him*?"

Miss Billups gave the bus driver a look they had never seen before, a look that, if it were paper, would have matched the hearts hanging from the ceiling. "Guilty as charged."

The four friends just stared, trying to fit this news into the world they thought they knew.

"And you — " said Salem, feeling the shape, the surface of the truth, feeling for the opening to the heart.

126

"Yes?"

"Was there one Love Line in *The Wurple*, by any chance, that wasn't from a student?"

"Bingo," said Bobo.

The teacher laughed and clapped her hands. "Yes!"

Salem pointed. "SB."

The teacher bowed. "Sarah Billups. Also known as Sally."

Salem turned, gaping, to her teacher's portly dancing partner.

"Students," said Miss Billups, "may I present Mr. Al Krumplik." She laid her head on his shoulder, she fluttered her eyes, she sighed romantically. "My valentine."

The hearts above seemed to swoon, woodwinds wooed.

"Let's go home," said Bobo. He grinned at the baby-sitters. "Unless you want to stay and dance with each other."

Sunny bolted for the door. "For-*get* it!"

In the crowded car, the kids all sat in back, hijackers on baby-sitters' laps.

"You weren't really mad at him at Valley Forge that day, were you?" said Pickles.

Miss Billups turned in the front seat. "No. In fact, he arranged to be the driver for the field trip."

"And he wasn't really sent to Late Room."

"Well," she chuckled, "he was, but not for being late. We happen to have a very nice and understanding and cooperative principal."

"And it wasn't a coincidence that you both just happened to be at the mall that Saturday."

"A well-organized plot."

Salem gasped. "That valentine candy box. You said — "

The teacher smiled and nodded to the driver. "My little nephew."

By the time they pulled up to the house, Miss Billups had told them how she and Bobo — "Al," she called him — had met one day when he honked his school bus at her.

"We never meant to keep it a secret from you kids forever," she said. "But for the time being, we thought it best not to announce to a school full of students that the bus driver and the social studies teacher were going steady."

The baby-sitters agreed that that was definitely a wise decision.

In the backyard, the fire had gone out. Bobo fetched every spare blanket in the house and, well before midnight, seven kids — three little, four big — were asleep in the tent.

Hours later Pickles awoke. He listened to the dark breathings around him. What had awakened him? He stood, keeping the patchwork quilt wrapped about him. He felt his way through the sleepers to the flap in front. He pulled it open. He looked. He put his hand out. He smiled. He whispered, softly as flakefall: "Snow."

29

There were a hundred sleds on Heller's Hill next day, but only one pickleboggan. And everyone wanted to ride it.

Pickles was generous, especially with the little kids. For one plunge down the endless slope, he managed to cram fifteen little bodies, besides himself, between the green panels.

Most of the trips, of course, were reserved for Eddie, Salem, and Sunny — plus a certain bus driver, a social studies teacher, and three former hijackers, all of whom happily showed up on the hill.

When Bobo rode, there was room left for only his girlfriend and the "Captain," which Pickles insisted on being called by anyone aboard the boggan. Whenever Bobo rode, the entire hill stopped to watch. His weight gave to the sled an unstoppable momentum that sent it faster and faster downhill until the silver runners blurred into the sun-dazzled snow.

While others cheered the speed and wonder of the great green rocket, Salem discovered something else — recovery — in the sight of Bobo and Miss Billups flying down the hill together. In their hugging and laughing descent she found the romance that she had so wanted for herself. Miss Billups' happiness, it turned out, was all the valentine she needed.

As for Sunny, her attention was directed elsewhere, namely off to the side, where Tuna Casseroli and his fellow nickelheads were rolling a ball of snow down the hill. By the time it got to the bottom, the ball was as tall as Tuna and twice as fat. A smaller, basketball-size snowball was placed on top. Stones made a doughboy face. A pair of pinecones became earrings. For the hairdo, someone brought a handful of small, round cookies. These were pressed all around the noggin, and presto — snow nickelhead!

Sunny could not resist. She dragged Pickles and his boggan over to the side. She pointed down the hill. "Can you steer this thing real close to that stupid snow jerk?"

"Watch me," he said.

They dragged the sled to the topmost point of the hill and began to push together. Within seconds, they were sprinting. They hopped aboard.

With Pickles manning the tiller, Sunny pulled herself onto the flanks so that one foot rested on the sideboard, one on the backboard. She stood, wobbled, extended her arms for balance, and let out a war cry.

When the nickelheads, who were gathered about their snowman, looked up, they saw a girl straddling Pickles Johnson's green monster like a trick rider in a circus — and it was all hurtling straight down at them. They scattered. As the boggan flew past, they heard the girl yell, "Hai-YAH!" and throw out her leg. The white head exploded in a splatter of cookies and snow.

The action threw Sunny from the sled. When she finally rolled to a stop and looked up, she found herself surrounded by nickelheads. She stood. She pointed at Tuna Casseroli. "That," she snarled, "was for Salem's hat."

What happened next surprised all who witnessed it. The fierce scowl vanished from Tuna's face, and suddenly he was booming with laughter at the sight of his headless snowman and the girl who did it.

Was it the blanketing, peacemaking power of the long-awaited snow? Was it the spell of Valentine's Day? Whatever, within minutes nickelheads were lining up at the top of the hill for rides on the pickleboggan. And every one of them called the driver "Captain."

About the Author

Jerry Spinelli is the author of several novels, including *Fourth Grade Rats*, *The Library Card*, *Do the Funky Pickle*, and the Newbery Medal–winning *Maniac Magee*. He lives in Phoenixville, Pennsylvania, with his wife and fellow author, Eileen Spinelli, and their children.

Any Way You Look At It,
LOUIS SACHAR'S
Books are Hilarious

___ 0-590-45726-8	**Sideways Arithmetic from Wayside School**	$4.99 US
___ 0-590-47762-5	**More Sideways Arithmetic from Wayside School**	$4.99 US
___ 0-590-46075-7	**Sixth Grade Secrets**	$4.99 US

Available Wherever You Buy Books or Use This Order Form

Take a Lesson in Laughte

from Newbery Award-winning author Jerry Spinelli

JERRY SPINELLI
Newbery-award-winning author of Maniac Magee

PRINCIPAL

REPORT TO THE PRINCIPAL'S OFFICE

SCHOLASTIC

JERRY SPINELLI

FOURTH GRADE RATS

SCHOLASTIC

_____	0-590-46277-6	**Report to the Principal's Office**	$4.99 U
_____	0-590-46278-4	**Who Ran My Underwear Up the Flagpole?**	$4.99 U
_____	0-590-45448-X	**Do the Funky Pickle**	$4.99 U
_____	0-590-45447-1	**Picklemania**	$4.99 U
_____	0-590-44244-9	**Fourth Grade Rats**	$4.99 U
_____	0-590-38633-6	**The Library Card**	$4.99 U

Available Wherever You Buy Books or Use This Order Form

Scholastic Inc., P.O. Box 7502, Jefferson City, MO 65102

Please send me the books I have checked above. I am enclosing $_____ (please add $2.00 to cover shipping and handling). Send check or money order—no cash or C.O.D.s please.

Name_____ Birth date_____

Address_____

City_____ State/Zip_____

Please allow four to six weeks for delivery. Offer good in U.S.A. only. Sorry, mail orders are not available to residents o Canada. Prices subject to change.

SCHOLASTIC and associated logos are trademarks and/or registered trademarks of Scholastic Inc.

 **SCHOLASTIC**

SPINELLIR

WHO RAN MY UNDERWEAR UP THE FLAGPOLE?

WHO RAN MY UNDERWEAR UP THE FLAGPOLE?

JERRY SPINELLI

SCHOLASTIC INC.

New York   Toronto   London   Auckland   Sydney
Mexico City   New Delhi   Hong Kong   Buenos Aires

ISBN 0-590-46278-4

31 30 29 28 27 26 25 24 23 22 21   4 5 6 7 8 9/0

Printed in the U.S.A.   40

For their contributions to this book
I would like to thank Jimmy Kerr, Drumore
Elementary (PA); Charles Patton, principal,
Unionville Middle School (PA); and Karen
Bretzius, whose desserts fueled the writing.

To Betsy Hoffman
John and Lila McCleary
Tom and Niki Reeves

WHO RAN MY UNDERWEAR UP THE FLAGPOLE?

1

Eddie Mott remained silent while the debate raged around him.

"He's never coming," said a tall red-haired boy named Wilson.

"He's just late, that's all," said a girl with a skirt on, the only skirted girl in class.

"It's twenty minutes already," said another.

"Maybe he's with the principal."

"Maybe he's sick."

"Maybe he's dead!"

A cheer went up from a dozen students who did not like social studies. Social studies was the subject, Mr. Hollis was the teacher, and he was late. Half the period had passed, and still no Mr. Hollis.

For the first ten minutes no one had said a word. The school year was barely three weeks old, but that had been long enough for the class to learn that Mr. Hollis was not a teacher to mess with. Mr. Hollis believed that kids these days were too pampered and spoiled, and he believed his mission in life was to put a stop to all that.

Physically, Mr. Hollis was perfect for the part: He was the tallest person in the school, his shoulders were wide as two student desks, he had a holler that could rattle glass three classrooms away, and he never, ever smiled. It was a historical fact — though not a surprising one — that Mr. Hollis had never sent anyone to the principal's office, for the simple reason that no one had ever dared to be bad in his class.

If such a student were destined to appear in the future, one thing was certain above all else: That student would not be Eddie Mott. Though he had been a middle school sixth-grader for three weeks now, Eddie was still a grade school kid at heart. He did not feel like a real member of the student body. In the hallways between classes, he felt uncomfortable, edgy, like an outsider among the mobs of clattering seventh-graders and huge, bellowing eighth-graders.

And now he was feeling apart from even his fellow sixth-graders. Where did they get the nerve to talk that way about the dreaded Mr. Hollis? What if he walked in right this second and caught Wilson, the tall redheaded boy, who now was — incredibly — telling the students that they had a right to leave when a teacher was this late?

"I have a brother in college," Wilson was saying, "and if a professor is fifteen minutes late for

2

a class — *zam!*" — Wilson flattened his hand and shot it toward the open door — "they're outta there."

Besides wanting to avoid trouble, Eddie had another reason for not wanting to get "outta there." The reason's name was Sunny Wyler. Ever since he had seen her on the bus heading for the first day of school, Eddie had had this feeling about her. The feeling seemed to be located in his eyes, for whenever she was around, he could not take them off her. And she was around right now. To be precise, she was seated directly across the aisle from him, to his right.

If Eddie could have had his way, he would have swung around, plopped both feet in the aisle, sat sideways in his chair, directly facing her, and stared at her for all forty-five minutes of social studies. Of course, the fearsome Mr. Hollis would never allow such a thing, and neither would Sunny Wyler. Not only did Sunny have no desire to look at Eddie, she did not even like him to look at her.

For the first couple weeks of school, she had been positively mean about it, scowling at him and once even pretending to flick a boogie at him. Then, after he rescued Humphrey, the school's mascot hamster, and returned him to Sunny, Humphrey's caretaker, Sunny had softened a little toward him. But not to the point of allowing him to openly gawk at her.

So Eddie kept his face pointing forward and

jammed his eyeballs to the right till they ached. He wished people came equipped with spare parts. He'd insert his spare eyeball into his right ear and, face forward, look at Sunny Wyler to his heart's content. Since that was impossible, the best he could hope for was to sit beside her for the full forty-five minutes of this period.

But the situation was quickly turning to mutiny.

"How many people have gym next?" demanded Wilson, now standing up front. Almost every hand in the class went up. Eddie, ever obedient, even to a fellow sixth-grader, raised his, too.

"See?" said Wilson. "Who could blame us? Do you think they *want* us to sit here doing nothing, wasting our time? Don't you think they would *want* us to go to the locker rooms now, so we could get a head start changing for gym, so we could be out on the field early, being healthy and all?"

Eddie wasn't surprised at Wilson's line of reasoning. He was known to be a sports fanatic. Even so, his argument seemed to make sense. Nobody was objecting. Eddie sincerely wished somebody would, for he longed to sit beside Sunny Wyler till the last second.

"Look," said Wilson, pointing to the clock, "there's only fifteen minutes left. Do you *really* think he's gonna show up *now*?" He looked over the class; no one answered. He went to the doorway, stuck his head out, looked both ways. He

4

pulled his head back in, swung it toward the class, grinned: "Nobody there."

Several kids giggled.

"I'll even call him, okay?" Wilson stepped fully into the hallway, so he was visible to only the first three rows. But everyone could hear his singsong voice, not as loud as a shout, but louder than a whisper: "Mister Hollll-is . . . Mister *Hollll*-is."

Five seconds of utter silence passed . . . ten seconds. The class, as one, held its breath.

Wilson strode back into the room, beaming, throwing out his arms triumphantly to show that he was safe, he was right. The class applauded.

Wilson seized the moment. He swept his books and gym bag from his desktop, he headed for the doorway, he punched his fist in the air. "Let's go!"

They went. Even Sunny Wyler. Even Eddie Mott, though he was the last one out the door.

Shortly, the boys were pouring into their locker room, the girls into theirs. Eddie found the locker room to be twice as crowded as usual, as the previous class was still there, changing back into school clothes. Eddie plunked his books and gym bag down, sat on the bench, and started getting ready. Like most of the kids, he didn't have to change his sneakers, as he wore his regular school sneaks for gym.

Shouting, laughing, horseplay — the commotion of fifty boys in a sweat-fumed locker room swirled in noisy riot until, in an instant, it stopped,

5

as if snipped by the first syllable of the megaton roar coming from the door: "SOCIAL STUDIES CLASS, THE PERIOD IS NOT OVER! GET BACK WHERE YOU BELONG! THIS INSTANT! *NOW!*"

The door closed upon dead, stunned silence.

Eddie took off. The man said *NOW!* the man meant *NOW!* He knew it, he *knew* he should never have listened to that Wilson, gone along with the crowd. Well, he may have been the last one out of the room, but he sure wasn't going to be the last one back in. He burst from the locker room, he raced down the hallway even as Mr. Hollis' voice roared into the girls' locker room: *"NOW!"* He careened around corners, flew up a stairway, tore into room 212, social studies, and slammed into his seat so hard he nearly toppled his desk over.

He was gasping, he was shaking, he was terrified — but he was also back, the first one back, where he was supposed to be. That should count for something.

Within seconds, Mr. Hollis returned. He glanced once into the room and parked his towering bulk by the doorway, just outside the room. As the other kids began to straggle back, each had to pass beneath his scorching glare. They were quiet and docile as lambs, not a peep, not even from Wilson, who in his haste had neglected to zip up his fly. In spite of the grim situation,

Eddie had to stifle a grin when he saw that.

Apparently others noticed, too, for as they took their seats, Eddie could hear giggles, faint and muffled so as not to reach the ears of Mr. Hollis. Eddie began to feel sorry for Wilson. Somebody should tell him, he thought.

And then Sunny Wyler was coming in, clutching her books, straight-faced — until she sat down and broke into a grin that grew and grew until her mouth was no longer big enough to contain it. Her whole body was shaking, her cheeks were bulging. She managed to do all this in silence, her hand clamped over her mouth, until a most ungirl-like snort, with nowhere else to go, blew out her nose. For his part, Eddie was delighted to see Sunny laughing, since she was usually so grouchy.

All noise and movement came to an abrupt halt as Mr. Hollis stepped into the room and slammed the door shut. He walked slowly to the front-center of the room and folded his arms. When his eyes fell on Eddie, his terrible stare seemed to soften a little. He knows I was the first one back, Eddie thought.

Indeed, as if to confirm this thought, Mr. Hollis spoke: "Never pull that again, people, no matter how late I may be. I want to see every one of you in here after school for a half-hour detention — everyone except" — he looked directly at Eddie — "what's your name, son?"

"Eddie Mott, sir."

"Everyone except Mr. Mott, who obviously was the only one to strictly obey my order to return at once."

Eddie's heart soared.

"Unfortunately," Mr. Hollis went on, "sometimes there's a small price to pay for obedience. Mr. Mott"— he looked not at Eddie but at the clock — "if that clock is correct, you have forty-five seconds before the bell rings and the halls are filled with people . . . forty seconds now to return to the locker room for what you forgot."

Forgot? thought Eddie. Forgot what? He looked from Mr. Hollis to his desk . . . his desk . . . his *empty* desk. No books! He forgot his books!

"Thirty seconds, Mr. Mott."

As Eddie turned sideways to get up, his legs came into view . . . his *legs*. His sneakers were there at the bottom with his socks, and at the top was his red-and-blue Superman underwear, but in between: nothing. *His pants were gone!* Back in the locker room, with his books, abandoned in the terror of Mr. Hollis' *"NOW!"*

"Fifteen seconds, Mr. Mott."

Eddie made it in ten.

2

"You're a witness," said Eddie Mott.

"You're loony," said his best buddy, Pickles Johnson.

They were in the alleyway behind Pickles' house after dinner.

"You got the matches?" asked Eddie.

"Yeah."

"The right kind?"

Pickles thrust a box of stick matches in front of Eddie's face. "Yeah, here — okay?"

"Just checking."

Eddie had asked for stick matches because he wasn't sure he could light one of the matchbook types without burning off half his fingers.

"So what do you think?" he said. "Should we pour some gasoline over them, or lighter fluid, or something?"

"Heck no," said Pickles. "Why don't we do it right? Let's steal some TNT and make a bomb and bomb 'em."

It took Eddie a second to realize Pickles was joking, and even then he barely cracked a smile. This business was simply too serious to joke about.

At their feet, by the side of the alley, sat a colorful rumpled bundle of underwear — underpants, to be exact. Eddie's entire underpants wardrobe: three Supermans, three Batmans, two Fred Flintstones, and a Casper the Friendly Ghost.

"What are you wearing now?" said Pickles.

Eddie hesitated, then whispered: "Nothing." Just uttering the word made him feel wicked, but grown-up, too, and *that* was the whole idea.

"You *are* loony," said Pickles.

Eddie's ears reddened. His nostrils twitched. It happened whenever he thought about the events of social studies class earlier that day. He poked a finger at Pickles. "Listen, *you* weren't sitting in class in your underwear. *I* was. *You* didn't have to go running through the halls that way. *I* did. It's not *you* everybody in school is laughing about. It's *me*."

"So what are you going to do," said Pickles, grinning, "go streaking down the hallway tomorrow with nothing on just to show everybody you don't wear Superman undies anymore?"

Eddie yanked a wad of dollar bills from a side pocket and thrust it into Pickles' face. "I'm buying new ones with this. I was saving up for comic books."

"So what kind are you going to buy?"

"I don't know."

"Where are you going to get them?"

"I don't know."

"You know anything?"

"Yeah, I know I gotta grow up. I gotta stop being a little kid."

"You *are* a little kid."

"But I *can't* be!" Eddie screeched. "I'm in the middle school now."

"So's everybody else. You're not the only sixth-grader at Plumstead."

Eddie threw up his hands. "Yeah, right, but I *am* the only one who did exactly what the teacher said and went right back to the room, in my underwear. Why didn't anybody *else* do that?"

Pickles grinned. "Because they're not as dumb as you."

Eddie swatted, but Pickles ducked, laughing. "Yeah, well, it's also because I was scared. And why was I scared? Because I act — and think — like a little first-grader. Starting right now — gimme" — he held out his hand; Pickles gave him the matches — "no more baby. No more being laughed at. No more jumping every time a teacher says jump. No more" — he struck a match — "Superman underwear."

He dropped the burning matchstick onto the jumble of underwear. The match burned along the length of itself, swallowed itself, and went out. Eddie struck another match and dropped it; then another and another. The underwear caught, flared. "Yahoo!" went Eddie. Fred Flintstone's face crumpled and dissolved. In less than a minute, the once-bright bundle was a dull, sooty gray, as though the flames had stolen its colors.

Pickles picked up the bucket of water that had been sitting nearby. "Now?"

"No, wait," said Eddie, fascinated to see his little-kidhood going up in smoke.

"That's long enough," said Pickles at last, emptying the bucket. The flames hissed and spat defiantly, then vanished.

"We'll leave it here to make sure it dies out," said Pickles. "I'll scoop it up and put it in a trash can later." He tossed the empty bucket into his backyard. He tugged at Eddie, who was still staring at the smoldering heap. "Come on, snap out of it. We're going to the Acme."

Eddie looked at him. "Acme?"

"Yeah, it's the only place I know around here where you can get yourself some new undies. Let's go, we're riding."

Eddie allowed himself to be steered to the pickleboard, his friend's oversized, custom-made, green, pickle-shaped skateboard. They took off down the alley, Eddie behind Pickles, each with his left foot on the board, right foot pushing, like a pair of oarsmen.

"If you really want to grow up," Pickles called back, "there's something you can try besides new underwear."

"What's that?" said Eddie.

"Go out for football."

3

Salem Brownmiller had a special reason for wanting to make the Plumstead Middle School cheerleading squad. Salem wanted to be a writer. Though strictly speaking, she guessed she was already a writer, if having your very own word processor and your own writing scarf and sitting down and writing practically every day of your life made you a writer — then, yes, she was a writer.

Perhaps you could say she wanted to be a published writer. But then, how about the poem she sent to the children's magazine *Lickity Split*? They had sent her an acceptance letter — she had even kissed the mailman when it arrived — and a month later there it was, on page 19 of *Lickity Split*. Yes, she was already a published writer.

To be really specific about it, what Salem Brownmiller wanted to be more than anything in the world was an *author*. To Salem, the very word itself was magic. *Author*. It meant someone who had written a book, a book that could be found in bookstores and libraries. In Salem's case, the book would be fiction, a story that she would create with her imagination but that would be inspired by real people and real life.

Salem knew that in order to write such books she would have to understand many different kinds of people. She knew that the best way to understand somebody was to put yourself in their place. And that's why Salem Brownmiller was trying out for cheerleading. She knew that the cheerleader was an important kind of person in today's world and that sooner or later she would be writing about one. And since she was not the cheerleading type herself — far from it! — she would have to become one in order to gain insights into the world as seen through the eyes of a cheerleader.

And that's why she had invited her new friend Sunny Wyler over to her house. Sunny was also out for cheerleading.

"I need help bad," said Salem, slumping onto her bed. "I'm the worst one out there. I know I'm not going to make the cut tomorrow." Her eyes rolled hopefully up to Sunny. "Am I?"

Sunny was giving herself a tour of the bedroom, this being her first time in Salem's house. She shrugged. "Probably not."

Salem beat the mattress with her hands and feet. "Ohhhh! You don't have to be so honest."

"You asked me."

"You could lie a little."

"You're the greatest cheerleader in the world."

Salem sighed. "What exactly am I the worst at?"

"Everything."

"Ohhh!" Salem clutched her heart as if mortally wounded. Even so, she was glad she had asked Sunny over. Sunny was the only person she could trust to be totally, brutally honest.

"Except maybe for smiling," Sunny added. "You're a pretty good smiler."

"My smile won't keep me from being cut." Salem lay on her back on the bed, staring at the ceiling. She took a deep breath, gathered herself, and sprang to her feet. "Well, let's get started. I brought you here because you're the best of all the sixth-graders. To tell you the truth, I think you're better than the seventh- and eighth-graders, too."

Sunny seemed oblivious to the compliment. She pulled from Salem's bedstead a length of black, silky material. "What's this?"

"My writing scarf," said Salem. "I always wear it when I'm writing." To demonstrate, she took the scarf from Sunny, flung it once around her neck, sat down at her keyboard, and pretended to peck away. "Tah-dah. I write my stories and poems here, then transfer them to my father's desktop publisher."

"You're goofy," said Sunny.

"Thank you," Salem replied primly. "I hope so. Actually, the word you're looking for is *eccentric*, which is what writers are supposed to be."

"And what's all the posters?" said Sunny, gazing at one.

"Paris. That's the Eiffel Tower. That one over there is the famous Left Bank."

"Famous for what?"

"Famous for writers. That's where all the American writers went back in the 1920s. A couple of years on the Left Bank, and they became famous. I'm just getting started in here. Pretty soon, when you walk in here you'll think you're right in the middle of the Left Bank of Par-*ee*."

"You're not goofy," said Sunny, "you're weird."

Salem got up. She tossed her writing scarf aside. "I am also going to be cut from cheerleading tomorrow if you don't help me out."

Sunny just stared at her. "Am I *that* hopeless?" Salem asked. Sunny kept staring.

Even considering Sunny's unusual first name — the official version of which was Sunshine — Salem sometimes wondered why she liked Sunny. Sunny's disposition was often anything but. She always seemed to be complaining or otherwise looking on the dark side of things. She was, to put it bluntly, a grouch.

And yet there was something appealing about her. Most of the time she made you want to laugh instead of being grouchy back. Two of Salem's other friends, Eddie Mott and Pickles Johnson, liked Sunny, too. In fact, Eddie *really* liked her, though Sunny was as cool to him as she was to all boys. I wonder if she likes me, Salem thought.

At last Sunny said something: "Coochy Coo."

Salem groaned. "Oh, no. That's my worst one."

"That's why you should work on it." Sunny snapped her fingers. "Let's go."

All of the routine was regular cheerleading moves except for the "Coochy Coo" lines of the chant. As Ms. Baylor, the cheerleading coach, had demonstrated, you had to do a wiggle while at the same time make a full-circle turn.

Salem stood in the middle of her room, un-moving.

"Let's go," Sunny repeated. "Coochy . . ."

Salem took a deep breath and plunged in:

"Coochy Coochy Coochy COO!
We're gonna win.
Well, it's TRUE!
Coochy Coochy Coochy COO!
We're gonna win.
We're gonna beat YOU!"

It ended with an aggressive stomp forward with one foot and a thrust of the forefinger at the other team, wherever they were. Sunny blinked for a while, looked at her feet, then at the wall posters.

"Well?" said Salem.

Sunny sniffed. "Your finger point wasn't bad."

"And the rest?"

Sunny held her nose.

"I *know* it stinks!" Salem cried out. "That's why you're here, to help me unstink myself. You have" — she looked at her digital clock — "an hour and fifteen minutes to make me a better cheerleader. Show me. Coach me."

Sunny stared steadily at her. "If I had to pick the worst of the worst, it would be the wiggle."

"Really bad, huh?"

"The pits. I've seen better wiggles on boys."

"Acchhh!" Salem flung herself back to the bed. "What's the matter with me? When I make myself into a character in a story, I'm always so graceful and elegant. Why can't I be like that in real life? What kind of a girl am I? Eleven years old, and I can't even wiggle yet!" She pounded her pillow and buried her face in it.

A silence followed. Then Salem felt the mattress sag: Sunny had sat on the bed. Then came Sunny's voice, in a flat, I'm-not-impressed tone: "Aren't you overdoing it a little?"

Salem couldn't help it, she laughed into her pillow. She swung onto her back. "That's what my parents always say, I overdo it. I guess if I weren't a writer I'd be an actress." She sat up. She was liking Sunny more and more, grouch or not. "But I really *do* have to make cheerleading.

So I can find out what makes a cheerleader tick. So I can get *insights*."

Salem looked down. She hadn't realized it, but she was clutching Sunny's arm, as if to squeeze the cooperation out of her. Sunny was looking back, still unsmiling, but with no sign of discomfort or disapproval. Salem knew that Sunny was not the type of girl that just anybody could touch, much less grab; yet Sunny sat calmly, patiently, and made no move to extract her squeezed arm. In that moment Salem began to understand the language upon which their friendship would be traded. Yes, she thought, she does like me.

4

Sunny tried. Salem tried. But it was not to be.
The following day, standing in the grass by
the sideline, the pads of the practicing football
teams thumping in the background, Salem listened in vain as Ms. Baylor called out the names
of the survivors. Sunny, of course, made it, despite Ms. Baylor's constant harping: "Smile, Wyler, smile!"

Sunny stayed close to Salem as the girls headed
for the gym to pick up their books. The lowering
sun, whose age was reckoned in the millions of
years, sat upon the roof of Plumstead Middle
School, not yet one month old.

"Now what?" Sunny asked.

Salem only shrugged.

The route to the gym took the girls along the
perimeter of the football field, which was occupied
by two teams: the varsity and the 100-pound. The
latter was made up entirely of sixth- and seventh-
graders.

The girls skirted the goalposts at one end and were coming up the opposite sideline when several players began dashing their way. The football had been fumbled and was wobblehopping over the grass, the players in frantic pursuit, as though chasing a rabbit. They all caught up with it at once, and the resulting collision of helmets and bodies caused several of the girls to stop and gasp.

The knot of players, each grasping for the ball, lurched and staggered like a drunken, many-headed creature. Suddenly the whole knot spun violently, and out of it came one of the players flying and landing with an "Oof!" at the feet of Salem and Sunny.

The player's number, 89, was so big for his body that the bottoms of the 8 and the 9 were buried in his padded pants. His glossy purple helmet also seemed enormous for the thin, pale stalk of a neck showing beneath it.

Number 89 groaned, a bleating, high-pitched sound that did not seem to go with the huge pads that bloated the shoulders of his shirt. He pushed himself to his knees, to his feet, and suddenly he was screaming, "I can't see! I can't see!"

At that point he was standing directly in front of Sunny, his voice coming through the purple plastic helmet, rather like that of a giant talking fly. "No kidding, you dummy," said Sunny, plucking the helmet from the head. "Your helmet got turned backwards."

"Eddie Mott!" exclaimed Salem.

Eddie Mott's eyes gaped as if he were newly hatched. "Sunny," he breathed.

Sunny dropped the helmet into his hands. "Here's your head back."

"You're bleeding," Salem said, rushing in. A gash across the bridge of Eddie's nose was spilling blood. "He's bleeding!" she called to the field. In an attempt to stop the flow, she pressed the short sleeve of her shirt to his nose. To someone at a distance, it would have looked like a girl giving a boy a whiff of her underarm.

In time Mr. Lujak, the coach, came clomping over, not exactly in a big hurry. "What now?" he growled.

Salem took her arm away. "He's bleeding. It's cut."

Eddie himself seemed not to notice the injury but kept gazing at Sunny.

"Great," said the coach. "I got a halfback over there who thinks he's got a loose tooth. I got a center who giggles every time the quarterback touches his rear end. And I'm supposed to get this team ready to play somebody two weeks from now." He looked up and down the sidelines. He shouted in the direction of the school, the ancient sun: "I need a manager!"

In a flash of recovery and inspiration, Salem Brownmiller shot her hand skyward. "I'm here!"

5

T. Charles Brimlow, brand-new principal of brand-new Plumstead Middle School, welcomed his guests into his office: Salem Brownmiller, Sunny Wyler, Eddie Mott, and Dennis "Pickles" Johnson. The Principal's Posse, he called them. He had invited these four sixth-graders to have lunch with him on the first day of school and had decided to make it a weekly occasion.

The first two lunches had been fancy, cafeteria-catered affairs. Now, over Salem's objections, it was just bring your brown bag and sit wherever you like.

Mr. Brimlow himself stood, leaning back against the front edge of his desk. Eddie Mott fished into his bag from his seat on the rug. "What happened there, Eddie?" said the principal.

Eddie touched the adhesive bandage that humped over the bridge of his nose and tailed under both eyes. "Football." He said the word

24

with a clear hint of pride, then added with a casual shrug, "No problem."

The principal assumed that this manly performance was for the benefit of Sunny Wyler, whom Eddie liked. As for Sunny, chomping a sandwich in one of the high-backed leather chairs, she was plainly unimpressed. So Brimlow, not wanting Eddie to go scoreless, raised his own eyebrows. "Football, huh? Tough sport."

"Nah," said Eddie, ripping a chunk from his Devil Dog as though he were an animal eating raw meat. "You gotta play with a little pain, that's all."

"He was bleeding all over at practice yesterday," said Salem, who had settled into the other leather chair. "He was *gushing*. I had to stop it with my shirt, which I had to throw away because it was half-dyed red. Ugh!"

"And what were you doing on the football field?" asked Mr. Brimlow.

"That's a long story," Salem said, and everyone knew that no one could stop Salem from telling it. "I was trying out for cheerleading so I could gain new insights so I could be a better writer, someday an author of books, as you know. I feel that as a writer, it's important to get into your main character as much as possible."

"She bombed out," said Sunny, munching.

Salem stared wide-eyed across the office at her

25

friend, blinked, turned back to the principal. "I didn't make the cut. I — "

"She can't wiggle."

"Sunny!" White bread specks flew from Salem's mouth. She fumed, glared, squeezed her sandwich, giving it a twist. At length she regained her composure and turned again to the principal. "I guess I'm not the most coordinated person in the world, at least not in a cheerleading kind of way. Anyway, I didn't make it, and practice was over, and we were walking around the field when — *pow* — there's this big collision of players, and one of them lands at our feet — of me and my *former* friend, Miss *Sun*shine Wyler" — she said, knowing Sunny hated that name — "and who was it but Eddie Mott."

"Bleeding," said Mr. Brimlow, hoping to hasten the story.

"Gushing," Salem nodded, "but we didn't know it at the time because he had his helmet on backwards, which my former friend pulled off. Then the blood. And the sleeve. And then Mr. Lujak, the coach, came over and complained that he needed a manager to help him out and I said, 'Hey, that's me!' "

"Now you're gaining insights into football managers," offered Mr. Brimlow.

"Exactly," said Salem, still holding a full sandwich minus one bite. "They may not be as impor-

26

tant in the world as cheerleaders, but that doesn't mean they're not interesting."

"Especially," snickered Sunny, "if the manager gets a load of Eddie's underwear."

Eddie nearly choked on the last bite of his second Devil Dog. "Hey, what's that supposed to mean?"

Sunny's eyes wandered over the ceiling. "It's a bird . . . it's a plane . . . it's — "

Eddie spluttered, "That was a mistake! I don't have Superman underwear!"

Sunny gave Eddie's beltline a sly, sideways leer. "Oh, no?"

"No!" squawked Eddie, rising to his knees and facing Sunny. His ears were red, his nostrils twitching.

Mr. Brimlow froze. Was the boy going to prove it?

"It's true," said Pickles, speaking for the first time. He sat in the principal's swiveling armchair, which he had wheeled out alongside the desk. His pickle-green sneakers were propped up at the heels and crossed casually on the carpet. "The underwear was an old pair left over from when Eddie was little. He only wore them that day because all the others were in the wash."

Eyes paddleballed between Pickles and Eddie. Brains computed this new claim.

No one really believed it, a conclusion voiced

by Sunny's sarcastic snort: "Yeah, right."

As far as Mr. Brimlow was concerned, believing it was beside the point. What touched him was Pickles' attempt to rescue his pal from ridicule.

Eddie, his face grimly set, was on his feet now. He went behind the high-backed chair in which Salem sat. Visible only from the neck up, he appeared to be twisting, doing something. A brief ripping sound was heard. Eddie emerged from behind the chair. He marched straight to Sunny and threw a small, white something into her lap. "Here."

Sunny looked at it. She burst out laughing. She flung the white thing back at Eddie. It sailed, as if on the wind of her laughter, past Eddie and came to rest at Mr. Brimlow's feet. He picked it up. It was the cloth label from Eddie's underwear. It read *FRUIT OF THE LOOM*.

"Well," Mr. Brimlow said, searching for words to put a lid on this episode. "This certainly has been a revealing lunchtime."

Sunny said, almost in a whisper, "He thinks he's all grown up."

Mr. Brimlow stared at her, his expression saying, Give it up, Sunny, back off; but she was speaking into her lap: "How big can he be if he eats his Devil Dogs first?"

She ended with a brief snicker. No one joined in. She snickered some more, alone. "Well, *I* think it's funny."

28

Eddie Mott sat alone on the carpet, staring blankly at an empty Devil Dog wrapper.

For once Salem was at a loss for words. Mr. Brimlow himself searched his mind for a way to repair the damage he has just witnessed. His impulse was to rush over to Eddie Mott and take the kid in his arms and tell him it was okay. Since the first day of school, when a group of eighth-graders had tossed him around the school bus, Eddie had been picked on — and now by no less than a fellow sixth-grader. And the boy was the timid type to begin with. Mr. Brimlow had the crazy feeling that if he did not say or do something useful in the next two seconds, Eddie Mott would dissolve, right before their eyes, into a puddle on the rug.

And then the matter was taken out of his hands. Pickles Johnson pulled a Devil Dog from his lunch bag. "Eddie," he called and tossed it.

Eddie stabbed at the pack one-handed, missed, picked it up. He looked over at Pickles, and something in his face changed. He unwrapped the Devil Dog. He stared at the chocolate sandwich. He pulled the halves apart, revealing the pure white creamy filling. He glanced once again at Pickles, stood, walked over to Sunny in her high-backed chair, and mashed one of the chocolate cake halves, creamy side down, into her face.

The bell rang as Pickles, Salem, and Eddie erupted into gales of laughter. They gathered up their lunch trash and dropped it into the waste-basket; then they hung around, still chuckling, while Sunny scooped filling from her face and licked away every fingerful. She nodded. "Mm . . . thanks." She pulled a napkin from her bag, wiped her face dry, got up, tossed her trash into the basket, and went out with the others.

For more than a minute the principal just stood there, trying to figure out what he had just seen. Where did Eddie get the nerve to do it? Why didn't Sunny retaliate? Why didn't she even seem to be upset? With his foot Mr. Brimlow pushed his swivel chair back behind his desk. Apparently he still had a lot to learn about sixth-graders.

6

"No! No! No! . . . This way! . . . *This* way!"
All afternoon the voice of Arnold Hummelsdorf could be heard braying over the playing fields of Plumstead, louder than the football coaches, louder than the cheerleaders. Hummelsdorf, known to generations of Cedar Grove students as Lips, was the school's music director.

Only two weeks before, Hummelsdorf had achieved the unbelievable: For the musical segment of the opening assembly, he had directed onstage a band that was composed of every student of the new school — all 340 of them, playing the likes of soda bottles, washboards, and rubber bands. The auditorium seats had been empty of everyone but teachers.

In the afterglow of that stunning achievement, Hummelsdorf had hatched another. Plumstead would be the first middle school in the county — or anywhere, so far as he knew — to put a marching band on the field during halftime of football games, especially 100-pound-team games. Well, he got his band, all right — all seven of them. A bugle player, a tuba player, a clarinetist, a triangle player, a flutist, a drummer, and a violinist. The violinist, of course, belonged in the school orchestra, but the kid volunteered to march, and Hummelsdorf was only too happy to get every warm body he could. He would have taken a flute-tooting duck had one presented itself.

Once, Lips Hummelsdorf had dreamed of leading 200-member bands before vast crowds in college stadiums. Instead he had come to this, trying to teach seven nincompoops how to march and play at the same time. Well, six actually; the bugler, the kid called Pickles, wasn't so bad.

The others were a horror story. The flutist was forever turning the wrong way and bumping into the clarinetist. At one point, the violinist dropped her bow. When she stopped and stooped to pick it up, the tubist, marching onward, went flying over her back and landed head-down into the gaping mouth of his own instrument. For a half second there, before the kid toppled over, it looked as though a student were being swallowed headfirst by a great white tuba.

The triangle player, a sixth-grader as tiny as the *ting* from his instrument, seemed in a total fog, as though he were supposed to be elsewhere, maybe Mars. In any case he kept marching off in odd directions — *ting ting ting* — and Hummelsdorf had to keep calling him back: ". . . *this* way!"

But worst by far was the drummer. To begin with, he was an eighth-grader, meaning he thought he owned the school and all surrounding property.

As if that wasn't bad enough, he was also one of these so-called nickelheads. The trouble kids went to these days to make themselves ugly, especially with their hair, was beyond Hummelsdorf. Glopping it, slicing it, spiking it, roasting it — he had seen hair in the hallways that would terrify a werewolf. And now these nickelheads, with their teddy bear cuts and circles gouged out right down to the skull. To Hummelsdorf, it looked as though an octopus had grabbed each of them by the head.

And now, recently, some of them had taken to painting the bald circular patches. If they wanted to be clowns, why didn't they go join the circus? And this one, the drummer, was probably the most ridiculous of all. His head circles were not only painted, they were numbered. All he needed was a cue stick and he could play pool with his own head. And in fact his nickname was Cueball.

The nickelhead imagined himself to be a drummer with a famous rock band and was totally out of control. He beat not only his own snare drum but anything else that came within reach: the triangle player's triangle, the tuba, the violinist's head, his own head. In the nickelhead's hands, the drumsticks became instruments of mayhem. He tickled Pickles' stomach as he was tooting, changing bugle notes to a horse's whinny. He stuck the tip of a drumstick into the clarinetist's ear and up the flutist's nose.

And now he was over by the cheerleaders, bothering them. The remaining six members of the band could not contain their curiosity. In the middle of the fight song, composed by Hummelsdorf himself and called "Hail to the Hamsters," the band stopped their marching and turned toward the cheerleaders. The notes from their instruments subsided to a trickle. "Play! Play!" ranted Hummelsdorf, but when he himself turned to see what was happening, the music ceased altogether.

What they saw were the cheerleaders doing their wiggle-waggle Coochy Coo number, and behind them the nickelhead thumping away on his drum and doing a wild, comical wiggle of his own. Then he sneaked up behind one girl in particular and started tapping with his drumstick where she wiggled. The girl whirled — it was Sunny Wyler — whacked him in the chops with a roundhouse right, and began chasing him over the grass.

"Don't come back, nickelhead — knucklehead — whatever your name is!" yelled Hummelsdorf. "You're off the band!" The only reply from Cueball was a shrieking cackle as he unhitched his drum from his belt and fled onto the

34

football field barely ahead of the raging cheer-leader.

Meanwhile Eddie Mott was doing some running of his own. He was playing second-string halfback against the first-string 100-pounders. He had taken the ball on a handoff from the quarterback and suddenly — miraculously — found himself in the clear, nothing between him and the goal line but thirty yards of green grass.

Just as he was beginning to believe in his good luck, it turned bad. Racing for the goal, his eye caught a movement beyond the edge of his bob-bing, too-big helmet. He gripped the ball tighter and turned, bracing to be tackled. But instead of a first-string 100-pounder in a football uniform, he saw to his amazement a nickelhead shrieking and waving a pair of sticks.

Since the first day of school, the nickelheads had been a pestilence upon Eddie. Time and again they made him pay a lunch tax, usually the dessert from his lunch bag. They took every other op-portunity to harass him. He had thought that on the football field at least he would be safe; but now, here was this nickelhead galloping straight toward him, and all Eddie could think was, Oh, no!

He forgot about the goal line, he forgot about the football — he flung it away and just took off in the opposite direction. If Eddie had looked back, he would have seen Cueball continue running across the field and toward the school. But he did not turn, he simply ran, sure that any moment now the nickelhead's hand would reach out and grab him by the neck. He did not realize that he was running onto the varsity team's portion of the practice field. Neither did he realize that a critical part of his uniform was coming loose.

By the time Eddie had belatedly come out for football, all the 100-pound uniforms had been taken. All that remained was one varsity uniform, intended for a 200-pound tackle, number 89. The tail of the shirt came down to his knees, the helmet felt as roomy as a watermelon, and the pants he could have wrapped twice around his waist. The pants did not use a belt but cinched with a drawstring — and Eddie had never been good at tying knots.

Now, unbeknownst to him as he fled the phantom nickelhead, the drawstring knot was coming loose. With every frantic step, it got a little looser. Eddie never noticed, partly because he was overcome with panic, and partly because his oversized football uniform had always felt loose as a tent. Consequently, Eddie was as surprised as everyone else when suddenly his pants collapsed about his ankles and sent him sprawling onto the grass.

The nearest varsity players to him at that moment were the defensive linemen, who were working out on the dummy sled. As Eddie spit out grass and turned, expecting to see a crazy nickel-head about to pounce on him, he saw instead the hugely grinning face of Richard "Tuna" Casseroli, the biggest player on the team, the biggest kid in the school, second in size only to the titanic social studies teacher, Mr. Hollis.

The next thing Eddie knew, he was being hoisted by his ankles, the early October air cool on his bare, white legs. To his eyes, inches from the ground, the world was a vast carpet of green grass, while far above, the voice of Tuna Casseroli boomed: "Hey, look — no Supermans! No Supermans!"

7

The late bus grumbled softly in the parking lot, awaiting the last of the football and field hockey players and cheerleaders and band members to climb aboard. Eddie had no intention of taking the late bus. After this latest disgrace, the last thing he needed was to board a bus and find himself staring into fifty grinning, sniggling faces.

He dawdled in the locker room, finding all sorts of little things to do before changing his clothes. By now he was positively paranoid about being undressed. His bare body was better known to his schoolmates than that of anyone except Humphrey the hamster, Plumstead's mascot. He imagined that eyes — eighth-grade eyes, nickelhead eyes — were constantly watching him, and that the instant he took off his clothes they would swoop down and scoop him up and fling him out into the middle of the football field for all the world to see.

And so he dawdled while the others horseplayed

and showered and changed. Finally the last one left. He was alone. Wasn't he? He checked the aisles of lockers, the showers. Yes, alone.

Even so, he decided to take as few chances as possible. Normally, for the last eleven years, or ever since he took over for his mother, his pattern was this: get totally undressed, then dress. No more. Never again. From this day forward, Edward Mott would never as long as he lived leave more than one body part exposed at any one time.

Thus he took off the right football shoe and sock, put on the right sock and sneaker; took off the left football shoe and sock, put on the left sock and sneaker; and so on. And even this he did as quickly as possible, glancing around all the while. Once he even stood on the bench to check out the tops of the lockers in case anyone was lying flat up there, waiting.

The parking lot was right outside the locker room. Several high, frosted windows were open, and through them Eddie could hear two voices in a most unusual shouting match:

"I said you're out!"

"Aww, come on, let me back in!"

"No!"

"I'll be good!"

"No!"

"Aww, Lips, please!"

"Never!"

The voices obviously belonged to a student and

to Mr. Hummelsdorf, the band director. Everybody called Mr. Hummelsdorf "Lips" behind his back, because of his plumlike lower lip, turned out and dangling from forty years of showing students how to play the trumpet, the trombone, and his favorite, the tuba. So far as Eddie knew, this was the first time anyone had ever said "Lips" to his face, and at the sound of it Eddie could feel the universe tense up. Certainly he himself did, pausing for the only time during his quick change.

When he finally left the locker room, he went to the side door and peeped out, just in time to see the late bus pulling out. Carefully, he opened the door and stepped onto the parking lot macadam. For half a minute he stayed there, near the door, like a mouse by his hole, alert, sniffing for any sign of the cats of his existence, eighth-graders and nickelheads.

All he saw was the flat, gray tableland of the parking lot; all he heard was the faint rush of traffic from the distant street. He clutched the drawstring sack containing his books and football shirt, took a deep breath, and ventured out. A clatter arose to his right, making him freeze; then a yelp; then from around the brick corner of the building came a sight out of a Saturday morning cartoon.

It was the same shape and color as the pickle-board — only much larger. It was the biggest, the longest skateboard he had ever seen. It had six wheels. It carried three people — Sunny, Salem, and Pickles — all of them laughing and yelping as Pickles guided the enormous green vehicle up to him.

All Eddie could say was, "Wow."

"Wow squared!" laughed Salem.

"What *is* it?" said Eddie.

With the tip of his sneaker, Pickles pointed to the yellow lettering on the curved, green side panel. It read:

PICKLEBUS

"Once was a surfboard," said Pickles. "Now it's our own private late bus. The four of us. I've been working on it for weeks. I just finished it last night." Pickles went on to explain that a friendly custodian had allowed him to park the picklebus in the basement. He slapped the side panel. "Climb aboard."

The two girls backed up, leaving a space between Pickles and Salem. Eddie climbed on. He could see now that only one side of the board had a side panel; the right side had been left open for shoe-to-sidewalk locomotion.

"Here we go!" called Pickles, pushing off from his pilot's position.

"Tallyho!" called Salem.

And off they went, three times in a wide circle around the parking lot — four legs pushing off like

41

oars in unison, a pickle-shaped galley on an asphalt sea — then once around the school and down the driveway to the sidewalk.

They cruised along slowly to the *clack-clack* of the sidewalk cracks, making the ride last. They were, from front to back: Pickles, Eddie, Salem, Sunny.

Salem tapped Eddie on the back, "Did you hear the argument?"

"Yeah," said Eddie. "It sounded like Mr. Hummelsdorf and some kid."

"That knucklehead jerk, Cueball," came Sunny's snort from the rear.

"Did I hear right?" said Eddie. "He called Mr. Hummelsdorf — " Eddie hesitated to say it.

"Lips?" Pickles nodded. "Yep. Cueball was on the bus, leaning out the window. Mr. Hummelsdorf was getting into his car. That's when they got into it. Cueball said it, right to his face, halfway out the bus window. Lips."

Eddie got the shivers just picturing it. "Wow."

"That's a nickelhead for you," said Pickles.

"That's one *dead* nickelhead for you," said Sunny.

"Ski jump!" shouted Pickles, and all four screamed as the picklebus flew off a high curb and landed five feet into the street, everyone teetering for balance but still aboard. "Yeah!" they cheered, pumping their fists in the air.

8

There was no ramp up to the next sidewalk, so the riders had to halt the picklebus and lift it over the curb. When they got back on, the order from front to back had changed. Now it was: Pickles, Salem, Eddie, Sunny.

The new order was no accident. At least, not on Salem's part.

When they reboarded the bus, Salem quickly inserted herself right behind pilot Pickles, leaving the third slot, in front of Sunny, open. Salem did this for a very clear reason: She knew that Eddie liked Sunny, so she figured she would arrange for him to be close to her.

As for Eddie, he knew that Salem knew that he liked Sunny; so when he saw that his place had changed, he didn't argue, he took it. As the Posse pushed off, Eddie put his hands on Salem's waist to hold steady, as Salem was doing to Pickles. He tingled, waiting for the touch of Sunny's hands on his own waist. A block went by. The touch never came.

Oh, well, Eddie wasn't surprised. Sunny was a notorious boy-hater, so what could he expect? He was glad she wasn't poking him in the ribs or jumping off and walking home. He was glad just to know she was right behind him, *that* close.

There may or may not have been another reason why Salem changed places when reboarding the bus — it was not clear, least of all to Salem herself. She thought all she was doing was a favor to Eddie. But then, when she found herself close behind Pickles as they hummed down the sidewalk, and when she put her hands on his waist, even she wasn't sure if she was doing it just to hang on.

"So," she said, blowing away her dimly disturbing feelings, "what did everybody think of the big announcement today?"

"About the cookie sale?" said Eddie.

"No," scoffed Salem, "the Halloween dance."

Principal Brimlow had announced that on the last Friday in October — otherwise known as Halloween — there would be a school dance. What the principal did not say was that the dance was intended to keep the older kids off the streets that night. Too many neighbors were complaining about rowdy teenagers merely holding masks in front of their faces and demanding unreasonable

44

amounts of candy. What the principal did say was that everyone who came in a costume would get a bag of treats.

"I'm not going," said Sunny. "Why would I want to go to a dance?"

"To dance with boys," Pickles called back, kidding.

"I'd rather dance with crocodiles."

"Eddie, how about you?" said Salem.

Eddie hesitated before finally answering, "I don't know. I'll have to think about it." Which was the truth. After hearing the announcement that day, Eddie had prompty forgotten it. It didn't seem to apply to him. He could not imagine himself going to something as grown-up as a dance. Sometimes it was hard to believe that he wasn't still back in grade school. Yes, this was going to take a lot of thinking.

"Well, isn't *anyone* going?" Salem whined. She tweaked the pilot in the waist. "How about you?"

"I don't know, either," said Pickles. "I hate to give up trick-or-treating. I'll think about it along with Eddie." He raised his right arm, then extended it to the side. "Right full rudder!" The picklebus veered to the right, rolled down a grassy slope, and coasted onto the asphalt playground of his old school, Second Avenue Elementary.

But Salem wasn't finished. Frustrated at her friends' unsatisfying answers about the dance, and discovering that something in her fingers liked the feeling of tweaking Pickles' waist, she began to tickle him.

"Hey," Pickles protested as the bus shimmied. "Stop!"

"Not until somebody agrees to go to the dance with me," said Salem, tickling harder.

"No . . . no!" Pickles laughed, trying to protect himself and control the bus, which now swung wildly, as though *it* were being tickled, four right paddle feet stabbing at the ground — "we're gonna — "

The crash came before the word; the bus yawed sharply, sailed atilt for two breathless seconds on the three left wheels, and plunged into a railroad tie at the edge of the grass surrounding the asphalt.

Three of them got up, unhurt.

"Sunny!" cried Salem.

Sunny had landed in a play area truck tire. Only her legs were sticking out. The other three raced over and peered into the round, rubbery well of the enormous tire.

"Sunny?" whispered Salem.

Sunny opened one sleepy eye. She groaned. "I'm dead."

Salem and Pickles laughed with relief. Eddie Mott did not. "What's so funny?" he scolded. "She's injured." Pangs of worry and a crush of love brought panic to his eyes. "We gotta get her to a doctor!"

He reached into the tire well, gripped Sunny under the arms, and pulled her to a sitting position on the tire's broad sidewall.

"Let her sit there. She's woozy, that's all," said Pickles, laid-back as ever.

"That's *all*?" screeched Eddie. "She could go into a coma any second. Look at her!" They looked at her. She did not look back. Eddie raised one of her eyelids. The three of them leaned in. "What do you think?" said Eddie.

Pickles shrugged. "It's an eyeball."

They stared at the gaping, blinkless eyeball for a while, but no one could think of anything more to say about it. Eddie let the lid drop. He had to hold her up, for her entire body was limp, without bones, it seemed. A groan came from deep inside her.

"That's it," said Eddie firmly. "I'm getting her to a doctor, with or without you people. Her brain could be losing oxygen right now. She could be a vegetable in minutes." He reached into the tire well, pulled out her legs, and swung them around till they hung outside the tire. He then crouched, leaned his shoulder into her midsection, wrapped his arms around her, and straightened up. He could hardly believe it — it worked! He was carrying her. She was draped over his shoulder, like a sack, just like in the movies.

Unfortunately, this was true only as long as he stayed still. As soon as he tried to move, he discovered that, due to the body on his shoulder, he was seriously lopsided to the right. He began to tilt in that direction. He threw out his right leg to brace himself, stopping the sideways tilt, only to find himself now tilting backwards. He planted his left foot and attempted to heave himself forward. He succeeded, but only with himself, for as his shoulders came forward, the slumped body continued its slide backwards, smoothly, unstoppably flowing over his right shoulder and down his back and onto the grass.

At this point Pickles made a move to intervene but was stopped by Salem, who was overcome by the exquisite romance of it all: Eddie Mott gallantly struggling to save the girl who rejected him. Practically in tears, she held Pickles by the arm. "Let them go. Let him try."

Eddie tried. Sunny was a groaning human puddle at his feet. This time he decided he would carry her the old-fashioned way, like men carry their brides over the threshold. He bent, he stooped, he squatted. He wormed his arms under her, one arm under her legs at the knees, the other under her back. He tried to remember how those Olympic weight lifters did it. He spread his feet, squared his shoulders, straightened his back. He braced himself, he took a deep breath, he lifted, he farted. Sunny never left the ground.

"That does it," said Pickles, pulling away from

Salem. He righted the overturned picklebus. "Help me out."

Together, Pickles and Salem lifted Sunny into the picklebus and started pushing her up the hill to the street. Eddie gathered everyone's books and followed.

Maybe it was the ride, maybe it was escaping Eddie's care — whatever, within a block Sunny was sitting up. Within two blocks she was her old self, grouching, "Did I *imagine* some dumbo dumped me on my head?"

9

When Salem Brownmiller became student manager of the Plumstead 100-pound football team, Mr. Lujak, the coach, outlined her primary duties as follows: "Wash the uniforms after game days, be ready with the first-aid kit, and just generally help out." That last part gave Salem all the leeway she needed. With it, she took student management to places where no one had ever taken it before.

It began the day after Eddie Mott lost his pants. Salem, who had witnessed the whole episode, knew what the problem was. As Eddie trotted onto the practice field next day, Salem called him over. She sat on the bench, made him stand in front of her, and started to untie the drawstring that cinched the waist of his oversized pants.

"Hey — " he protested, slapping her hands. "What are you doing?"

She pushed his hands away. "I'm tying you a good knot."

Eddie glanced about nervously. "You can't." The last thing he needed was to have other guys see him being dressed by someone else, a girl no less. He pushed her hands away.

Salem grabbed his arms by the wrists and clamped them to his sides. "*Listen* — do you want me to tie you a knot that won't come undone, or do you want your pants to fall down again today?"

Eddie squeaked and fidgeted in frustration, but he let her tie the knot. The moment she finished, he took off — and then it happened. Quite unexpectedly, before she could rise from the bench, Salem found herself facing another football player. It was Raymond Milford, a sixth-grader and one of the littlest kids on the team.

"Salem," he said, holding out his drawstring to her, "would you tie mine, too?"

Salem tied Raymond Milford's drawstring. And before the day was over she also tied knots for Jeremy O'Bannion, Bobby Troop, Sam Bukowski, and Damon Ross. All of them had the same problem — tying knots; and the same dread — that what happened to Eddie Mott might happen to them. Several of them had already had a nightmare in which Tuna Casseroli was holding them upside down and pantless by the ankles.

A short while later, after practice had begun,

Raymond Milford came running over to Salem on the sideline. His little face was lost in his helmet. His chin didn't stick out far enough to touch his chin strap.

"What is it, Raymond?" said Salem.

"Ah, nothing," said Raymond, his mouth dragging manfully, "just an injury."

"Oh?" Salem looked him over. "Where?"

Raymond looked at her from deep inside his helmet. His eyes grew wide and watery, his lower lip trembled. "My f-f-*finger*!" he bawled, thrusting his hand out to her. "It g-got bent b-b-*back*!"

Salem placed his hand as gently as possible in hers. She inspected the wounded finger, touched it.

"Is it b-*broke*?"

Salem pressed it ever so slightly. "I don't think so. Let's see if it'll bend."

"Do we h-have to?"

"I'll be careful." She pressed on the fingernail and very slowly bent the finger till the tip touched the palm. "There, it's not broken."

Raymond searched her eyes. "But it still *hurrrts*!"

What Salem did then came without thinking, from tearful and tender moments between her and her mother. She lifted the wounded finger to her lips, kissed it, patted it, smiled, and said, "That better?"

Raymond blinked, as if emerging from a dark

room into sunlight. He swallowed a sob, sniffed, looked at his finger. He reached his other hand into his helmet and wiped tears away. He sniffed again, took a deep breath, set his lips, and trotted back onto the field.

Ten minutes later, when Damon Ross came limping off the field with a stubbed toe, Salem said, "Okay, but no kisses."

So it began. And so it happened that as the days passed, bump by bump and ache by pain, Salem Brownmiller became more than a manager.

It happened because of who Salem was, and because of who the 100-pound football team was, which was mostly sixth-graders. It did not take long for these sixth-graders to make a very useful discovery: With Salem they could be themselves in a way that they could not be with Coach Lujak. With Coach Lujak they could not complain. With Coach Lujak they could not admit they were afraid to get tackled or run over. With Coach Lujak they could not show that they didn't care whether they won or lost. With Coach Lujak they could not cry.

With Salem, they could. They did. Salem and her first-aid kit became a healing oasis.

If a kid came to her hurting, she would keep him on the bench and try and fix him. If he didn't get better, he didn't go back into the action, simple as that.

For some players it was a conflict. "But I *have*

to go back!" Jeremy O'Bannion screeched one time, even though he was still obviously sick from the knee he had received in the stomach.

"*Have* to?" scoffed Salem. "What do you mean, *have* to? Look at you. You're sick. You're *green*."

"It doesn't matter," groaned Jeremy. "You can't be a baby. This is football. If you can't play with a little pain, you should go out for the pattycake team."

Salem raised her eyebrows. "And who says?"

Jeremy nodded toward the field. "You know who."

Salem brought her face practically into Jeremy O'Bannion's helmet. "Is that so? Well, you go tell Coach Lujak that when you're out there on the field, maybe then you belong to him, but when you step over that line" — she pointed to the chalky stripe that marked the sideline — "you're mine. And as long as I'm here, the only thing green on that field is going to be the grass."

Salem could see the relief in Jeremy O'Bannion's face. He argued no more. He simply went behind the bench and gratefully threw up.

Each player learned to use Salem in his own way. Raymond Milford, for example, used her to cry. Almost once a day Raymond showed up in front of Salem, his back to the coach, lip quivering. At first he would fight it. "I c-can't," he would stutter. "Not ag-gain."

Salem would slap him in the shoulder pads. "Oh, hogwash. Sure you can."

"But I'm not even h-hurt. He only h-hollered at me."

"*Hollered* at you? That's even worse. Feelings hurt more than bones. You have to let it out, don't you know that? You boys are so dumb. Listen, you know how you feel better after you throw up?"

Raymond nodded. "Uh-huh."

"Well, crying is like that. Tears are like your feelings throwing up. You'll feel better. Come on now, I'll cry with you. Let it out."

Salem would work up a sniffle, and Raymond would let it out.

With Butchy Wallace, Salem became Sigmund Brownmiller.

"I hate that guy," Butchy would seethe.

"Why is that?" Salem would say calmly.

"He thinks I'm no good."

"Tell me about it."

"He won't let me be the kicker."

"Why not?"

"He says I don't kick it far enough."

"Is he right?"

"No, he's a liar."

"The rat."

"He's stupid."

"He makes a worm look brilliant."

"He stinks."

"I can smell him all the way over here. He smells worse than the droppings of a thousand elephant seals. I'm going to put in an order for gas masks. He's a pollution violation all by himself."

Butchy Wallace would stare at Salem, and sooner or later the fury would drain out of him. He would relax, snap on his chin strap, and trot back onto the field.

Salem personalized her service as much as possible. She tried to meet the needs of every player, every situation. Mark Halley, for example, had a sinus condition, his nose was always running. Mark was one of the few kids in school who carried a handkerchief. But there were no pockets in his football uniform, no place to put a hankie. Salem saw his problem and brought a box of tissues from home.

Then there was Mickey Schultz and his pet horsefly. He brought it to school every day in an old half-pint coleslaw container, with tiny holes poked in the clear plastic lid. Mickey took the horsefly around to classes with him, but he was afraid to leave it unguarded in the locker room during football practice. So for two hours each afternoon, Salem became keeper of the horsefly. It was the biggest thing with wings other than a bird or airplane that she had ever seen. She pitied the poor spider that ever met up with it. She didn't even want to imagine what Mickey Schultz fed it.

Brian Blittman tipped the scales right at the limit of 100 pounds, and he believed that if he ate a mini-box of California raisins halfway through each practice, he would be stronger than the other linemen. Salem was his grocer.

Of course, the first-aid kit was not nearly big enough to hold these extra items, so Salem brought a small suitcase from home. She told Coach Lujak she just needed more room for her first-aid supplies.

Salem saw herself and her sideline as giving the 100-pound warriors a little touch of home during their brief respites from battle. And then one day she brought home out onto the field.

10

It began on a Monday, three days before the first game. In order to give the players a taste of the real thing, Coach Lujak had declared an intra-squad scrimmage. First string against second string. They would play it just like a regular game, from kickoff to final whistle, four quarters long, including time-outs.

Coach Lujak called the first time-out midway through the opening quarter. Salem was sitting at her usual place on the bench, munching on a granola bar, and peering across the football field to where the band was practicing, trying to locate Pickles, when several voices yelled at once: "Manager!"

Salem yipped, "Oh!" She jumped, she lunged for the first-aid kit, she dashed onto the field. What she found were two groups of players standing around, one on either side of the ball, which looked rather ignored and forlorn by itself on the grass. She stopped at the ball, looked at both teams. "Who's hurt?"

Snickers and outright laughter broke out. "Nobody's hurt," said Mr. Lujak. "It's a time-out. You bring out the yellow buckets." He pointed to the sideline. "Yellow buckets."

Salem looked at the sideline. She looked at the coach. "Oh," she said, and wagged her head and chuckled at her own silly mistake. "Sorry, Mr. Lujak. I guess you can tell how many football games I've seen. In fact, I don't think I've ever seen a single one. Come to think of it — wow" — she thought for a second or two — "this is the very first time-out of my entire life. I was never on any kind of team, unless you want to count the spelling team in grade school. I'm not exactly the most coordinated person in the world, as the cheerleaders can tell — "

"Miss Brownmiller!" roared the coach. "The yellow buckets! Now!"

Salem raced to the sideline, knocking her knee three times with the first-aid kit. She limped back with two yellow buckets. Each contained three squeeze-type water bottles with plastic straws, plus several towels. She dropped one bucket off with the first-stringers and one with the second-stringers. That's where she stayed, since Coach Lujak was with the first-stringers.

No one moved.

At last Jeremy O'Bannion spoke up. "Well, come on, Salem."

Salem looked at him. "Come on what?"

"Do your manager thing."

"What's that?"

Several players gave exasperated sighs. "Don't blame her," said Eddie Mott. He pulled a water bottle from the bucket. "Here, do this." He raised the bottle, tipped the straw toward himself, and squeezed. A jet of water streamed into his mouth. He handed her the bottle. "You do it."

Salem raised the bottle, tipped it, squeezed, and watered her own nose.

"No! No!" groaned half the team.

"You do it to *us*," said Jeremy O'Bannion.

"Oh," said Salem.

At which point Coach Lujak blew his whistle, ending the time-out. Eleven second-stringers scowled at Salem. She snatched up the yellow buckets and got out of there before they decided to assassinate her.

By the second time-out, she was ready. So were the second-stringers, having gone unnourished during the first time-out. They stood with their helmets in their hands, their hair plastered with sweat, their mouths open, like eleven guppies waiting to be fed.

Salem flipped two of the bottles to others, kept the third herself and started shooting water. She caught lips and chins on the first few tries, and from then on hit them dead-center in the back of the tongue.

"Towel," called Jeremy O'Bannion.

Salem pulled a towel from the bucket. She offered it to him. He frowned and shook his head. "Face."

Salem blinked, smiled. "Ah!" She mopped his face with the towel, then the ten other faces. When she finished, she felt smiled at and thanked, even though no one came right out and did either. Only Damon Ross spoke, staring pointedly at her, as if delivering a dispatch that she should carry to the home front: "It's murder out here."

The whistle blew: Time-out was over. Salem gathered her goods and returned to the bench, feeling closer than ever to the players and wishing there was more she could do.

By the end of the scrimmage, the two sides had practically plowed each other into the ground. They dragged themselves off the field, muttering things like, "Who needs this?" and "I'm quitting." They threw their helmets down. They spit. They cursed. Five of them lined up to have cuts and scratches tended to.

Bobby Troop had an ugly red, brown, and green skinburn on his arm, the result of a meeting with the first-string fullback and his wall of blockers. He was fighting back tears. "I'm outta here," he told Salem bitterly. "This stinks." Then he screamed aloud as Salem tried to wash the dirt from his wound.

Salem winced, "Oh, I'm sorry, Bobby. I wish I were a better doctor." Her own eyes were welling up.

"It's not your fault," said Raymond Milford, who was next in line. "It's just that we used to play tag football in grade school. Who knew tackle was gonna be like this? The coach thinks we're pros or something. He makes us do everything ten times. He bops us on our helmets. I'm getting a headache."

"We're dog meat," groaned Zachary Riley, flexing his sore knee. "That's all. Dog meat."

"Plus we stink," added John Rankin. "We're gonna lose our first game a hundred to nothing."

The others muttered and nodded.

Salem held up a water-soaked cotton ball. "Hey, wait a minute, that's not true. You guys are *not* dog meat. And you *don't* stink. And you're *not* going to lose a hundred to nothing."

"Right," snickered Zachary Riley. "*Two* hundred to nothing."

"Listen," said Salem, "the first game is Thursday. You can't go into it thinking like that. You have to have a better attitude."

"I gotta have a better *life*," said Zachary Riley. He kicked his helmet ten feet. "I'm quitting."

Salem grabbed his arm. "No!"

Zachary stared at her. "Why not?"

"You don't want to be a quitter, do you?"

"Why not?"

"Then you'll start quitting everything. You'll go through your whole life just giving up every time something gets a little hard."

"A *little* hard?" laughed Zachary. "Why don't *you* go out there and get *your* butt massacred? You sit over here, where it's all safe, eating candy bars. Football used to be easy. It used to be fun. Now it's not. I *hate* it."

"Me, too," said another.

"It wasn't candy," said Salem lamely, "it was a granola bar." She couldn't think of any more arguments, any new way to persuade Zachary and the others not to quit. She had never seen such low morale. How could she, how could anyone, ever change it? "Well, just don't," was all she could say.

Raymond Milford stepped forward. "Why not?" he demanded. "What do we get out of it except beat up, especially us second-stringers? We get the most massacred of all." For once, there were no tears in his eyes.

Salem looked at Raymond, at Zachary, at them all. As a writer, she had always prided herself on her creativity, her imagination. But now, just when she needed it: zero. Her head was as empty as a classroom two seconds after dismissal.

The players began to slump and straggle off to

the locker room. "Wait!" she called. "Don't quit now. Wait till the first game at least. Okay?"

Zachary Riley looked back. "Why should we?"

Salem stomped her foot in frustration. "I don't *know*! Just do it, o-*kay*?"

They did not answer. They resumed their motley plod to the locker room.

And Salem was asking herself, Now, why did I say that?

Salem thought about it all that night and all the next day at school. How could she keep them from quitting? How could she raise their morale? Nothing came to her. She was sure that a true author would never suffer such an appalling lack of ideas. This was worse than the occasional case of writer's block. This was pure brain block, a total eclipse of the mind.

The day was rescued from absolute disaster when, to her great relief, Salem saw Zachary Riley and Raymond Milford and the rest of them heading for the locker room for Tuesday's practice. She tied drawstrings and baby-sat Mickey Schultz's horsefly and did all her other usual duties, then sat on the bench to think some more.

She unwrapped a granola bar and broke off a bite. She gazed about. The cheerleaders were off beyond a set of goalposts, practicing the cheers that she would never lead. As usual, Ms. Baylor was yelling at Sunny: "Smile, Wyler, smile!"

Straight ahead, on the far side of the field beyond the football players, the world's smallest band was marching — or rather bumbling — to the animated directions of the kidney-bean shaped Mr. Hummelsdorf. To Salem's surprise, she noted that Cueball the nickelhead was back, rattling away at his drum and everything else in sight. In fact, the band had grown by two. There were now nine members.

As before, Pickles was the only one who seemed to know what he was doing, marching erect and sure, his arms high, his elbows flared, bugle to his mouth as proudly as if he were in the Rose Bowl Parade. In some strange way, the sounds from his bugle fell upon her as his voice, as notes about to become words.

When Salem's eyes shifted to the football action, she came out of her reverie to find that all but one bite remained of her granola bar. For the first time (other than sleeping) in nearly twenty-four hours, she had not been thinking about the problem of the players. And as often happened — in this case, as she stared at the remaining bite of granola bar in her hand and remembered something Zachary Riley had said — the answer came only when she stopped looking for it.

11

Thursday was a day of surprises for Eddie Mott.

His first surprise was finding himself named as starting free safety for the Fighting Hamsters' opening game against Tarrytown Middle School. Eddie wasn't kidding himself; he knew he wasn't that great a player. And he knew the reason for his promotion from second string was that the usual starting safety, Ned Povich, had cracked a finger against somebody's helmet and was out for the season.

Still, Eddie was determined to make the most of his opportunity. If only he could get lucky, he thought, intercept a pass and return it for a long touchdown, maybe everybody would forget about the underwear business. Maybe they would stop calling him "Supe" in the hallways. Maybe Tuna Casseroli would stop pointing to him from the varsity practice area and laughing and raising his hands as if holding someone upside down by the ankles.

Eddie was told about his starting role by Coach Lujak in the locker room before the game. He got his second surprise as he trotted out to the field with the team. The Hamster Band was there, marching off a last-minute rehearsal for their half-time show, and Eddie was flabbergasted to see that the drummer was none other than the crazy nickelhead, Cueball. In fact, there were two other nickelheads in the band. One played a soda bottle, blowing across the mouth to produce a breathy, mournful sound; the other played a kazoo.

Eddie was not aware of why this had come about. He did not know that after the shouting match in the parking lot that day, Lips Hummelsdorf had had second thoughts about kicking Cueball off the band. The problem was numbers. Now that he had committed himself to fielding the county's only middle school football marching band — and very likely the world's smallest — he calculated that he needed at least ten members to make it work.

Why?

The letter P. What good was a marching band if it could not form the school's initials on the playing field during the halftime show? Michigan State University, for example, Lips' college alma mater, formed a colossal MSU that went practically from sideline to sideline, goalpost to goalpost. Of course, they had 200 members, as did many college bands. Easy for them. Even Cedar

Grove High School had enough members to make a respectable CGHS on the field.

Hummelsdorf knew that a three-letter formation — P(lumstead) M(iddle) S(chool) — was out of the question. The best he could hope for was a P for Plumstead. But after banishing the crazed nickelhead, he was left with four short of the ten people necessary to form a readable P.

And so, despite the lunatic drummer's insubordination, when he came around the next day whining to be let back in the band, Hummelsdorf swallowed his pride and said okay. On one condition: if the kid brought along three more band members. Well, he came up with two — fellow nickelheads, it turned out — bringing the count to nine. And on Thursday morning, with the first football game mere hours away, Hummelsdorf came to the decision that he had hoped he would never have to make: He himself would become the tenth Marching Hamster. He himself would complete the Plumstead P.

Eddie Mott, of course, did not know all this. All he knew was that a nickelhead had dared call Mr. Hummelsdorf "Lips" to his face and not only lived to see the next day, but was readmitted to the band — along with two more nickelheads! Was there nothing these guys couldn't get away with?

Before the game Salem came over to him. She smiled. "Nervous?"

"Nah," he answered as casually as he could.

"Want me to tighten those pants some more?"

"Nah." He knew what she was thinking. It was bad enough for his pants to fall down during practice, but for them to drop in front of the bleachers full of students, teachers, parents . . . He shrugged. "Well, okay, if you insist, go ahead."

Salem gave the drawstring a double knot. She was grinning.

"What's so funny?"

"Oh," she said, giving the knot a final tug, "I was just wondering why you never let me do anything but this."

Eddie stepped back and adjusted his hip pads. "What do you mean?"

"I mean you never ask me to help you, like the other guys. There's nothing in my suitcase for you. I saw you get hurt a couple of times in practice, but you didn't even come over to get first aid."

Eddie looked around. The Tarrytown team was warming up across the way. "I got a game to play," he said. "Ask me later."

She grabbed his chin strap. "I'm asking now."

He glared at her, took in a whistling breath. "Look, you want to baby those guys, that's your business."

"They seem to like it," she said.

"Fine. That's their business. That doesn't mean I have to like it."

She flicked the tip of his nose with the chin

69

strap. She was enjoying this. "Don't you know I'm your mother out here on the football field? Mr. Lujak is your father, and I'm your mama."

He slapped her hand from his chin strap. "Not *my* mother, you're not. I got one mother, that's enough. That's the reason I came out for football. I'm trying to get away from mothers, so I can grow up. This is football, y'know, not pattycake." He walked off.

"Well ex-*cuuuze* me," said Salem, pretending to be huffy. Then she called, "Eddie!"

He stopped but did not turn. "See you at the first time-out!" he heard her sing.

Whatever that meant. Eddie had more important things on his mind, like Tarrytown. He joined the other players for a final huddle with Coach Lujak, who told the players this was what they had all been working and sacrificing for. Now it was time to show what they were made of. Time to toughen up! Time to kick some tail! Time to go down in history! Time to give Plumstead Middle School its first-ever victory in sports!

"Yeah!" shouted Eddie, piling his hands onto the others in the huddle. He raced onto the field, yelling and pumping his fists, ready to kill. Then he discovered his mistake. Plumstead was receiving the kickoff, meaning they would be on offense. He was a defensive player; he didn't belong on the field. He ran off.

The Fighting Hamsters failed to make a first

down and had to punt to Tarrytown. Eddie and his defensive mates took the field. As free safety, Eddie was the farthest back from the line of scrimmage, the last line of defense, the last hope. If a Tarrytown player managed to get through all ten of the other Hamsters, it was Eddie's job to stop him. There was nothing behind Eddie but the goal line.

As he waited for the play to begin, he heard a voice: "Hey, Supe!" The voice was coming from a bunch of varsity players, heading for practice on another field. He saw an upraised hand, a flash of red. Tuna Casseroli was waving a pair of Superman undershorts in the air and laughing and pointing. "Hey, Supe! Hey, Supe!"

Eddie turned away. "I'll show ya," he said through gritted teeth, "I'll show ya."

Tarrytown ran its first play and — oh, no! — it was Eddie's worst nightmare. The Tarrytown line opened a hole big enough for an elephant. The Tarrytown fullback charged through and into the Hamster backfield. He stiff-armed Damon Ross, ran right past Sam Bukowski, and steamrollered over Zachary Riley as if he were no more than a dandelion — and now he was heading Eddie's way. Eddie planted his feet wide, crouched, ready to go left or right, but one look at the frightening sneer on this guy's face and Eddie knew he wasn't going anywhere but straight ahead. Eddie froze. The last he saw of the fullback was the sneer —

he could even smell his breath — and then Eddie was flying, and then he was on his back looking up at a dinosaur-shaped cloud in the sky, and then the rest of the Tarrytown team was stampeding over him on their way to mobbing the fullback in the end zone.

The extra point was good. Tarrytown 7, Plumstead 0.

When Eddie got back to the bench, Jeremy O'Bannion pointed to Eddie's chest and said, "Hey, look!"

Eddie looked. Stamped across the 8 of his number 89 was the perfect footprint of the Tarrytown fullback. Eddie groaned and slumped onto the bench. But not for long. Within a minute Tarrytown had the ball again, and he had to go back out on defense.

This time it took Tarrytown three plays to score. And this time Eddie never even touched the fullback, as he was obliterated by a pair of blockers.

Tarrytown 14, Plumstead 0.

When Tarrytown threatened to score again a few minutes later, Coach Lujak called from the sideline: "Time-out!"

All the Hamsters but Eddie took off their helmets and flopped to the ground. "Come on," Eddie told them. "Don't let them see you like that. We gotta be tough."

"*You* be tough, " said Zachary Riley. "I'm not

even waiting till after the game. I'm quitting at halftime."

"Who's waiting till halftime?" said Mickey Schultz, lifting himself painfully to his feet. "I'm taking my fly and going home now, while I'm still alive."

As Mickey Schultz turned to walk off, he bumped into Salem, who said. "Where are you going?"

"Home, to play pattycake."

Salem grinned. She had her usual yellow time-out bucket with her, but she also had a suitcase, a different one than before. It was old and beat up, but it was a lot bigger, and painted on its side in tall white and purple letters were the words FIGHTING HAMSTERS. "You'll be sorry," she sang.

From the gleam in her eye and the tone of her voice, Mickey Schultz could tell she was right. So he stayed.

Salem stepped in among the eleven players and set down the suitcase. "Hamsters," she said brightly, "behold — the dawn of a new age in time-outs."

She opened the suitcase, laid its two sides flat on the ground. Twenty-two eyelids shot up like tiny shades. Twenty-two eyes gaped in wonder at what they saw.

12

There were chocolate-chip cookies. There were graham cracker, chocolate, and marshmallow s'mores. There were Rice Krispies squares and chocolate-covered pretzels and peanut-butter fudge and chocolate-walnut brownies and cupcakes with icing and candy beads and bite-size squares of Sicilian pizza, some with a pepperoni circle, some with a mushroom.

Salem pulled the straw-top plastic bottles from the yellow bucket. It wasn't water in them. "Hawaiian Punch," she said.

She picked up a round chocolate-cake sandwich with white cream in the middle. She held it out to Mickey Shultz. "Guess what this is called?"

"Pattycake!" exclaimed Mickey and snatched it from her hand.

The team attacked the suitcase — except for Eddie Mott.

"C'mon," said Salem, "don't be such a pooper.

You're missing the world's first gourmet time-out."

Eddie growled at her. "You're just making a joke out of everything. This doesn't have anything to do with football."

Salem moved closer to Eddie. She whispered, "It does if it keeps them from quitting the team. Now stop being such a jerk. Eat."

Eddie just glared at her as the official blew the whistle, ending the time-out. Salem closed the suitcase, nearly snipping off a few lingering fingers. Mickey Shultz quickly jammed a cookie into his pants. Zachary Riley stuffed a s'more into his shoulder pads. As the players pulled on their helmets, their cheeks bulged like chipmunks'.

Salem glanced back with a flirtatious wave. "See ya next time-out, *boyzzzz.*"

Nothing about the football game changed. Tarrytown scored a third touchdown two plays later. They continued to score at will.

The difference was, none of the Fighting Hamsters, except Eddie Mott, was very upset about it. They were thinking more about the next time-out than the next tackle. Their problem was no longer the Tarrytown team, but how to eat and play football at the same time.

On the play after the first time-out, for example, Mickey Schultz took a body block that crushed his cookie. For the rest of the half, Coach Lujak believed Mickey was especially lively on his toes, dancing this way and that to make blockers miss him. The truth was that the chocolate-chip cookie crumbs in Mickey's pants were driving him crazy.

Then there was Sam Bukowski. Sam had pigged out more than anyone else during the first time-out. In less than two minutes he was seen to wolf down three cupcakes, five chocolate-covered pretzels, two brownies, and half a bottle of Hawaiian Punch. Then, as Salem was closing the suitcase, he grabbed a handful of bite-size Sicilian pizza squares, which he dumped into his helmet before pulling it on.

Within minutes, Sam became very sluggish. He dropped into his crouch on the line of scrimmage and never really rose out of it. He was involved in plays only if by accident they happened to come straight at him. On those occasions, the slightest bump was enough to send him reeling onto his rump. At one point during the action, one of the pizza squares slid down and began to ooze red and cheesy through the ear hole of his helmet, causing the Tarrytown player who had just blocked him to cry out in horror: "I just knocked his brains out!"

The Tarrytown player fainted and had to be revived and helped from the field. As for Sam Bukowski, the referee discovered what was really protruding from the helmet hole and ejected Sam from the game.

Sam refused to go.

The referee's eyes boggled. He seethed. He blew his whistle, called an officials' time-out, pointed to the Plumstead bench, and commanded: "Out!"

"No, please!" begged Sam. "I'll be good from now on! Look — " He took off his helmet and dumped the remaining pizza squares to the ground. "See, they're gone."

"Out!" roared the referee.

Sam fell to his knees. "No! Please don't kick me out!"

In all his career as a football official, the referee had never come across a player who refused to be kicked out of a game. Spitting out his whistle, he took three strides toward the Hamster bench and yelled: "If somebody doesn't come out here and remove this player from the field, this game will be over and declared a forfeit to the visiting team!"

Coach Lujak himself then ran onto the field, as did Salem. As Sam was dragged from the field, he kept looking back at the huddle of his teammates and the suitcase unfolding. "No, Coach," he kept crying, "let me play! I love football!"

With a minute to go in the first half, Tarrytown scored its seventh touchdown for a 44 to 0 lead. The Plumstead offense took their positions on the field to receive the kickoff. They were a happier bunch than when they had started the game. They had had three of the most wonderful and delicious time-outs in the history of football, and looked forward to an equally tasty second half.

As the two teams spread out across the field, awaiting the referee's whistle, they could not have looked more different. The Tarrytown players were clenched and snarling, anxious as horses in the starting gate, hungry for more points, eager to wrest the ball from Plumstead and score yet again.

The Hamsters, on the other hand, were a picture of contentment. Life had suddenly become very good to them. From their side of the field came languid smiles and the gentle sounds of burping and stomachs gurgling.

In the meantime, the Fighting Hamsters marching band had come down from the bleachers and lined up in the end zone behind the Hamster players. Director Hummelsdorf thought he remembered it being done this way from his days at Michigan State. Beyond that, however, he was strictly guessing. Hummelsdorf knew about tubas and flutes and any other instrument you could name, but he didn't know a thing about football.

The referee raised his whistle to his lips. In that moment before the kickoff, the field was quiet, the sidelines were quiet. The bleachers were not. There was a commotion, shouting. Distracted, the referee took the whistle from his mouth and turned to see what the problem was.

13

What the referee saw was a Plumstead cheer-leader, in her white sweater and purple-and-white pleated skirt, pointing to the bleachers and yelling loudly enough to be heard from one end of the field to the other: "That's it, nickelnose! If you're gonna sit in front of me, you're gonna cheer!"

"I'll cheer when I feel like it!" the spectator with a strange haircut yelled back. "It's a free country!"

"Love it or leave it, polka-dot head! I'm not here for my health! You cheer or you clear out!"

"I'll cheer when you start smiling, you grouch-bag! Who ever heard of a cheerleader who don't smile?"

"You wanna come on down here and make me, butt-face?"

"Yeah, yeah, I'll come down and make ya!"

As Sunny Wyler stood squarely before the bleachers, as the spectators gaped in amazement, the nickelhead came down, stopped on the front row, leaned down, thrust the forefingers of each hand into the sides of Sunny's mouth, and pulled upward and outward.

"Have a nice d — " the nickelhead managed to get out before Sunny slapped his nose sideways. The nickelhead yelped and took off behind the bleachers, Sunny lit out after him, and the referee returned his attention to the game. He blew the whistle.

At the sound of the whistle two things happened: (1) the Tarrytown kicker began running toward the ball; (2) Lips Hummelsdorf blew *his* whistle, and the Fighting Hamster band began marching forward. Only one of these things was supposed to happen.

Director Hummelsdorf, unacquainted with football as he was, thought the referee's whistle meant the end of the first half, so he in turn ordered his troops forward. As the ball left the foot of the Tarrytown kicker, the band moved from the end zone onto the field.

The ball sailed end over end to the twenty-yard line, where it was caught — to everyone's surprise — by Sam Bukowski. Still stuffed and woozy but determined not to miss any more time-outs, Sam had sneaked onto the field with the offense. That made him the twelfth player on an eleven-member side, but no one was counting.

Sam made the mistake of catching the ball more

with his stomach than with his hands. He took two running steps, stopped, said, "Uh-oh," and dropped the ball.

"Fumble!" yelled the oncharging Tarrytown players. Three of them dove for it just as Sam barfed, coating the ball with a warm Sicilian pizza and chocolate-chip soup.

The ball, quite slippery now, squirted from the grasp of the three Tarrytown players, who then began screaming and clawing madly at the grass. Players from both teams — at least, those who did not yet realize that the ball was covered by more than pigskin — picked up the chase. A player from Plumstead would scoop up the ball, discover what he had in his hands, scream, and fling the ball away. A Tarrytown player would then scoop it up and go through the same thing.

Meanwhile, the band was up to the forty-yard line, only to find themselves surrounded by players darting this way and that after the bounding ball. Seeing that it would be just as difficult to retreat as to press on, Director Hummelsdorf thrust his baton forward and commanded, "Onward, Hamsters!" Flying football bodies took their toll on the band. The flutist fell at the forty-five-yard line, the triangle player at the fifty; but the band, led by the blare of Pickles' bugle and the rattle of Cueball's drum, marched on.

By now, half of the twenty-two players on the field were screaming and clawing at the grass. The remaining players, fully understanding the situation, had no intention of touching the contaminated ball — at least, not with their hands. So they began to kick it, and suddenly the game looked more like soccer than football.

At first the players kicked aimlessly at the ball. Then it seemed to dawn on all of them at once: The thing to do was kick the ball all the way into the other team's end zone, then, somehow, pick it up and thus score a touchdown.

In the meantime the zebra-shirted officials were trying to wave the band off the field while whipping out their rule books to see if interference by barf or bands was covered. The referee, eyes on stopwatch, blew his whistle when time expired — not that it made any difference, for the play in progress had to be allowed to run its course.

The officials waved, the band marched, the "soccer" game played on, and Sam Bukowski, feeling better now but awfully tired, lay down and went to sleep between the twenty-five- and thirty-yard lines. A thundering kick by a Tarrytown player sent the ball sailing toward the Plumstead goal. It landed on the twenty-yard line and rolled into the end zone and sat there, a touchdown prize for the first Tarrytown player to reach it.

A Tarrytown linebacker, from forty yards away, began a dead sprint for the ball at the same time that Sunny Wyler's nickelhead came tearing back around the bleachers with Sunny on his tail.

Screeching and flapping his arms like a goose taking off, the nickelhead circled the field down to the Plumstead end, veered sharply, and headed onto the field itself. He dashed under the goalposts, through the end zone, and collided at the goal line with the Tarrytown linebacker just as he was about to reach for the ball.

As the nickelhead and the linebacker lay dazed on the field, the next player on the scene happened to be Eddie Mott. All this time Eddie had been planning what to do if he ever got near the barfed-on ball. Now was his chance. He yanked off his helmet and stuffed it like a sleeve down over the ball till only the tip of the ball was sticking out. Holding the helmet by an ear hole, he began running in the opposite direction. He ran past the band, he ran past the officials, he ran past the players on both sides. He ran 103 yards, all the way to the Tarrytown goal line. He stood in the Tarrytown end zone, jumping and yelling and waving his helmet.

The referee came running. He saw, he thrust his arms to the sky: Touchdown!

The first half was over.

14

There was plenty to talk about on the picklebus ride home that night. The two headliners were Eddie and Sunny: Eddie because he had scored the Hamsters' only touchdown in Plumstead's 84-to-6 loss to Tarrytown, and Sunny because she had been kicked off the cheerleading squad for attacking a fan.

"That's what Ms. Baylor called him," snorted Sunny. "A fan. He's no fan. If he was a fan, he would've been cheering. He's a jerk."

"He's a hero, too," said Salem. "Everybody's saying if it wasn't for him crashing into the Tarrytown guy, they would have scored the touchdown and we would have had zero."

"And Crazylegs Mott never would have had a chance to be a hero himself," added Pickles as he guided the green bus the long way home to give them more time to talk. "Who would have ever thought it — Eddie Mott has something to thank a nickelhead for."

"So I guess I should thank Sunny then, too," said Eddie, who rode the third slot between Salem and Sunny. "If she didn't chase the nickelhead, he never would've crashed into the Tarrytown kid."

"He's lucky he crashed into the kid," said Sunny. "If I caught him he wouldn't have got off so easy."

The four pickleteers laughed. The bus rolled on.

"I warned you," Salem called back good-naturedly. "You can't be a grouch and a cheer-leader at the same time."

"So what are you going to be now?" said Pickles. "A hit girl? Carry a club to each game, bop everybody on the head who doesn't cheer?"

More laughter.

When quiet returned, Sunny said, "I already know what I'm going to be."

Three heads turned, waiting.

"I'm going to be the mascot."

"We already have Humphrey," said Eddie, referring to the school's pet hamster and the inspiration for the football team's nickname.

"Humphrey can't come to the games," Sunny pointed out. "And even if I brought him, he wouldn't do any good. He's too little. Nobody would take him seriously. What this joint needs is a *big* hamster to whip these people into shape."

"Nobody says a hamster has to smile, right, Sunshine?"

"Right," said Sunny, who allowed only these three friends and the principal, Mr. Brimlow, to call her by her given name.

"Nobody says a hamster has to be nice."

"Exactly."

"Don't you need permission?"

"From who?" said Sunny. "Mr. Brimlow? He won't care. This is school spirit. Who's gonna say no to that?"

"The nickelheads?" suggested Pickles.

"Wanna bet?" said Sunny.

Nobody took the bet.

Pickles held up his hand. "First stop coming up — Brrrrownmiller rrrresidence."

"Oh, no," Salem protested. "It's too soon. Go around the block once."

"I have homework," said Pickles.

"I have dinner," said Sunny.

Salem climbed off with a groan and sulked away. Suddenly she brightened, she turned. "Hey — if we can't go around the block, let's have a party. My house. Saturday. What do you say?"

"Don't go," said Eddie. "I was at her house once, and she made me drink this punch from hell, and I was sick all the next day."

"It was Periwinkle Punch," sniffed Salem haughtily, "and this child made himself ill by eating everything in sight."

"I'll be there," said Pickles. "I'll drag the Mottster along."

"Me, too," said Sunny.

Salem clapped her hands. "Good! Once I get you there, I'm going to convince you all to come to the Halloween dance with me. See ya." She dashed into her house.

Pickles called, "Next stop, the Wyler rrrresidence."

Eddie said nothing all the way to Sunny's house. He just concentrated on knowing that she was mere inches behind him on the picklebus.

Pickles left off Sunny and headed for Eddie's.

"Did you ever stop and think about what you did today?" said Pickles.

"Sure," said Eddie, "I scored a TD. A hundred and three yards long."

"Right, but it was more than just that, you know."

"What do you mean?"

"It was a first, Motto. That's what makes it really special. Look, who was the fourteenth president?"

"I don't know."

"Who was the first?"

"George Washington."

"Who was the first man to walk on the moon?"

"Michael Jackson."

Pickles threw up his hands. "No, no, Mottster. Michael Jackson was the first to *do* the Moon*walk*. Neil Armstrong was the first to *walk* on the *moon*."

"Right," said Eddie. "I knew that."

"So, who was the second man to walk on the moon?"

"Michael Jordan." Pickles groaned and looked back at his passenger. "Just kidding," said Eddie. "Actually, I don't know."

"Neither do I," said Pickles. "See, that's what I mean. Nobody knows who was second or third or seventy-seventh. Just the first, that's who everybody remembers. That's what goes down in the history books."

Eddie gasped. "*History* books?"

"Sure. When somebody does something for the first time, it's historic."

"Wow," went Eddie. He tried the word himself. "*Historic.*" His shoulders tingled.

"That's how it is with first things," said Pickles, pulling up to Eddie's house. Eddie stepped from the bus. "Look at it this way — if Plumstead lasts for a thousand years and the hundred-pound football teams score a million touchdowns, even if the universe lasts forever, there can only ever be one first touchdown scored at Plumstead Middle School, and — "

Pickles handed the rest of the sentence over to Eddie. Eddie finished it in a dry, awestruck whisper: " — and I scored it."

Pickles saluted him. "Bingo. And not only that. You're probably the first person — shoot, you're probably the *only* person — ever to score a touchdown by carrying the ball in his helmet, in the history of *football*, period." He thumped Eddie's shoulder. "Think about it."

The two shared a reverent minute of silence at the very thought of it.

"Well," said Pickles at last, "gotta go. See ya at the flagpole." Pickles and Eddie, by appointment of Principal Brimlow, had the job of raising the flag at the school every morning.

"See ya," Eddie answered absently and went inside.

That evening Eddie had trouble concentrating — on dinner, on taking a bath, on homework. What Pickles had said kept replaying in his head, especially the word "*historic . . . historic.*" Instead of focusing on his division problems, he kept imagining a history book of the future. In his mind he flipped the pages . . . here was George Washington crossing the Delaware . . . here was Neil Armstrong stepping off the ladder of the lunar module onto the dusty surface of the moon . . . here was Edward A. Mott, scoring the first touchdown for Plumstead Middle School. Washington. Armstrong. Mott. He got the chills.

He imagined that one day there would be a monument at the football field, perhaps just beyond the goalposts where he began his historic 103-yard run. Perhaps the monument would be a tall, diamond-tipped obelisk, like the Washington Monument. Or maybe it would be a statue, showing him running, helmet in hand, the tip of the ball barely sticking out.

He imagined, years from now, his teammates bringing their children to the field, showing them the monument and saying, "Yes, Junior, it's true. I knew Eddie Mott personally. We played on the very same team together. I was here that day. Saw it with my own eyes. I can tell you, it was an honor just to be there. He was the greatest player I've ever seen. He was truly historic."

Maybe then the old teammates would take their kids inside the school, to the trophy case. They would stand there silently, respectfully, looking at the jersey. "That's his, all right," an old teammate would say, wiping away a tear of remembrance, "ol' number eighty-nine."

When Eddie finally got to sleep that night, he was thinking about how great it was to be finally rid of that Superman underwear stigma. He was thinking of what to say to the reporters and TV crews who were bound to be waiting when he showed up at the flagpole the next day. He was wondering whether to give Neil Armstrong a call.

15

Riding to school the next day, Salem could not have been more pleased with herself. She had succeeded beyond her own hopes, which had been simply to keep morale high enough so the players wouldn't quit. Well, not only were the players staying, they had to be the happiest team in all of football. Chattering, laughing, cheering. By the end of the game, their morale had been so high — their only complaint was that the game was over — you would have sworn they had just won 84 to 6, not lost. And then to see them charging at her, sweeping her and her magic suitcase onto their padded shoulders, giving her the ride of her life across the field and into the school, begging her to be their manager forever — it was all she could do to keep from breaking down and bawling like a baby, she was so happy.

Of course, there was the little matter of the coach. After looking up to see her riding the shoulders of the team, he babbled something about "hopeless pattycakers" and announced that as of that moment he was quitting. He stomped off to his car and drove away. Nobody begged him to stay.

Right then everyone began wondering who the next coach would be. Some suggested it should be Salem. Salem laughed it off and told them she was having too much fun being student manager. Besides, she didn't consider getting a new coach a problem. From what she had seen of football, practically anybody could coach it. It was a simple enough game, especially if you were properly fed.

These happy thoughts were on her mind as she got off her bus in the school driveway. Normally, she would not have noticed the flagpole, but today, with kids looking up and laughing, she followed the pointing fingers to the top. Her first impression was of a flash of red and blue; she thought that odd, since Eddie and Pickles didn't usually raise the flag till everyone was in homeroom.

Then, shielding her eyes from the sun glare, she saw that it was not the flag at all, but underwear — red-and-blue Superman underwear — hanging from the top! Salem's heart sank. Oh, no, she thought, she ached, poor Eddie!

Pickles was running out then, running out with his bugle and the triangle-folded American flag under his arm, pushing through the giggling gawkers to the pole. Salem rushed over. "Let me help," she said, taking the flag and bugle. In a blur Pickles unwrapped the ropes from the metal cleat and — *zing!* — pulled the underwear down so fast it seemed weighted with lead. Pickles fastened the real flag to the rope, raised it so that it came blooming red, white, and blue out of Salem's hands, then gave her one rope and said, "Pull slow." As she did so, he raised the ancient, dented bugle to his lips and, as he did every morning, played reveille.

By the time the flag reached the top, the crowd of kids was hushed. Then they applauded and whistled while Pickles and Salem went into the school. Pickles stuffed the underwear into his pocket.

"Did he see it?" said Salem.

Pickles nodded grimly. "Yeah. He took off. I don't know where he is."

Salem sniffled, "He felt so good yesterday, so proud of himself. I thought this was all over."

"So did I."

They both looked down the long hallway, at the kids draining into their homerooms.

It was midway through third period when Mrs. Oates, the home skills teacher, brought the bald young man into the principal's office. She was decidedly nervous and no doubt relieved to be handing the boy over.

"I found him in my supply closet," she said. "I almost stepped on him. He was just sitting there on the floor. Almost scared me to death." She glared at the boy, retasting her anger. She gave the principal a hopeless look, shrugged. "Won't tell me his name. Won't speak."

The principal nodded. "Okay, thank you. I'll see to it."

"Hair all over the floor of the closet."

"Mm."

"Guess I'll get stuck with cleaning it up."

The principal's eyes shifted toward the door. The home skills teacher left.

Mr. Brimlow smiled. "How are you doing, Eddie?" He got up, pointed to the two high-backed leather chairs on the other side of the office. "Have a seat." In certain situations he made a point of getting out from behind the desk, where the appearance was Me Big Authority Figure, You Little Student Nobody.

The boy was still standing. Mr. Brimlow sat. "Eddie, come on." Eddie sat.

Mr. Brimlow had arrived at school well before the first bus, as usual, and had not noticed the flagpole. Only later, from his office window, did he hear and witness the episode. He was proud of the way Pickles and Salem handled things. He was especially sensitive to anything involving his Principal's Posse. And now he hurt for Eddie Mott.

Seeing Eddie in the high-backed chair reminded Mr. Brimlow of the first time he had ever laid eyes on him. It was the first day of school, and his first job as principal had been to coax this frightened sixth-grader from the back of the school bus. He didn't want to come out because some eighth-graders had tossed him around on the way to school. And now this.

He decided not to meet the issue head-on. Not an easy job, considering the sight before him. Eddie's scalp was not bald in the strictest sense. At its shortest, it was about a quarter-inch long. Here and there brown tufts cropped up. It looked ragged, more chewed than cut, as if he had been locked in that closet with a hungry goat. Add to that the most sad-sack face Mr. Brimlow had ever seen, and the principal managed to keep a straight face only because of equal pressure to both laugh and cry.

"So, Eddie," he said as casually as possible, "I hear you really did a number on that Tarrytown team yesterday. People are still talking about that touchdown you scored."

"I want to go to Alaska," Eddie muttered in a monotone.

The principal tried to keep his eyes planted on the boy's face, not his Charlie Brown dome. "Why Alaska, Eddie?"

"They hate me here. I cut my hair. I can't go home. I can't face anybody. I want to go to Alaska."

Mr. Brimlow took a deep breath. He needed

95

help. He looked at his watch. "Tell you what," he said, "you just sit here for a little while. This isn't our usual Posse lunch day, but maybe we'll call a special session."

Mr. Brimlow went to the outer office and gave directions to the secretary, Mrs. Wilburham. Not long after, as the bell rang for lunch, the other three Posse members walked into the office.

"Eek," went Sunny when she saw Eddie.

"Oh," went Salem.

Pickles said nothing.

Salem went right over and sat on the arm of Eddie's chair.

Sunny just stood there.

Pickles turned to the principal. "I think you'd better let us handle this."

The principal thought for a moment, nodded, and left the office. He heard the door close behind him.

Ten minutes later Pickles came out, walked briskly through the outer office, and down the hallway. He came back with a roll of gauze, white tape, and scissors.

After another ten minutes Brimlow heard laughter on the other side of the office door.

When the bell rang to end lunch, the four of them emerged chattering and in every other way normal, except for the bandage bowl that capped Eddie's head. The principal and the secretary just stood there staring as the sixth-graders breezed on by. Pickles gave a thumbs-up sign, Salem whispered in passing, "Tell you about it later," and they were gone.

Knowing how much Salem loved to talk, Mr. Brimlow was confident she would keep her word. Sure enough, within seconds after last bell, she was standing before his desk, huffing, glancing at the clock. "Okay, Mr. Brimlow (huff, huff). Only have a minute. Have to get to foot (huff) ball practice. First of all (gulp), you know Eddie, *always* overreacting, right? Well, we can't change that. His personality's set, probably for life. He's an overreactor. So (sigh) we're just — 'we're' meaning Sunny, Pickles, and I — we're just going to have to be around to clean up the messes he makes of his life, right? . . . Right?"

She expected an answer.

"Yes, right."

"Right. So, here's what we did. Two-part plan. Part one — Pickles' idea — bandage his head and make it look like he got injured in the football game yesterday. That's what we'll tell people. What this will do is, capital A under part one, it will hide what he did to his hair, in school, anyway. We can't stop the grief he's going to get at home. Capital B, it will get him some sympathy from the other kids. And capital C, it will draw their attention away from his underwear, which, personally, is what I think he was trying to do subconsciously when he cut his hair in the first place."

She took a deep breath, glanced at the clock. "Gotta go. Part two, quick. My idea. I told myself we have to give him something to live for, something to make him happy. What could that *be*? I asked myself. Then it came to me. I whispered it to him so no one else could hear, and presto!" — she snapped her fingers — "he was cured." She looked at the clock. "Yikes! Gotta go."

She started off. Mr. Brimlow grabbed her by the book bag. "Hey, you can't leave me hanging like that."

She stared up at him, blinking, thinking, in a rare reluctance to speak. She gave a sheepish smile. "Well, it's sort of personal."

He released her book bag. He said nothing more, demanded no more information, knowing full well it was not in her power to keep her mouth shut.

Again she glanced at the clock. Then glanced around. She moved in close to him, did not look up, whispered to his chest: "I'm having a party tomorrow. I told him I'd fix it so he could kiss Sunny." She ran. " 'Bye!"

16

"Forget it," said Sunny. "No way. *Nada*. N-O-P-E."

"Oh, Sunny," said Salem. "don't be such a poop."

"If I want to be a poop, I'll be a poop."

"It's not going to kill you."

"Oh, really? So that means I should do it? Just 'cause I'm not gonna die?"

"The *point* is, you don't have to *do* anything. All you have to do is let *him* kiss *you*."

"No."

"Sunny, it's a good cause."

"So's Save the Whales. I'll give to that. I'll let a whale kiss me."

"Sunny, I promised."

"Fine. Then let him kiss you."

Salem shook her fist at the ceiling. "Ouuu . . . you are incorrigible."

"Don't curse at me," said Sunny. "And besides, you lied. You told me to come early to help you

69

get ready for the party, and all you're doing is telling me I should let some bald-headed kid who thinks he's Superman put his lips on me. Some friend you turned out to be."

Salem sighed mightily. "He is not bald. He does not think he is Superman. He burned his Superman underwear. All he is is a person who was really feeling rotten, and here you have a chance to make him feel really good. You can turn his whole life around. It's in your power. And it's not like he's some stranger, you know. He's the person who pulled you out of the tire when the pickle-bus crashed. He's our friend. He's *your* friend."

Sunny crunched a potato chip. "He's also a boy." She crunched another chip. She almost grinned. "Anyway, I know what you're really up to."

Salem's eyebrows arched. "Do tell? And what might that be, if I may ask?"

Sunny reached for another chip. "I've seen you look at Pickles. You just want to get something started so you can lay a wet one on him."

Salem was dumbstruck. She stared speechless at Sunny for a painfully long time, listening to Sunny chew chip after chip but hearing the crunching of her own private life. Then came the merciful sound of the doorbell. "It's them," she said and opened the door for Pickles and Eddie.

Pickles was carrying a plastic bag. "What's that?" said Salem.

"You'll see," said Pickles. He handed the bag

to Sunny. "A little present for you."

Sunny pulled a mask from the bag. She frowned at it. "Huh?"

"It's a hamster," said Pickles. "Didn't you say you were going to be a hamster at the football games from now on? So, here's your hamster face." He took the mask from her. "See, it used to be Bugs Bunny. I made it for Halloween a couple years ago. Eddie helped me. We clipped off the ears, painted the face light brown, like Humphrey. We kept the whiskers." He turned it to Salem. "What do you think it looks like?"

Salem threw up her arms. "Why, it's a *hamster*!"

Pickles put the mask over Sunny's head. She looked at herself in the mirror. "I'm working on the rest of the costume," said Pickles. "It should be ready by next game."

The hamster head nodded. "Okay, but it still looks half-rabbit to me."

"No problem," said Pickles. "Call it a ramster."

"When do we eat?" said Eddie, now wearing a baseball cap instead of a bandage.

"*Maintenant*," said Salem.

"Huh?"

"That means 'now' in French." Salem ushered them into the dining room.

"Wow," said Pickles.

"Double wow," said Eddie.

The table had been exquisitely set by Salem, to

whom every event was an occasion. There was a sky-blue tablecloth, and contrasting pure white porcelain dishware, and fine, fancy silverware. There were eight white bowls containing the following: strawberries, pineapple chunks, banana slices, potato chips, pretzels, pound-cake squares, vanilla wafers, and pieces of peanut-butter granola bars.

In the center of the table were two larger items. One was a clear crystal bowl, huge and half-filled with a pink punch in which floated an iceberg of sherbet. The other item was a metal, copper-colored pan, resting several inches above the tablecloth on a wiry base. In the center of the base sat a short, fat candle throwing a blue flame onto the underside of the copper pan.

"Is that what I think it is?" said Eddie, staring straight down into the pan.

Salem nodded. "Behold, *le chocolat*."

"Melted?"

"And warm."

"To *drink*?"

Salem sighed. "To dip. It's fondue."

"Great!" exclaimed Eddie, and immediately dipped his right forefinger into the warm, liquidy chocolate.

If Salem had not screamed, Eddie might not have flinched, and a drop of chocolate might not have flown from his finger onto the sky-blue tablecloth. But Salem did scream and Eddie did flinch, and now she ran to the kitchen and returned with a dishcloth and started scrubbing frantically at the dark-brown spot, muttering, "Cold water. Cold water takes out stains, if you get it soon enough. If. If. Please, cold water, please . . ."

After a full minute of scrubbing and muttering, only a large dark-blue wet spot remained. But Salem wasn't finished. She now began removing all items from the table to the floor, muttering all the while: "They're gonna spill chocolate on my good tablecloth, my mother said. No they won't, I said. They will, she said. They're kids. Kids spill. They won't, I said. If they do, you're dead, she said. They won't, I said. They did . . ."

When all items were off, she swept the blue cloth from the table and stomped away. Within seconds, a washing machine could be heard churning to life. Salem returned with a stack of newspapers. She spread them over the table, then began transferring the items back from the floor. "*Little* kids spill, I said. *All* kids spill, she said. Not *these* kids, I said. My friends? Spill? Never. Hah! Ho-ho. I'm dead. Exterminated. I look like I'm alive. Here I am putting dishes on the table, but actually I'm a corpse. I am a dead eleven-year-old. Here lies Salem Jane Brownmiller . . . she trusted . . . she trusted . . . she's dead. . . ."

The last thing she did was return the four white

name cards to their former places. Except for the newspapers, the table now looked exactly as it had before.

The three guests, who had backed into the living room, dared return. Pickles applauded; Eddie and Sunny joined in. Salem took a deep breath, smiled for the first time in five minutes, and bowed briefly.

"You always get goofy when you're upset?" said Pickles, now staying well away from the copper pot.

"Only when I'm about to be executed by my own mother," said Salem. "Also, it helps me get things out of my system so I can return to normal."

"*Return* to normal?" Sunny chuckled. "How can you return if you were never *there*?"

Sunny laughed. Salem laughed. They all laughed.

"Find your places," said Salem. "It's time to eat."

17

Salem explained: "As I said, it's called fondue. You dip stuff in — *not* fingers. Look." At each place was a long, thin, two-pronged fork. Salem picked up hers, stabbed a strawberry, dipped it into the copper-potted chocolate, and held it up for all to see. "*Violà!*" She ate it. "Mmm-mm."

For the next five minutes the only sounds were the chewing of four mouths and the drip of chocolate onto newspaper. As the initial feeding frenzy slowed down, Pickles took time between bites to observe, "I am fond of fondue."

Eddie said as he downed the last of the pound-cake squares, "How did you know what to put out for dunking?"

"Chef's choice," said Salem. "I just decided what would go good with chocolate. And you're not dunking, you're dipping."

Eddie devoured his dripping dark-brown pound-cake square. "You mean you're allowed to dunk anything? It doesn't have to be what's here?"

Salem saw what was coming. She considered her answer carefully. *"Allowed?* Yes, you're allowed. There's no fondue law that says what you can and cannot dip. I mean, you're *allowed* to dip an eraser in the fondue. But that doesn't mean you *would*. That doesn't mean it would taste good." She decided to call his bluff, challenge him directly. "You wouldn't dip a brussels sprout in it, would you?"

Eddie made a face as he dipped a pretzel. "No *way*. Ugh."

"Well," said Salem, feeling a small puff of triumph, "it's all a matter of good taste."

Eddie licked chocolate from the pretzel before taking a bite. "How about pepperoni?"

In that instant, Salem knew she had brought a monster to life. She tried to ignore him. She gave no answer.

"Well?" said Sunny, grinning like a gremlin. "The boy asked about pepperoni."

Salem glared daggers at Sunny. "If the boy means is it *allowed* to dip pepperoni in chocolate fondue, yes, it is *allowed*, even though no sane or insane member of the human species would ever actually *want* to do it."

"I would," said Eddie cheerily.

Salem slumped. "No."

"You said there's no law."

"I also said it's a matter of good taste."

Eddie dipped a granola piece, then held it above

106

his open mouth to capture drippings. "Chocolate has good taste."

"Can't argue with that," Sunny added.

"Eddie," said Salem, "do you happen to remember a certain Saturday last month when you were here at this same table?"

Salem was referring to a lunch meeting she had called to discuss the question of a mascot for the new school. Eddie, the only one of the Principal's Posse to show up, had eaten virtually everything on the table and had wound up sick that night and all the next day.

"It wasn't the food I got sick on," said Eddie.

Salem jabbed her finger at him. "Don't you go saying it was my Periwinkle Punch."

Eddie shrugged and dipped a potato chip. "Okay, I won't say it."

Salem steamed. Eddie munched. Sunny watched. Pickles whispered to himself, "Periwinkle Punch."

Finally Salem began to slowly nod her head. "Okay . . . okay . . ." She got up from her chair, muttering, "Why should I care? It's not my life. Anyway, I'm already dead." She left the room. In a minute she returned with a saucer of pepperoni slices and a bucket. She placed the saucer in front of Eddie and the bucket on the floor beside him. She took her seat.

Eddie looked at the bucket. "What's that for?"

"For you to throw up in," Salem replied matter-of-factly, "if you'll excuse me ending the sentence with a preposition. When you fill that one up, I'll bring another."

Everyone but Salem laughed; Eddie ate. When he finished the chocolate-dipped pepperonis, he requested, and received, permission to check out the kitchen for further possibilities. He returned with string cheese, marshmallows, chocolate-frosted mini-donuts (They're *already* covered with chocolate! Salem thought but did not say), roast turkey, and a Swedish meatball.

"Yeuch!" went Sunny. She reached for the bucket. "He doesn't need this. I do."

Within a minute, Sunny, Salem, and Pickles had all retired to the living room. When Eddie finally joined them, the only sign of stomach distress he showed was a burp.

"Pig," said Salem.

Eddie took a seat in the recliner, pushed it back, put his feet up, burped again, and smiled contentedly. "So, what games are we going to play?"

"Games?" echoed Salem. "Do we have to play games? What is this, a first-grade birthday party?"

"Well, what did you have in mind?" said Sunny. "Sit around and discuss our favorite textbooks?"

Howls from Pickles and Eddie.

"So what do you want to play?" said Salem directly to Eddie. "Pin the tail on the donkey?"

"How about pin the tail on the hostess?" said Eddie.

More howls.

"How about pin the *kiss* on the hostess?" said Sunny.

Silence.

Quiet enough to hear Salem sizzling. Pickles noted her red face. "Sunnyburned?" he said.

Salem turned quickly to him, searching his face for meanness, but found only his usual friendly grin. She had to do something, change the picture. She popped up. "Egad, almost forgot! Sunny already saw my room but you guys didn't. First one who guesses what city it's supposed to be gets a copy of my first published book." She headed up the stairs. "Come on . . . come on . . . ."

By the time she led them back down the stairs (Pickles had quessed Paris), Salem had regained her composure. ". . . so we all expected the new coach to be another old macho gruff guy like Mr. Lujak, right, Eddie?"

"Right."

"So who shows up? Mr. Foy."

"The art teacher?" said Sunny.

"Exactly. And you knew he wasn't Mr. Lujak when he started out, 'Good afternoon, children.' "

Salem plopped onto the sofa. She shivered visibly. "Ouuu — don't you just hate to be called children?"

Eddie stretched out on the recliner. "Never thought about it."

"Well, we are, aren't we?" said Sunny.

"Who isn't?" said Pickles. "A hundred-year-old man is somebody's child."

"I know, I know," said Salem. "I'm not saying we aren't, technically. But you know what I mean. Like, they say a person becomes what you tell them they are. So if you call kids children and keep treating them like children, well, they'll act like children."

"That's so bad?" said Sunny. "I wouldn't want to act like some of the grown-ups I've seen."

"The point is," said Salem, "we're not in grade school anymore, where we were surrounded by little children. We're in middle school now, which means we'd better start growing up. Who knows what grown-up things are going to happen to us by the time we graduate from Plumstead three years from now. I say we start getting ready for grown-upness so it doesn't take us by surprise."

"So what should we do," said Pickles, "grow mustaches?"

Sunny said, "I know what she wants us to do." All heads swung to the dark-haired girl sitting cross-legged before the fireplace. "She wants us to start kissing."

18

This time Salem was ready.

"Listen to her, she keeps bringing up this kissing business. I was just thinking of the Halloween dance. That shows what's on *her* mind." She turned to Sunny. "Is there somebody in this room you wish to kiss, Miss Wyler?"

"Not me," said Sunny. "I'm too young for that stuff."

"Well, what are you going to do if some boy likes you? If he does kiss you?"

"He'd have to get close to me first, and that ain't gonna happen." Sunny tilted herself till she was lying on her side, her right arm propping up her head. "Unless he has five-foot-long lips."

Pickles roared at that one. Eddie laughed, but more carefully.

Salem jumped up, looked down at Sunny. "But what if he sneaks up on you, real quiet, from behind — " She demonstrated, playing the part of the boy with an invisible Sunny. "And then suddenly he goes — " She darted forward and planted a kiss on invisible Sunny's cheek.

Said the visible Sunny, "He'd be dead."

Eddie squirmed. Salem threw up her hands. "Well, see, that's what we're up against here. How can you have progress with that kind of attitude? You probably giggle every time somebody says the word *sex*."

"Don't you?"

Giggles from Eddie and Pickles.

"No," said Salem, "as a matter of fact, I don't. What's there to giggle about? It's nature. It's natural as trees and cows. Do you giggle when somebody says trees or cows?"

"If the tree tries to kiss the cow," said Sunny, "sure, absolutely."

Howls.

Salem gave a shrug of surrender. "Okay, okay, funny people, you win. I can see there's no point in trying to say something a little serious around here, not with a roomful of giggling little children." She returned to the sofa. "I guess I'll just go to the Halloween dance by myself. You'll probably be busy playing with your Tinker Toys anyway."

Salem folded her arms and stared grumpily at the floor.

Sunny sat up. She bobbed her head and batted her eyelashes. "I have an idea," she said perkily.

"Let's be big. Let's play spin the bottle!"

"Sunny," said Salem. "you can quit the act. Nobody believes it. And anyway, playing spin the bottle isn't being big."

Sunny stuck out her tongue at Salem.

Salem said, "My, my, such maturity. You know, Sunshine, you are a disgrace to your own sex when you act that way."

Sunny kept her tongue out while replying: "Ith that tho?"

"Yes, that's so. Everybody knows that girls mature faster than boys. It's okay for them" — she waved in Eddie's and Pickles' direction — "to act like babies, at least up to a point. They don't know any better." Eddie and Pickles looked at each other. "Something must be holding you back. Are you still eating Pablum by any chance?"

"No way," said Sunny, reeling in her tongue. "I eat mashed bananas. Doesn't everybody?"

"Hold it there," Pickles piped. "Back up a minute. That sounds like an insult to me. Who says I'm a baby?"

"You know what I mean," said Salem. "I didn't mean it as an insult. It's just nature's way. Girls mature faster than boys. In fact, women are usually more mature than men. That's why young women marry old men."

"Okay," said Pickles, "let's see who the baby is. Do you sleep with a night-light on?"

Salem scoffed, "Of course not." Suddenly she and Pickles locked eyes: Both had the same idea. "Hey," she said, "let's — "

" — ask everybody."

Salem stood. "Okay. Raise hands. Be honest, everybody. And anybody can ask a question. All right, same question: Who still sleeps with a night-light on?"

All four looked around. One hand was in the air: Eddie's.

"Okay," said Pickles, "who's afraid to go down to the basement all by themselves?"

All eyes swung toward Eddie. Eddie's hands were gripping his chair. Then surprisingly, it was Pickles' hand in the air. "There's no use playing if we're not going to be honest."

The other three hands went up.

"All right," said Salem, "confession is good for the soul. Now we're getting somewhere." She thought. "Okay, how about this: Who still puts catsup on their scrambled eggs?"

Eddie raised his hand, puzzled. "What's wrong with that?"

Sunny said, "Ask him if he uses chocolate syrup."

Salem didn't ask, but the uncomfortable look on Eddie's face hinted at what the answer to that question might be.

"Next question," said Pickles. "Who still believes in the tooth fairy?"

No hands. Nevertheless, Salem, Sunny, and Pickles looked at Eddie and began to laugh. Again his face, especially his twitching nostrils, had given him away.

"*Who*," said Sunny, fixing her eyes on Salem, "is supposed to be a big-deal lady but can't even wiggle yet?"

Salem fumed at Sunny, then replied with a sniff, "The question has to apply to everyone in the room." She leaned toward Sunny. "*Who* . . . sticks out their tongue at people?"

Sunny smiled cheerfully, waved her hand in the air, and stuck out her tongue.

The questions came fast.

"Who eats peas with a spoon?"

Eddie raised his hand.

"Who gets sauce on themselves when they eat spaghetti?"

Eddie, Sunny, and Pickles.

"Who gets carsick?"

Nobody.

"Who cries when they get hurt?"

Everybody.

"Who sleeps with a stuffed animal?"

Eddie.

"Who," said Eddie, posing his first question, "has ever kissed a member of the opposite sex?"

Eddie shot his arm into the air, this time with pride. But so did the others.

"My father," snickered Salem, "you goof."

Eddie's hand came halfway down, he frowned; then his face brightened, his arm shot back up. "A member of the opposite sex who is not a relative!"

Sunny's and Pickles' hands went down. Salem's stayed up. "My mailman. When he brought me the letter that said I had a poem accepted in *Lickity Split*."

Eddie's arm strained for the ceiling. "A member of the opposite sex, not a relative, *your own age!*"

Everyone gaped at Eddie, whose chair had suddenly become a throne of triumph. Salem's hand went down. "Who?" she growled.

"Flossie," beamed Eddie.

The other three combed their brains.

"How old?" said Salem.

"Eleven, same as me."

"Lives in Cedar Grove?" said Pickles.

"Yep, definitely. Oh, yeah, I almost forgot — " Eddie put on a face of casual smugness — " *on the lips.*"

Stunned, staring silence was his tribute.

At last Salem rasped, "Flossie who?"

Eddie blinked, shrugged. "Flossie Mott."

Salem shrieked. "You said not a relative!"

"She's not a relative," said Eddie, and then it burst from him in howling laughter: "She's a *dog*! She's the same age as me and she kisses me all the time" — he pointed to his lips — "right *there!*"

Pickles cracked up. The two girls threw pillows at Eddie.

When things quieted down, Salem said, "All right, let's separate the adolescents from the babies. *Who* . . . will allow themselves to be kissed by another person in this room" — she glared at Sunny — "of the *opposite* sex, and in doing so will show he or she is the most mature person here?"

As Salem raised her hand, she looked about. No one else moved. "Well, I guess that settles that."

Sunny sat up straight. "No, I guess that *doesn't* settle that. Saying you'll do it doesn't prove anything. If somebody came over to give a big liplock, how do we know you wouldn't turn chicken and run off screaming in the other direction?"

Salem stared at Sunny. Salem stood. "Very well." She swallowed. "Okay." She swallowed again. She pinned her eyes on the picture hanging on the opposite wall; it was an oil painting of a clown with a sad face. She cleared her throat. "If someone would care to kiss me at this particular time, you may."

Somewhere outside little children squealed at play. In the Brownmiller living room, among the four still figures — three seated, one standing — all was as silent as the sad clown on the wall. As the silence grew longer, Salem fixed her eyes ever more on the picture. She sensed the distance between herself and the others increasing at an alarming rate, till they seemed no closer than orbiting moons. She had never felt so alone in her life. As her eyes began to water, the plump, drooping mouth of the clown blurred and overflowed and, perversely, seemed to turn up slightly as if beginning to smile.

And then someone was taking her hand — she turned — Pickles! — taking it and lifting it to his lips and kissing it — a light touch of his lips on the back of her hand, in the middle between her knuckles and wrist, letting her hand go then and returning to his seat.

For the next several moments Salem floated in a hazy daze. When she came to her senses, she found herself back on the sofa, and Sunny was standing before the fireplace, sneering, "Hah! That's nothing. You want to see *mature*? I'll show you *mature*. What's the big deal *allowing* yourself to be smooched? That's just being the smooch-*ee*. I want to know who's big enough to be the smooch-*er*. Who's got the nerve to walk over and lay a big wet one right on somebody's opposite-sex face right here in this room? Let's go — hands."

Salem did not move. Pickles did not move. Eddie did not move.

Sunny grinned. "Well, well." She raised her hand slowly, like a flag. "Looks like I'm surrounded by little kiddies."

What happened next happened very quickly. There was no time to react, only to stare wonderstruck. With a yip and a yelp, Sunny snatched up the hamster mask, rushed across the room to the boggle-eyed Eddie Mott, plunked the mask over his head and laid a loud, long, juicy smacker right on his three-inch whiskers. She then wheeled and hip-whipped back across the room, one hand fluffing up the back of her hair, fluttering her eyelids, crooning, "Just call me . . . Miss Ma-tur-i-tee . . ."

That's when everyone cracked up.

19

Halloween night!

Pickles was behind schedule. He had told the others he would pick them up at seven, and here it was already 7:05. He hadn't expected problems transferring his old bicycle headlight to the picklebus. Well, at least now it was done and working, ready for the dark.

What really got shortchanged was his costume. It had no distinctive finishing touches. He pulled the long green shroud over his head and let it fall to the floor. He pulled his arms in through the side slits. He looked in the mirror. He was not happy. Only a very sloppy eye would pass him for a pickle. He could just as easily go as a cactus, a cucumber, a green banana, or a moldy hot dog. Oh, well, there just wasn't time in a day to do everything right.

As Pickles pushed off toward Eddie's house, trick-or-treaters were dashing up the sidewalks and driveways, some with parents, some with bags as big as themselves. All along the street, doors were opening to reveal the silhouettes of tiny ghosts and goblins.

Pickles was torn.

On the one hand, he sort of agreed with Salem that they should all go to the dance. He agreed that they ought to support their school and that they were not little kiddies anymore and that the Halloween dance was as good a place as any to start growing up. Yes, he agreed with all that. Sort of.

But on the other hand, he would be lying if he said he didn't wish he were one of those kids dashing up and down the street. He asked himself what he would rather be holding that night: a girl on the dance floor or a bag full of candy? It was no contest.

That's what he was most uneasy about: the dance. And Salem. He had been uneasy for the three weeks since Salem's party, since he had kissed her hand. He kept wondering if she realized he had done it only to keep her feelings from being hurt. He wondered if she realized he wasn't ready yet to start messing around with girls.

Eddie stood before the bed in his Fruit of the Loom underwear. On the bed lay two Halloween costumes: Superman and a hobo. It was seven o'clock, Pickles would be here any second, and still he hadn't decided which one to wear.

It was amazing that Superman was even in the running, considering the flak he had caught over his red-and-blue underwear. But the fact was, Eddie had recently begun to calm down about the whole thing. Maybe it was cutting his hair that did it, getting it out of his system. Or maybe it was Sunny kissing him — well, the mask — even if she was joking. Or what Pickles had said to him one day: "Hey, man, stop trying to be somebody you're not. Be yourself."

Eddie had applied his best pal's advice to football. He stopped taking the game so seriously — not hard to do with Mr. Foy as a coach. Eddie didn't even object when Salem put happy face decals on everyone's helmet. And he joined the rest of the team in gorging himself silly during Salem's gourmet buffet time-outs. One game — incredibly! — she even brought chocolate fondue onto the field. Who cared that the Fighting Hamsters had lost their first four games by a combined score of 213 to 6?

As for goodies on this night, Mr. Brimlow had announced that there would be treats for the kids who came to the dance. Maybe so, but Eddie was willing to bet that they wouldn't give him enough stuff to cover his bed with, as he had done last year, and the year before that. He remembered wistfully how he had filled up his bag three times and had to keep coming back to the house to unload. He recalled fondly how sick he had gotten.

Every year, as far back as he could remember, he had gotten sick the day after Halloween. And why not? It was a tradition. What good was Halloween without enough junk to get sick on?

Ooguh! Ooguh!

Eddie heard the new picklehorn. He looked out. He couldn't see Pickles too well in the dark. The headlight switched on and off several times. "Pickle pickup!" came the call.

Eddie whirled to the bed. Be yourself, Pickles had said. Okay — who was he tonight? Superman or a hobo?

Superman!

He was dressed in thirty seconds and out the door.

Sunny was waiting on her front steps. The neighborhood was crawling with demons and monsters. What to be tonight had been no problem for her. She loved her hamster suit, even if the body part of it was a pair of Pickles' father's long underwear dyed caramel-brown and otherwise disguised. Her sole regret was that she had been allowed to wear it for only one game.

Ah, but what a game. It was against Harry S Truman Middle School. As the official Fighting Hamster, unseen behind her costume, she could get away with stuff that as a cheerleader she could not. In fact, shenanigans were expected of a mascot. So she roamed and cavorted at will, along the

123

sideline and even into the bleachers. She led the cheers, she commanded the cheers, and if somebody wasn't cheering, she smacked them with her paw — and they laughed and cheered!

If only she could have confined herself to the spectators. If only she didn't want her school to win so bad. If only that Truman player wasn't laughing. There he was, running down the field, not a Hamster within twenty yards of him, heading for a sure touchdown with his team already ahead 47 to 0 — and he was *grinning*. That's what did it. Leading 47 to 0 and looking over at the Plumstead bleachers and grinning, rubbing it in. Well, he wasn't grinning when the four-foot-nine-inch hamster tackled him on the two-yard line.

Of course, they had to allow Truman a touchdown anyway. And of course Sunny had to be fired from her job. She wasn't too surprised at all that. What did surprise her, and disappoint her, was that the whole bleachers hadn't emptied and joined her in burying that Harry S Truman grinner.

Ooguh! Ooguh! "Pickle pickup! Pickle pickup!"

Still a block away, the picklebus clattered down the sidewalk, its headlight like a low-flying star. Sunny ran out to meet it.

Two years before Salem had been William Shakespeare. Last year she was Louisa May Alcott (even if nobody realized it). And this year: a beatnik poet, all black from her floppy felt hat to her cape to her boots. She seldom fooled anyone on Halloween. Everyone knew that the Brownmiller girl would be the one in the writer's getup.

Lately, Salem was wondering if she had been fooling herself. When Pickles kissed her hand at the party, she had been stunned. No surprise there. But there had also been a second reaction, and it *was* a surprise: fright. It had scared her to be that close to a boy, to wonder what was next, to have used her female powers to cause a boy to act.

Until then, she had only imagined what it would be like to be more than just friends with Pickles. Now she had discovered that imagination could not always be trusted. It frightened her to think that she could be responsible for someone else's feelings, for making them happy or sad. It scared her to think that things might get complicated at the dance tonight. What if Pickles tried to kiss her again, this time not on the hand? What could she say to him without hurting him? How could she make him understand that she liked the two of them just the way they were? How could she tell him that she wasn't ready yet to start getting personal with boys?

Ooguh! Ooguh!

Salem opened her front door. All three of them yelled: "Pickle pickup! Pickle pickup!"

For a moment she just stood there. What a

sight: two pickles — one horizontal, one upright — a superhero and a hamster. She couldn't help giggling. What was there to be afraid of?

"What are you supposed to be?" called Sunny. "A lump of coal?"

"I'm a beatnik!" called Salem. She shut the door behind her and climbed aboard.

The Pickle Posse was still five blocks from school when Eddie cried out: "Ou-ou, stop!"

The bus came to a halt.

"*That* house." Eddie pointed to a house across the street. The door was open. One group of Halloweeners was leaving, one group could be seen in the living room, one was waiting on the porch, and another was heading up the driveway. "They give the best stuff," Eddie gushed. "They give candy, and not the mini-sizes. The *regular* sizes. And if you ask for two, you *got* it!"

"You come this far for Halloween?" said Pickles.

"I go everywhere," said Eddie, who already had both feet on the sidewalk. "I know that house. I gotta go." He looked at his friends. "I *gotta*."

"Well," said Sunny, "if you gotta, you gotta." From somewhere inside her hamster suit she pulled a pillowcase. She handed it to Eddie. "And if *you* gotta" — she pulled out three more and waved them in the air — then we *all* gotta!"

Everyone cheered and grabbed a pillowcase.

The picklebus zoomed across the street.

As they headed for the open door, Eddie raved on: "And I know another great house on Beech Street . . . and one on Woodbine . . ."

The picklebus never made it to the school dance.

About the Author

Jerry Spinelli is the author of several novels, including *Fourth Grade Rats*, *The Library Card*, *Picklemania*, and the Newbery Medal–winning *Maniac Magee*. He lives in Phoenixville, Pennsylvania, with his wife and fellow author, Eileen Spinelli, and their children.

Any Way You Look At It,
LOUIS SACHAR'S
Books are Hilarious

ake a Lesson in Laughter
rom Newbery Award-inning uthor erry pinelli

JERRY SPINELLI
Newbery-award-winning author of *Maniac Magee*

PRINCIPAL

REPORT TO THE PRINCIPAL'S OFFICE
SCHOLASTIC

JERRY SPINELLI
Newbery-award-winning author of *Maniac Magee*

FOURTH GRADE RATS
SCHOLASTIC

REPORT TO THE
PRINCIPAL'S OFFICE

**Look for these other great books
by Jerry Spinelli**

Fourth Grade Rats
Do the Funky Pickle
Who Ran My Underwear Up the Flagpole?
Picklemania
The Library Card

REPORT TO THE
PRINCIPAL'S OFFICE

JERRY
SPINELLI

SCHOLASTIC INC.

New York   Toronto   London   Auckland   Sydney
Mexico City   New Delhi   Hong Kong   Buenos Aires

ISBN 0-590-46277-6

32 31 30 29 28 27 26 25 24 23 22 21   4 5 6 7 8 9/0

Printed in the U.S.A.   40

For their contributions to this book,
I would like to thank
Pat Carbone, teacher;
Judy Anderson, teacher;
and Jennie Singleton, kid.

For Sherwood and Rowena Mercer
Marion Baker
and Mardie Bell

1

Sunny Wyler opened her front door and stepped out of her house. Directly across the street, Hillary Kain came out of her house. The instant the two best friends saw each other, they burst into tears.

They met on the sidewalk in front of Sunny's house.

"Come on," sniffed Hillary, "I'll walk you to the bus."

They walked as slowly as they could.

"Look at this," said Sunny, picking at the sleeve of her DEATH TO MUSHROOMS T-shirt. "Same rag I wore last year. I'm gonna wear it every day till we're back together again."

"Won't you have to get it washed?"

"I'm not gonna."

"You'll start to smell."

"Good," grumbled Sunny. "The worse I smell, the faster they'll kick me out and transfer me to your school."

1

"Now I feel guilty," said Hillary.

"Why?"

"Here I am with my new clothes. I should give up more, like you."

"Don't be a moron," said Sunny. "You know me. I overdo everything. You're doing the hair. That's enough."

"You think so?"

"I think so."

The girls had vowed that from that day forward, they would never again wash their hair till they were back in the same school.

For seven years — preschool, kindergarten, grades one through five — Sunny and Hillary had gone to the same school. In fact, at Drumore Elementary, they had always shared the same classroom. They became best friends. They went on vacations with each others' families. And to top it off, they lived directly across the street from each other. They were meant to be together. Nothing would ever break them up.

But something did.

Two sinister forces were at work during those seven years. One force was population movement. More and more families were making their homes in Cedar Grove.

The other force was babies. People were having more of them than before. Newspapers called it the "Baby Boomlet." Even so, babies alone were not the problem. The problem was, they got older.

The problem was, sooner or later the babies became sixth-graders.

The problem was, Cedar Grove Middle School could not hold them all.

The *problem* was, they built a new middle school — Plumstead — to hold the growing population.

The PROBLEM was, when they drew the line on the town map to decide who goes to Cedar Grove and who goes to Plumstead, they drew it smack dab down the middle of the street that Sunny Wyler and Hillary Kain lived on.

Hillary would go to the old school, Cedar Grove. Sunny would go to the new one, Plumstead.

"I feel like I'm walking to the gallows," said Sunny.

"Me, too," said Hillary. She fished around for something helpful to say. "Look on the bright side. You're going to a brand-new school. New desks, new everything. I hear they even have air-conditioning."

"I don't *want* air-conditioning," Sunny grumped. "I just want to go to Cedar Grove."

They looked at each other. More tears came. And, in the case of Sunny, something else.

"Your nose is running," said Hillary.

Sunny sniffed. The runner retreated like a turtle's head.

"It's the baby boomlet's fault," said Hillary.

"It's our parents' fault," said Sunny. "The rats."

3

Hillary nodded. It was true. Their very own parents had been among the worst offenders of the boomlet. Each girl had two younger siblings — Sunny, two brothers, and Hillary, a brother and sister.

"We should've stopped them," Sunny said. "We should've put our foot down. 'No more babies.' "

"Then you wouldn't have any little brothers," Hillary pointed out.

A wicked grin curled Sunny's lip. "Yeah, too bad." Little brothers were not Sunny's favorite people.

"Your nose again," said Hillary.

This time Sunny did not sniff. "Let it run. I'm never gonna wipe it. I'm not gonna smile. I'm not gonna talk, not even if a teacher asks me a question. They'll be so disgusted with me and my bad attitude and my stinky shirt and my greasy hair, they'll *have* to transfer me. They'll *beg* me to go. They'll hire a limo to take me away."

If anyone else had said this, Hillary would have cracked up. But she knew her friend was perfectly serious and in no mood to be laughed at.

"We're here," said Hillary.

Sunny walked on. "I think it's the next corner." If she could only keep walking, she would never be there, it would never happen.

"Sunny," called Hillary, "*this* is the corner."

Sunny stopped. She slumped, beaten. A sigh of

4

utter desolation rose from her heart. She returned to Hillary.

The two friends stood grimly, silently, by the stop sign. Two blocks away, a yellow bus turned onto the street. Suddenly Sunny felt emptied of everything inside. She grabbed onto Hillary and felt Hillary squeeze back.

The bus should have come slowly, creeping, respecting her feelings. Instead, it roared to the curbside and, without the slightest hesitation, flung open its door.

"Oh," peeped Sunny.

The two friends hugged, inches from the yawning door. Sunny did not notice, but Hillary's hug was slightly lopsided. As much as she loved Sunny, Hillary did not care to have her new shirt become a handkerchief for Sunny's runny nose.

"Let's go, girls," called the bus driver. "I got a lotta people to pick up."

Sunny wasn't surprised at the remark. She had already decided that the Plumstead bus drivers would be despicable gorillas.

She parted from Hillary, mounted the steps, and before she could wave to her friend, the door had shut, and the bus was roaring away. Okay, she thought, one final word before I shut up forever. She paused beside the bus driver. Sure enough, there was hair growing out of his ears. "Gorilla," she said, and walked down the aisle.

2

Eddie Mott watched the girl come down the aisle with a growing dread. The seat next to him was empty. He had been hoping it would be filled by someone friendly and talkative, someone who would help take his mind off the fact that this was his first day of middle school.

But the girl looked anything but friendly. He had seen her glare at the bus driver and say something to him. Now, as she came nearer, he got a full view of the scowl on her face. It was worse than anything he had ever seen on a TV wrestler. And then he spotted the gleam under her left nostril.

This girl's got problems, he thought. Please don't let her sit here.

But sit there she did. Plopped herself right down next to him, scowling straight ahead.

Up till now, things had gone about as well as could be expected. Eddie had been determined to break the bonds of little boyhood and take that

6

first big step into a more grown-up world. Every school day for five years, his mother had walked him to Brockhurst Elementary. But last night he had said, "Mom, I want to walk to the bus myself." And he had.

He had picked out his own clothes to wear. Middle school clothes. The Daffy Duck pin that he had worn every day last year lay back in his bedroom dresser.

Leaving his memories behind was not so easy. At just about this time of the morning every day last year, he and Roger Himes would be raising the American flag outside Brockhurst. That had been his job all through fifth grade.

But now he was a sixth-grader, and doggonnit, he was going to fit in. That's why he had made up a three-point plan:

1. Be friendly.
2. Wear the right clothes.
3. Avoid eighth-graders.

The last point was advice from Roger Himes, whose older brother was now entering high school. "Stay away from eighth-graders," warned Roger. "They'll get you in trouble. They run the school."

Things had been going well until the sourpussed girl plopped down beside him. Now he began to feel his control of the situation slipping away. All morning he had been wearing an especially friendly face. If only she would turn and see how friendly he was . . .

"Hi," he said.

The girl didn't move an inch. She continued to stare glumly at the back of the seat in front of her.

Maybe she has a hearing problem, he thought. He couldn't see a hearing aid. Maybe it was in the ear on the side away from him.

So this time he tapped her lightly on the wrist when he said it: "Hi."

Still she didn't move. Was she hypnotized? In a trance?

The half of her face that he could see was the side with the running nostril. Actually, it wasn't running at all. It was simply sitting there, a gleaming little puddle, as though it had just crept out to have a look around. And it was really starting to bother him, Eddie being a very neat kid. It was all he could do to keep from whipping out his hankie and wiping it away. Maybe if he brought it to her attention in a nice way. . . .

"Got a cold there?" he said as pleasantly as possible.

Slowly the girl's head turned — he had never seen a head turn so slowly — till she was fully facing him. He froze. She raised her upper lip till she looked like a snarling Doberman. She sniffed.

The gleamer zipped back into her nose. She turned away.

Eddie allowed himself a breath. Now that the first move was over, he decided it hadn't really been so bad. After all, she did turn, she did respond to him. Must have been his friendly face. Maybe he should say something a little meatier this time.

"I hear the new school has air-conditioning," he said.

Again the head slowly turned. The girl spoke. "The next person that tells me the new school has air-conditioning is gonna get a punch in the face."

For the rest of the ride, Eddie looked out the window.

When the bus arrived at school, Eddie made sure to let the grump get well ahead of him. It was slow going down the aisle, as the bus had been filled to the gills. Eddie was scrunched front and back. He held his lunch bag to his chest. Everybody towered over him.

There was a commotion up front, bringing the aisle to a standstill. Kids up front were yelling to kids in back — all eighth-graders, no doubt. The kids up front were calling for their football. The kids in back were saying they didn't have it. The kids up front said they weren't getting off till they got it. The bus driver was calling them all delinquents and telling them to get off his bus, he had a job to get to.

"Throw the ball!" yelled the guys up front.

"Okay," yelled the guys behind, "you asked for it!" And suddenly Eddie was off his feet, hands under him from ankles to shoulders. He was horizontal, on his back, staring straight up at the white ceiling of the bus. "Here!" yelled the voices below him, and he was flying — *flying!* — down the aisle — *above* the aisle — clutching his lunch bag, landing in a squirmy bed of hands.

"Hey," yelled the new voices, "*this* ain't our ball!" And he was flying back down the aisle. At that point, the bus driver went totally wacko and started tossing kids off the bus.

When Eddie came to his senses, he found himself alone on the backseat.

3

T. Charles Brimlow was as ready as he would ever be. Fifteen minutes before the first bus arrived, he was out front wearing a smile as wide as his bow tie. And why not? He was a brand-new principal in a brand-new school. Talk about a fresh start! And he was determined to make the most of it.

The town, the architects, the taxpayers — they had given him all any principal could ask for in the way of a facility. The most modern this, the most up-to-date that. High-tech electronics from boiler room to kitchen. But without people, it was just a brick-and-glass skeleton. Students, teachers, staff — they would bring it to life, give it heart and soul.

And it was he — T. Charles Brimlow — more than any other person, who would determine the quality, the character of that heart and soul. He could only be successful, he had decided, if he and the students worked together as a team. Or even better, as a family. That was the key word: family. He intended to keep that word constantly in mind as he guided these 340 kids through their three years at Plumstead.

All summer long Mr. Brimlow had studied their records and profiles and pictures, so that now, beaming as the buses began to arrive, he felt as if he already knew them. It was a stitch, watching the surprise on the kids' faces as he held out his hand and greeted many of them by name.

"Good morning, Jennifer. Welcome to Plumstead."

"Hiya, Robert. You look like you've gained weight over the summer."

"Morning, Claudia. Still want to be a pilot?"

Now here was a dark-haired girl he couldn't place. Of course, that might be because her face was contorted into one of the most miserable frowns he had ever seen. He felt an instant need to make this child happy.

"Hello, there," he said cheerfully. "I'm Mister Brimlow. What's your name?"

"Butthead," replied the girl and breezed on past.

By the time Mr. Brimlow recovered, the girl was long gone and another stood in front of him. This one had long, curly hair, a thin, interesting face, and large eyes that seemed on the verge of astonishment. Slung over her shoulder was a green book bag. Her name was about to come to him, but she was first to speak. "You're Mister Brimlow, aren't you?"

"I am," he said, still somewhat dazed by the first girl.

"The principal?"

"So they tell me."

She smiled broadly and thrust out her hand. "Nice to meet you. I'm Salem Brownmiller."

He shook her hand. "Salem *Jane* Brownmiller, to be exact."

Her wide eyes widened. "You *know* me?"

"I know your school profile."

She sagged a trifle — "Oh" — then perked up again. "So you know I'm a writer."

"Indeed I do. You won the story contest at Hillmont last year."

She beamed. "I won a gold pin. The story was called 'The Squirrels of Pauline.' It's about this fifth-grade girl and two baby squirrels she meets when lightning strikes a tree in the playground and they fall from their nest. Would you like to read it?"

"I certainly would," replied the principal.

In a flash the girl whipped out some stapled sheets from her book bag and thrust them into his hand. "I carry copies of my stories everywhere I go. You never know when somebody might ask for one. Or suppose my house burns down with all my manuscripts in it."

Mr. Brimlow was considering the horror of it

when a short, portly man with hair in his ears tapped him on the shoulder. "You the bus monitor?"

"No, I'm the principal. Can I help you?"

"Yeah," said the portly man. "I got a kid here won't get off my bus."

4

The mashed stump of a cigar moved about the mouth of the portly, hairy-eared man as though it had a life of its own. "I could drag the kid off," he went on, "but I don't need to get sued. I already put my hands on enough of 'em. In ten minutes I gotta be to the gas station. This ain't my only job, chief."

Mr. Brimlow nodded. "Lead the way."

Salem Brownmiller tugged on his sleeve. "Oh, Mr. Brimlow, can I come, too? I'm writing a story about a girl's first day in middle school, and this could make a really neat subplot."

The principal faced her sternly. "Miss Brownmiller, whoever that is in the bus, it is a person, not a subplot."

For once, the girl was slow to speak. Those wide eyes stared up at him. "I didn't mean it that way, Mr. Brimlow."

15

The principal softened. "All right. Keep your distance, and don't interfere."

The boy was in the backseat of the bus. His head was slightly atilt. A brown lunch bag rested on his lap, held by both hands. The toes of his new sneakers pointed toward each other. They did not reach the floor.

The principal walked halfway down the aisle and stopped. The boy seemed to be staring at a point in space, about a foot in front of his own face. Mr. Brimlow remembered the face . . . Brockhurst . . .

"Edward?" he said gently. In the background the first bell rang. Students yelped, streamed past the bus windows. "Edward Mott?"

No response.

"Brockhurst? . . . Flag boy?"

Edward Mott's head remained still, but his eyes rolled upward.

"I'm Mister Brimlow, your new principal." He sat on the edge of a seat. "Would you like to come up here and sit with me?"

No answer.

The principal moved one seat closer. "You know, Edward — do your friends call you Eddie?" The boy shrugged. "You know, Eddie, we have something in common, you and I. Can you guess what it is?"

Eddie Mott shrugged.

"Well, I'll tell you. This is *your* first day as a sixth-grader, and it's *my* first day as principal. How about that?"

The answer came from the front of the bus. "I don't get outta here, this is my *last* day at the station. There's a mechanic down there can't work on cars 'cause he gotta pump *gas* because *I* ain't there to pump gas."

Mr. Brimlow stood. He clapped his hands. "Okay, Eddie, what do you say? Ready to go?"

Eddie Mott finally spoke: "No."

"That does it," growled the driver. The door swung shut, the engine rumbled to life, the bus lurched down the driveway.

"Hey!" said Principal Brimlow.

"We're being hijacked!" piped Salem Brownmiller, not unhappily.

The bus roared right on past the school bus parking lot and did not stop till it humped up to the restroom of the Texaco station on the corner of Grant and Mudd.

The driver flipped his hand as he jumped off. "You wanna fire me, fire me."

It was now 8:10 A.M., ten minutes into the first period of the first day at Plumstead Middle School, and a lot of people didn't know where a lot of things were. The gym teachers couldn't find a foot-

17

ball, the geography teacher couldn't find a map, and the math teachers had no chalk. And no one knew where the principal was.

Mrs. Wilburham, the school secretary, was going batty. People were calling her on the brand-new, high-tech, state-of-the-art intercom system, but darn if she could figure out how to answer them. She flipped switches all over the fancy console, but the best she could do was connect the kitchen to the teachers' lounge.

The office was getting more and more crowded. Teachers, students — everyone had a problem or a question for her, as if she were the answer lady. She didn't even know how to work this new-fangled telephone, with its million buttons and lights. If she did, she'd be calling the police right now to report a missing principal.

First period was nearly over, the German teacher was trying to figure out the intercom, the nurse was studying the telephone, and the entire history department was at the counter asking for books — when in strolled the principal himself, along with a boy and girl. And taking their sweet old time about it, too: laughing, jabbering, couldn't care less that the school was falling down around the secretary's ears.

"You're late," said Mrs. Wilburham, not even trying to disguise her displeasure.

The principal pretended to be shocked. "We *are*?" He looked down at his accomplices. "Well," he shrugged, "I guess we'll all have to go to Late Room."

The three of them broke up laughing. He then looked up the kids' schedules, scribbled out a late note for each, and sent them on their way — but not before shaking hands with them and saying with a wink, "See you at lunch."

Mrs. Wilburham bit her tongue. She had trained five principals in her lifetime. Apparently this one was going to take some doing.

She had to admit, though, once he decided to show up, things did get done. Within five minutes, the gym people got their footballs, the geography teacher her map, the mathematicians their chalk, the history department its books. He showed her how to get an outside line on the telephone, and he played the intercom console like Liberace at the piano.

There were only five minutes left of first period when he flipped the toggle labeled ALL RE-CEIVERS and made his opening remarks to the school:

"Good morning, everyone.

"I apologize to you all for not speaking to you during homeroom. I had some pressing business elsewhere.

"Let me make it plain that this is not my official greeting. That will come in a couple of weeks, when we have our opening assembly in the new auditorium. That's when all of us will meet all of you and when we will learn the identity of our school mascot, the selection of which you will be involved in.

"In the meantime, let's you and I and Plumstead get to know each other. Over the last couple of years, we've all felt a little like orphans now and then, haven't we? Not enough seats. Not enough classrooms. Shifting school boundaries. We were never really sure where we belonged, were we?

"Well, I'm here to tell you that's all over. I'm here to tell you now we have our own place, our own house. I'm here to say . . . welcome home."

The principal flipped the toggle off, laid down the mike, and went into his office.

Someone was there.

5

The boy had his back to the door, but Mr. Brimlow knew at once who it was. The green sneakers, the pickle-shaped skateboard . . . it could only be . . . "Dennis Johnson, I presume?"

The boy turned, smiled. "You can call me Pickles."

The principal smiled back. "I'll work on it."

They shook hands.

Mr. Brimlow did not need a school record to inform himself about this student. For the past several years, Pickles Johnson had been perhaps the most famous grade-schooler in Cedar Grove.

Pickles Johnson was an inventor. He invented everything from gadgets to excuses.

One day in Second Avenue Elementary, for example, Pickles had a problem. It was the day of the weekly spelling test, and he hadn't studied for it. He had to get out of taking it.

As the test was about to begin, the teacher noticed Pickles madly scratching his chest. When she unbuttoned his shirt, she saw a hundred little red spots and heard Pickles groan, "Chicken pox." She sent him to the nurse.

Five minutes later he was back, escorted by the nurse, who handed the teacher the cause of the "chicken pox": a red felt-tip marker.

For punishment, Pickles had to stay after school and write "I will not lie to my teacher" one hundred times on the blackboard. Only then could he go home.

The teacher left the room for no more than five minutes. When she returned, to her utter amazement, the sentences were on the board. Pickles was gone.

The teacher did not suspect that she had fallen victim to one of Pickles' first inventions: the chalk glove. It was a contraption made of clothes-hanger wire. It had ten "fingers," each one of which held a piece of chalk. Placing all ten fingers against the blackboard at once gave Pickles the ability to write ten letters — ten words — ten sentences at the same time. By actual count, he had written 120 sentences before taking off.

The next day he proudly showed his invention to the teacher, who was too amused and impressed to punish him further.

Pickles' most famous inventive moment, and the one which earned him his nickname, happened over Christmastime when he was seven. From the moment his mother and father brought home the Christmas tree, little Dennis wanted to decorate it. He kept begging, "Let's do it now!" But Mr. and Mrs. Johnson always did the trimming on Christmas Eve, which was still two days away. And they wouldn't even tell him where they kept the balls and tinsel.

So little Dennis took matters into his own hands. The next time Mr. and Mrs. Johnson came into their living room, they found the tree had been trimmed — with pickles. Dill pickles, to be exact, from the jar in the refrigerator. They hung from the tree limbs on hooks made of paper clips.

Mr. Johnson knew history when he saw it. He called a friend who took pictures for the Cedar Grove newspaper. By the time the photographer arrived, Mr. and Mrs. Johnson were practically as green as the tree from inhaling the mixture of pickle and pine fumes. The photographer snapped the picture and said, "I think your son just made himself a new nickname."

Now, as this same Pickles Johnson stood before him, Mr. Brimlow already suspected he was going to like this kid. Unlike most kids, this one looked him right in the eye.

"Well," said the principal, "were you ordered to my office, or did you just decide to pay me a visit?"

"I was ordered," said Pickles.

The principal pointed to the pickle-shaped skateboard. "Would your problem happen to have anything to do with that?"

"My teacher said I have to keep it in my locker," said Pickles, "but it won't fit in my locker."

Mr. Brimlow reached out. "Let's see."

Pickles handed it over. It was quite a piece of work. A casing had been carved from wood, much like a miniature canoe, painted green, and fixed to the sole of the original board.

"Got a name for it?" said the principal.

"Pickleboard."

The principal placed the board on the floor. He rolled it back and forth with one foot. "Smooth," he said. "Good wheels."

Pickles nodded. "The best."

The principal had seen the boy tooling around town on this green footmobile. He had to admit, it *did* look like fun. He pushed off and let it carry him slowly across the office, stopping with a mild bump at the bookcase.

"Always wondered what it was like," he said.

"It's the best fun," said Pickles. "But you have to give it a longer ride than that to *really* tell."

Their eyes locked. They were both thinking the same word: *hallway.*

"Your teacher's right," said the principal. "School is no place for this thing."

"What could happen?" said Pickles.

"What could *happen?*" echoed the principal as

he wobbled through the doorway and into the outer office, where he collided gently with the back of Mrs. Wilburham's swivel chair.

Mrs. Wilburham pitched forward. "What in the name of — ?" She looked up in time to see her boss set a course for the doorway, sail out into the hall, and bump into the far wall.

Pickles followed. "When you really get going," he said, "it's like you're flying." He looked down the long length of the hallway, at the shiny, newly waxed linoleum. "Especially on a new floor like this."

The principal pushed off — one push, two, three — picked up his push foot, wobbled, wobbled, pushed again, climbed on, and went sailing past the startled nurse who was stepping out of the infirmary. Past the library he sailed, faster and faster, the wheels humming like a blender on puree.

Behind him, running now, the boy yelled, "Yahoo!" Ahead of Mr. Brimlow loomed the end of the hallway, the door to room 101, Mrs. Volker's geography class. "How do I stop this thinnnnnnnnng?!" he yelled just as the bell rang, just as Mrs. Volker opened her door, just as he shot past her nose and into the room, swatting the huge globe of the planet on his way to a crash landing with Mrs. Volker's desk.

In the stunned stillness that followed, the only sound was the whir of the globe, spinning like the earth gone mad. The class, many of them frozen halfway out of their seats, gaped in mute wonderment as their principal rearranged a few things on Mrs. Volker's desk, stood tall, straightened his bow tie, cleared his throat, pointed out the door and down the hallway with the pickle-shaped skateboard, and bellowed sternly: *"That's* what could happen!"

Moments later, in the crowded hallway, Mr. Brimlow whispered to Pickles, "That was *some* ride." Then he told Pickles he would not be allowed to bring the board to school anymore. He could pick it up in the main office on his way home.

And then he invited him to lunch.

6

Back in his office, Mr. Brimlow took off his jacket. What a morning! Many times he had imagined his first day as principal, but never did he picture himself getting hijacked in a yellow bus and then hoofing it back to school with a pair of sixth-graders.

It was the best beginning he could have had. Not only was he not going to fire the portly, hairy-eared bus driver, he intended to thank him. He had gotten to know Salem Brownmiller and Eddie Mott better than he would have in three years from behind his desk. In fact, walking and talking with them, he had been struck with the inspiration to invite them to lunch. Then the Johnson boy. Yes, indeed, he was already getting a Plumstead family feeling.

He now turned his attention to a little matter that had been nagging him all morning: the sour-pussed girl, "Butthead."

Starting with the A's, he went through the

sixth-grade records, looking for that face, trying to imagine it with a smile. It didn't show up until the W's, and even then the smile was pretty skimpy. Her last name was Wyler, her first name was Elizabeth. And her middle name — surprise, surprise — was Sunshine.

Sunny Wyler was on her way. She was sure she would be the first kid ever transferred out of poopy Plumstead. In first period math, the teacher had made them write out all twelve times tables. She made sure she got every one wrong. For example, she wrote 2 x 2 = 94. And 5 x 5 = 1. And 7 x 3 = 23,962.

And that wasn't all. She did them in her super-subminiature writing. This was one of Sunny's great talents. She could make numbers and letters so small that at first glance they all looked like dots. Most grown-ups found them impossible to read. Wee writing, she called it, and it was perfect for secret notes to her best friend Hillary. And maybe also for getting herself kicked out of here and transferred to Hillary's school, Cedar Grove.

She had squeezed the entire set of tables — one hundred and forty-four multiplications — into the lower right-hand corner of the paper in a space about the size of two postage stamps. Of course, a pointy pencil was essential to wee writing, so she made a further nuisance of herself by going to the pencil sharpener exactly nineteen times.

And now she sat in second-period English. The teacher, Ms. Comstock, had given them an in-class writing assignment: "My Most Interesting Day Last Summer."

Sunny wrote:

my most interesting day last summer happened on the 4th of july. my little brother was liting a cherry bomb and it went off and blue his noze off. he was groping around for it but he couldnt find it becauz it flu in thru the kitchen window and into a bowl of serial that my father was eeting. only he wasnt looking. then he took a spoon full of serial and screemed. a noze!! i just bit into a noze!!!! yuck!!!!!!!!!!! and the ambulince came and took my brother to the hospittle and they took the noze along in a plastic bag focl of ice kubes so it wouldnt rot and they sood his noze back on. but the problem was when my brother cam outside it was raining reely hard and he drounded becauz they sood his noze on upside down!!! yes it sure was the most interesting day around here in a long time.

Sunny signed not only her name, but her home address and telephone number as well. She wanted to make sure the school authorities could reach her as soon as they decided to expel her.

When she finished, she looked up and found someone smiling at her. It was the dodo from the bus. What was it with this kid?

He was two seats up in the next row, too far to smack or kick. Then she thought of a trick she often used to get rid of her little brothers when they were bugging her. She stared straight back at the dodo, stuck her finger up her nose, and pretended to pull out a boogie. She rolled the pretend boogie between her thumb and forefinger into a perfect little pretend boogie ball. She sat the pretend boogie ball on her thumb, dug the nail of her middle finger in behind it, and while the dodo's eyes got round as quarters, she fired. The dodo ducked, almost falling out of his seat. Sunny almost forgot herself and laughed.

Shortly before the period ended, Ms. Comstock was called to the classroom door. She came back in holding a small white piece of paper. She looked over the class. "Elizabeth Wyler?" she said.

Sunny raised her hand. Ms. Comstock came down the aisle and gave her the piece of paper. The teacher's face revealed nothing. The bell rang.

Sunny turned in her essay and gathered up her books and joined the mob heading out. She unfolded the piece of paper. She read it:

Elizabeth Wyler —
Please report to the principal's
office at lunchtime.

Already!

Did the math teacher run down to the office with her tiny terrible times tables? Was the brand-new school bugged? Did a hidden camera in the ceiling record her essay as she wrote it, or catch her flipping the pretend boogie ball at the grinning dodo?

The principal's office. She couldn't believe it. Things were going faster and easier than she had even hoped. She could picture herself washing her hair tonight. Heck, before the day was over, she might be sitting alongside Hillary Kain in Cedar Grove Middle School!

7

Eddie Mott left Ms. Comstock's English class in a daze. Shattered were his hopes that his first day of middle school would go smoothly. So far he had been threatened by a grumpy girl, used as a football, hijacked, stranded at a gas station, and targeted by a boogie-shooter, none other than the same grumpy girl. What was the matter with her, anyway? Come to think of it, what was the matter with him? Why did he keep looking and smiling at her?

And this changing class business. Boy, things were sure a lot simpler when you just went to one room in the morning and stayed there all day. Luckily, he hadn't had to find his first class, because that's when he was walking halfway across town with Salem Brownmiller and the principal (the only good part of the day so far, and of course it happened outside of school). For second-period English, the principal himself had given him directions.

The stampeding herd carried him down the hallway. He looked at his schedule. Next was science in room 117. He looked up. He was passing the boys' gym. He had no idea where he was. He needed help.

A boy was bending over a water fountain, taking a drink. Eddie tapped him on the back, "Excuse me."

The boy kept drinking. He tilted his head. One eyeball rolled upward till it was staring at Eddie, while the boy's mouth continued slurping water. Eddie waited.

At last the boy finished and stood. Eddie came up to his shirt pocket. "What?" said the boy.

Eddie gulped. "I — uh — I'm looking for room one-seventeen. Do you think you could show me the way?"

The giant boy blinked a few times, then he smiled. "Sure. You in sixth grade?"

"Yeah," said Eddie. "First day in middle school." He hoped his voice wasn't shaking. Actually, he felt more at ease now that the boy was smiling.

The boy reached for the schedule. "Can I see that?" Eddie handed it over. The boy studied it, nodded. "Yep . . . ol' one-seventeen all right. Okay." He gave the schedule back. He leaned down. He put one hand on Eddie's shoulder and pointed with the other. "You go down these stairs here. When you get to the bottom, you turn —

let's see — right, yeah, and then there's a door, and you go through that, and you're there."

Eddie looked up. He smiled back. "O-*kay*. Thanks a lot."

"No problem," said the boy, his smile really big now. "Good luck, dude."

Eddie sailed through the door and down the stairs. *Dude — wow! An eighth-grader called me dude. They're not so bad after all. All you have to do is be nice to them.*

The bell rang. The other kids were gone. Uh-oh, he must be late! At the bottom of the stairs he turned right and looked for the door. There it was. He opened it . . . and instead of desks and students and a teacher, he saw pipes. Big pipes, little pipes, running up the walls, across the ceiling. And squatting on the floor were two big metal things. Well, it *did* look kind of scientific.

He peered back outside. Another door across the way. He tried it. It was a small room. A long-nosed man was sitting at a desk, drinking from a mug.

Eddie blurted out, "This isn't room one-seventeen, is it?"

The man was rising, saying, "What?" but Eddie already knew the answer. He dashed back to the stairway and up as far as he could go. He pushed through doors and into a long, deserted hallway. A mile of lockers and doorways and silence. His heart thudded against the English book he held to his chest. He had a vision of every classroom and locker door swinging open and faces leaning out of every one and braying: "YOU'RE LATE, SIXTH-GRADER!"

He took only a couple of steps before realizing he could never walk into room 117 this late, even if he ever found it. Somewhere nearby he heard horns and drums . . . then steps, coming from up ahead. Then a voice within: *Hide!*

8

Eddie barged through the nearest door. He found himself in the back of a wide, spacey room, a music room. Up front, kids were honking and thumping and plinking on instruments. There was an open door to his right, against the back wall. He ducked into it.

It was a large closet. It was shadowy, but light from the big room revealed it to be a storage area for musical instruments. Everywhere round brassy mouths gaped fishlike at him, threatening to blare and give him away. He picked his way as carefully as possible through the instruments and cases to the back of the closet. Here, in the corner behind a tuba, it was dark. He sat on the floor, his knees up to his chin.

Twice during the period, someone reached into the closet for an instrument. But no one came for the tuba.

Outside he could hear the instructor saying over and over: "Your lips go like this . . . like this . . .

okay now . . . blow." This would usually be followed by silence, followed by, "no . . . like *this*," followed by what sounded like the squawk of an animal whose tail had been stepped on.

Confusingly, there were other sounds, too, but not like any instrument he had ever heard: twangs, tweets, and bonks. This was *music*?

But all this was background to the feelings churning inside Eddie. There was no use pretending anymore that he wanted to be a grown-up middle-schooler. What he really wanted was to be back at Brockhurst Elementary. He wanted to stay in the same classroom all day. He wanted stars and turkeys on his spelling tests. He wanted to wear his Daffy Duck pin. He wanted recess.

And now, suddenly, he wanted to go to the bathroom. Oh boy! He clenched his teeth. He tried to think about other things, like baseball and raising the flag every morning with Roger Himes. Oh, life used to be so simple. You had to go, you raised your hand, and a minute later: relief. Now, he didn't dare move till the end of the period. It didn't help that against the wall a couple of feet away stood, invitingly, a saxophone.

The bell!

Eddie shot out of the closet, out of the music room, down the hall, around the bend, down the stairs, up the hall, searching for a door that said BOYS. . . .

There!

He burst in. There was a sound, a sound he had heard before, a sound that he himself had sometimes made before:

"hhhh-Thooo!"

Just as he realized it was the sound of a hocker loading and firing, he was hit. Smack in the left ear. He froze.

Someone said, "Hey, that don't count. He got in the way."

Somebody else said, "It counts, man. My turn . . . *hhh-Thooo!"*

A second hocker grazed his chin.

He was caught in the crossfire of a spit fight.

"I got him in the ear, man! That's two points!"

"It's no points! It's only a sixth-grader!"

"Yer cheatin', man!"

"Yer cheatin'!"

"Yeah?"

"Yeah!"

"hhh — "

"hhhh — "

"THOOO!"

"THOOO!"

Eddie bolted for the nearest stall and locked himself in. There was no longer any question of going to the bathroom. His bladder had turned to ice. His only concern now was walking out of here alive.

He pulled off some toilet paper and mopped out his left ear. He wished he knew more about the human ear. He knew there was an eardrum in there somewhere. He had always pictured it as a tiny bongo drum. Would it halt the seepage? Or would the hocker ooze on through, deeper and deeper into the dark catacombs of his ear? Would he lose his hearing? Horrible scenes came to him, pictures of people at supermarket checkout lines, gawking in wonder and disgust at the fat-lettered headlines in the *Star* and *Midnight*:

BOY'S BRAIN
TURNS TO
MUSH!

HOCKER BLAMED!

EIGHTH-GRADERS
SOUGHT IN
BATHROOM MURDER!

Frantically, he cocked his head and thumped the side of it, trying to jettison the runaway ooze. As he did so, there came a rattle and a bumping upon the door of his stall. He looked down, into a grinning, upside-down face occupying the space between the bottom of the stall door and the floor. "Hi, there," said the grinning face. Eddie looked up and saw the toe ends of a pair of sneakers hanging over the top of the door. One of the spitters was hanging upside down on his stall door.

He heard the telltale intake of breath, the loading: "Hhhh — " He glanced down. The mouth was no longer grinning. It was puckered. It occurred to him how much a mouth about to hockerate resembles a mouth about to kiss, but he felt certain he was not about to be kissed.

"THOOO!"

Eddie's English book flew to his face, just in time to catch the missile. The bell for next period rang. The face and feet disappeared. A moose call, a Tarzan yell, a gush of hallway noise as the door opened, and then silence. Merciful silence.

Eddie tore off some more toilet paper and wiped off the intercepted hocker. He was beginning to wonder if he had made some kind of terrible mistake. Maybe he had gotten on the wrong bus that morning. (Served him right, telling his mom to stay home.) Maybe he had boarded the bus to Hell. And now he was going to miss yet *another* class.

"Is that you, Eddie?"

He clamped his breath. He froze. Who was speaking?

"Eddie Mott?"

The voice seemed to be coming from another stall. Where had he heard that voice?

"Eddie."

He leaned down till he could see beneath the side panel of his stall. Two stalls up was a face, smiling, upside down, long curly brown hair pooling on the floor.

40

"Salem *Brownmiller*?"

"In the flesh."

"What — what — ?"

"It's a long story. Let's get out of here first."

Which they did. Fast.

9

In the hallway, Eddie went to the nearest locker and began knocking his forehead into it. "I'm in trouble," he whined. "*Big* trouble."

Salem pulled him away. "You're going to be in bigger trouble if you don't stop that. What's the matter?"

"What's the *matter*? Every time I look around, I'm in an empty hallway. I missed two classes so far, and the only one I went to, somebody flicked a boogie at me. And now I'm missing *another* class. I'm lost. I don't know where I am. I wanna go home."

"Whoa!" said Salem, whipping out her notepad and pen. "What was that about a boogie?"

Eddie just stared at her — a glazed, vacant look if she ever saw one. If he was going to do her any good, she was going to have to nurse him along. Hurriedly she jotted in her notepad:

flicked boogie
glazed, vacant look

Then she spoke gently to him. "It's okay, Eddie. First-day jitters, that's all. Let me see your schedule."

He handed it over.

"Hey, same as me! Art in one-oh-three."

"I don't know where it is."

Salem returned his schedule. "We'll find it together." She took his arm. "Come on."

They walked.

"Okay," said Salem, "go ahead, ask me."

"Ask you what?"

"What was I doing in the boys' room?"

"I don't care. I just want to be in class. *Any* class."

"Okay, I'll tell you anyway." She pushed a door open. "Down these stairs. But first you want to know *how* I did it, right? So say how."

"How?"

Salem pushed open the door at the bottom of the stairs. They were in another deserted hallway. Salem reached into her book bag and with a flourish drew out a long, black, silky scarf. *"This"* — she bunched up her hair and wrapped the scarf about her head, like a turban — "is how."

Eddie cooperated just enough to grant her a grudging glance. Sure enough, she could have passed for a boy.

"It's my writer's scarf," she said, unwrapping and returning it to the book bag. "I always wear

43

it when I'm writing. But sometimes it comes in handy for other things, too. At first I was going to get a white one, but then I thought, Nah, that's too common, just what you'd expect a girl to pick. So I got black. Mysterious, huh?"

No response from Eddie, who plodded straight ahead while Salem bounced sideways down the hall beside him, jabbering.

"So, now you want to know *why* I did it, right? Well, in a word: research. I've decided to write my story about a boy's first day in middle school instead of a girl's. So I asked myself: Where do you go to find out about boys? Answer: a boys' room, of course. I had study hall last period, so — presto! — there I was." She waved her notepad. "Taking notes. I'll tell ya, you boys are *something*." She said this with a sly grin and a nudge to Eddie's arm, trying to get a rise out of him, but he just plodded on, vacant, glazed. One thing she had decided not to tell him was that she had chosen him to be the model for the boy in the story. From the moment she had seen him sitting in the back of the bus, she knew he had to be her main character.

"So," she said, "what's it like to be a boy?"

No answer. And no wonder. Too general a question. Make it more specific. "So, what's it like to get spit on?"

He wasn't listening. He was glancing about at the room numbers. "Where's one-oh-three?" he demanded.

"Oh, it's down that way," she pointed. "We passed it a couple times, but we were having such a good dialog — "

"No! . . . No!" he screeched and once again began butting a locker.

This is wild, thought Salem. Now he's in an uncontrolled rage. Maybe he's got a multiple personality. That was every writer's dream, to know such a person. She remembered reading about a lady in Minnesota who had seventeen different personalities inside the same body. So far, she had counted two in Eddie Mott:

1. *Glazed, vacant*
2. *Uncontrolled rage*

She wondered if there were more. She wondered if she could bring them out. What a story! But for now, she pulled him away from the locker and tried to calm him down. It was then that they heard a yell from up the hall: "Stop that hamster!"

A small brown furry bundle was racing down the hallway at them. Around a corner several kids came careening, sneakers squealing like Michelins on the brand-new floor. "Stop it!"

Eddie just stood there, half expecting the furball to leap up and rip his throat out; it was about the only thing that hadn't happened to him. Meanwhile, Salem quickly dropped her book bag to the floor, set it on its side, and held it open, right in the path of the oncoming animal. The harboring darkness, the crannies formed by the papers and books within — it was too inviting for the hamster to resist. Into the green tunnel it scooted, into the back and bottom of the dark.

Salem lifted the book bag and slung it over her shoulder. The pursuers, three of them, came sneaker-squealing to a halt. "He in there?" the tallest one asked, catching his breath.

"He is," replied Salem.

"Well, fork 'im over. He's ours."

Salem's eyebrows arched. "How do *I* know that?"

The boy snarled, "Because I said so."

Eddie edged behind Salem.

Salem sniffed, "That isn't a reason."

The boy looked at his sidekicks, back to Salem. "We found it outside. It's ours." He put his hand out. He snarled, "Here."

Salem snarled back, "I wouldn't give *yyyew* a carbuncle off my nose, if I *had* a carbuncle."

The tall boy's face got downright ugly. He thrust his hand in front of Salem's face. "Girl, the hamster. *Now.*"

Salem embraced her book bag with both arms. She tried to make the same gargly sound that the spitters in the boys' room had made. "*hhhh* . . . one more inch, and I'll spit in your face." She pulled Eddie up to her, she put her arm around him. "And so will he."

The next movement came from up the hall —
a door opening, a teacher calling: "Hey, there, get
where you're going. No loitering."

Salem and Eddie started walking. The boys,
clearly eighth-graders, started walking, right behind them, inches behind them. Down to the end
of the hallway, turn left, down another hall. Even-
tually art 103 loomed ahead, and so did the question: Which was better, walk into class with half
the period over, or continue this nerve-wracking
parade?

Salem thought about it. Eddie didn't think. Eddie couldn't think. It was all he could do to remain
conscious. All he knew was that a pack of scowling
eighth-graders was following him down a deserted
hallway, and that they had been told that he would
spit in their faces. He was sure that if it were not
for Salem wrapping her arm around his and pulling him along, he'd be lying back up the hallway
by now, the eighth-graders finishing him off, a
carcass, buzzard meat.

And then they were veering into . . . a familiar
place . . . the office, where they had been this
morning. There was the secretary, and there went
the eighth-graders right on down the hallway.
And there was the principal, Mr. Brimlow, coming
out of his office with a big, surprised smile, saying,
"Well, well, look who's early for lunch!"

10

Mr. Brimlow was delighted that two of his lunch guests had showed up early. Especially Salem Brownmiller, who seemed to know what was required better than he, so he simply put her in charge, and soon both he and Eddie Mott were following her orders — dragging in a table from the guidance counselor's office, running to the cafeteria for napkins and utensils and such.

It was in the cafeteria that Miss Brownmiller looked up at him and said, "It *is* going to be catered, isn't it?"

The principal stared at her. "Catered?"

"Yes, from here. Somebody will bring our meals to your office on a big tray, or maybe a cart with wheels, with silver lids over our meals to keep them warm — " She stopped; with a look of rising horror she studied the blank expression on his face. "Mister *Brimlow*, we weren't going to brown *bag* it, were we?"

Mr. Brimlow gulped. "Oh, no . . . of course not."

And so Mr. Brimlow made arrangements with the cafeteria manager to have five hot meals delivered to his office at 11:50 sharp.

The hot entrée for the day, they discovered, was sloppy joe fajitas. "Great!" chimed Salem on the way back to the office. "We'll have a Mexican theme. You should always have a theme for a catered luncheon, don't you think?"

Mr. Brimlow cleared his throat; he nodded, "Oh, yes . . . quite."

As it turned out, there was barely time enough to set the table, much less decorate à la Mexico, for lunchtime was upon them.

Eddie Mott could not believe it. The girl standing in the office doorway was Miss Grumpy herself. He had wondered who the other place settings were for, but he couldn't imagine anyone inviting The Grump for lunch.

He watched in amazement as Mr. Brimlow went right up to her all jolly and shook her hand. "Well, hello, Miss Wyler. I see you got my note. Come on in."

The Grump looked confused. She took one step and stopped. She looked at Eddie. She looked at the table. She said, "Aren't I in the wrong place?"

"I don't think so," said the principal. "Where do you think you ought to be?"

She looked straight up at him. "Cedar Grove?"

Now it was the principal who was confused.

"Cedar Grove? Why should you be there?"

"Because of the stuff I did."

Mr. Brimlow studied her. He jiggled one wing of his bow tie. He folded his arms. "I see. Well, what stuff might that be?"

The Grump counted them off on her fingers. "In math class I wrote the times tables so small that the teacher will probably go blind trying to see them all. In English class I wrote something ridiculous about my most interesting day last summer. It was all lies. And" — she pointed to Eddie — "I flicked a boogie ball at that dodo." Everyone froze, as if fearing, waiting for her hand to go to her nose. "*And*," she concluded, "I've had a rotten attitude ever since I got on the bus."

There was silence and stillness, except for the slow nod of Mr. Brimlow's head. At last he said, "I see. Well. What do you think we should do about you?"

The Grump answered at once. "Expel me. I'm a rotten apple. If I hang around much longer, I'll probably infect the whole school."

Eddie glanced over at Salem. She was writing furiously in her notepad, the tip of her tongue peeping from the corner of her mouth.

The Grump took another look at the table. The confused expression returned to her face. "I *am* being expelled, aren't I? Isn't that why I'm here?"

Mr. Brimlow gave a small, regretful shrug. "I'm

afraid not, Sunny. The brutal truth is, you've been invited to have lunch with us."

Sunny, Eddie repeated to himself. *Sunny?*

And then Mr. Brimlow was bringing her over. "Sunny Wyler . . . this dodo also goes by the name of Eddie Mott." Shaking hands with her, trying to avoid her vicious scowl. "Sunny Wyler . . . Salem Brownmiller." Salem's eyes lighting up, as if she had just opened a great birthday present, pumping the girl's hand: "*Pleased* to meet you, Sunny."

And then the smell of sloppy joes filled the room. In rolled a double-decker cart pushed by a white-aproned cafeteria lady.

"*Olé!*" piped Salem.

Mr. Brimlow clapped his hands. "All *right!* Time to eat. Let's sit down, gang."

Salem, Sunny, and Eddie took their places. Mr. Brimlow started to help the cafeteria lady, but she waved him away. "Oh, no, Mister Principal. You sit." She was crisp and efficient and dignified, she wore her hair in a bun with a butterfly barrette, and she obviously knew her stuff. Perhaps she had once worked in a major hotel or a millionaire's mansion. Mr. Brimlow sat.

The cafeteria lady distributed plates. "Will there be another?" she asked, noting the empty place setting.

"We hope so," said the principal.

She laid down a fifth plate. Then came the food. From the upper rack of the cart she took three large, covered bowls and placed them on the table. With a flourish not unlike that of a matador, she removed the lids to reveal: a tossed salad . . . a steaming vat of sloppy joe . . . and a tall stack of tortillas.

"*Olé!*" said Salem.

"*Sí, sí!*" said Mr. Brimlow.

Sunny said nothing, though her head swiveled slowly toward the other girl.

The cafeteria lady then provided each place with a half pint of milk and two plastic-wrapped chocolate chip cookies. She stepped back to consider her work. Her finger went up. "Ah — straws." She plunged her hand into the deep pocket of the apron, almost to the elbow — her hand shot back up with such force and speed that it smacked her in the chin; her eyes were suddenly big as tortillas.

As the principal and three students watched in wonder, the apron pocket began to move — to the left, to the right, a rumpled, dumpled, bulgy ball of movement — and then the dignified cafeteria lady was tearing off her apron and flinging it into the air. The apron landed on the tortilla stack and went swooping about the table, knocking plastic forks and plates until it draped itself over the salad bowl and at last was still. And now a faint rustling could be heard beneath the ghostly apron, and another, tinier sound, like chewing.

"Don't worry," Salem told the others, "it's only a hamster." She pulled the apron away —

"It *is* a hamster!" exclaimed the principal, as the dignified lady fled.

Salem reached for it, the principal reached for it, and the hamster took the only escape route available, which happened to be into — and out of — the sloppy joe bowl. It leaped upon Sunny's shirt and onto the floor. Dripping orange and shedding hamburger bits, it dashed in frantic patterns about the office while Brimlow, Brownmiller, and Mott gave chase.

"The door!" cried the principal, but not soon enough, for the sloppy joed rodent already had a nose in the outer office, and then — miraculously — it was in the air, snatched by a hand that appeared as if from nowhere. And then the rest of the body appeared — a boy with green sneakers.

Mr. Brimlow hurried to him. "Welcome, and great catch there!" He pumped the boy's free hand and turned to the rest of them. "Friends, may I present our other guest for lunch today, Mr. Dennis Johnson."

11

Within five minutes the squirming hamster was cleaned up and deposited in an unused fish tank borrowed from the science lab.

At that point Sunny Wyler nodded to the sloppy joe bowl and announced, "I am not eating anything a hamster crawled through."

"What?" said Mr. Brimlow, looking shocked. "That gives it flavoring."

Sunny just stared at the principal until he laughed. He reached out and tweaked her nose. "Just kidding." He wondered how long it would take before he saw a smile on this kid's face.

Another five minutes passed as Mr. Brimlow called the kitchen and had a new batch of sloppy joe and tortillas delivered, forget the salad. This time the food was brought in by a man. He said the dignified lady had come back trembling and had told the manager she was returning to her old job at a private boarding school. The straws were still in the pocket of her abandoned apron. The man took them out, tossed them onto the table, and left.

"I'm not using any straw that some animal's lips were on," declared Sunny Wyler.

"Fine," said the principal, "you have my permission to drink straight from the carton." He was beginning to think she was serious about being expelled from school.

For some time after Mr. Brimlow said, "Dig in," no one spoke. He decided to break the ice himself with a question to the Johnson boy. "So, Dennis, considering your nickname, you must be pretty fond of pickles, huh?"

Pickles had not folded his sloppy joe filling into a tortilla, Mexican style, as had the others. He had instead laid a tortilla flat on his plate and spread a layer of sloppy joe over it, creating a sort of small pizza. He cut the pie into neat, equal-sized wedges.

"I hate pickles," he said.

"Really?"

"Yeah. I think they're neat-looking, and I like how the name sounds, but I can't stand the taste. My mother was always giving me one with my sandwich. That's why I put them on the Christmas tree, to get rid of them."

Mr. Brimlow filled in the other kids on how Pickles got his name.

Salem snickered. "Good thing you didn't decide to hate bananas."

"Bananas Johnson," giggled Eddie.

Trying to include Sunny Wyler, Mr. Brimlow said, "What food would you hang on a Christmas tree, Miss Wyler, if you had to?"

"Monkey brains," said Sunny Wyler. While the rest of the kids laughed, her sneer made it clear what she thought of this silly conversation.

Salem Brownmiller was jotting again in her notepad.

"Now, Miss Brownmiller," said the principal, "there must be a story behind your name as well. Don't tell me you're a witch."

Salem laid her pencil down. "That's not far off, actually. My mother and father met each other in Salem, Massachusetts. My father says she bewitched him. He said he wanted his firstborn to be named Salem, whether it was a boy or girl. I happen to think it's better as a girl's name, but of course I'm prejudiced. Actually, I didn't like my name at first; that is, when I got old enough to realize I *had* a name, of course. I loathed it. But then when I decided to be a writer, I started liking it, and now I *love* it. I mean, if you're a writer you need a name that people will remember when they see it with all those other names on the bookshelves, right? As for my last name, I don't know, I'm still debating whether to change it or not. I mean, Brown? Miller? *Together?* How common can you get! Sometimes I have nightmares about marrying somebody named Jones and hyphenating my name. Can you see it? Salem Brownmiller-Jones? Egad!"

"Egad, indeed," echoed Mr. Brimlow quickly, seizing the chance to silence Miss Brownmiller lest she talk the entire lunch period away. "And now Miss Wyler — " All heads turned toward the sour-faced girl with the DEATH TO MUSH-ROOMS T-shirt, now also featuring a tiny orange paw print from her brief encounter with the hamster. "Salem loves her name. How do you feel about yours?"

"I think it's dumb," she said.

"Is there a story behind it?"

"No."

"Well," the principal smiled, "it didn't fall down out of the sky and land on your birth certificate, did it?"

Salem and Eddie Mott snickered; Sunny glared. Mr. Brimlow decided not to be so flip with Wyler.

"It's not a *story*," Sunny snipped.

All were silent.

She waved her fajita. "It's just dumb. When I was born, my mother said it was like a little ray of sunshine."

Before Eddie Mott realized what was happening, the words were out of his mouth: "So what did she name you? Little Ray?"

This time it wasn't snickers, it was outright

laughter. Salem thumbed back to a previous page in her notepad entitled *Mott Personalities* and wrote:

3. Comedian

"Yeah?" Sunny snarled. "Well, the joke was on her, 'cause I'm a black cloud everywhere I go. If you let me hang around long enough, pretty soon everybody'll be going off to the shrink, they'll be so depressed." She ripped a bite from her fajita. She looked up at the faces around the table; she settled on Mr. Brimlow's. "See? Already I'm ruining your lunch."

Brimlow chomped on his fajita. "Not ruining *my* lunch." He polled the others. "Is Sunny ruining anybody's lunch here?"

Everyone shook their heads no, Eddie Mott a trifle belatedly.

"Mister Mott — " said the principal, and almost regretted it when he saw the boy tense up.

"Eddie, you and I seem to be the only ones here today without unusual names. I'll tell you, I almost feel positively boring."

Salem spoke, with a kindly glance toward Eddie. "You don't need an interesting name to be an interesting person."

Mr. Brimlow nodded. He smiled. "You're absolutely right, Brownmiller. Let that be the amen for this little discussion."

A warm tide rose in Mr. Brimlow's breast. He really liked these kids. He wanted more of them. "Mister Mott," he said, "as I recall from your record, you were a flag-raiser at Brockhurst. How would you like the same job here at Plumstead?"

The boy's expression barely changed, but for a moment that lost look was gone. "Okay," he said with a slight shrug, and Mr. Brimlow knew it was more than just okay.

"And you'll need help, right?" said the principal.

Eddie nodded. "You should always have two people, one to hold the flag and attach it and the other to pull the rope. Sometimes when my partner was absent, I did it all by myself, but it's pretty tricky. You have to be careful never to let it touch the ground."

"Right," agreed Mr. Brimlow. "Well, how about if you work with Johnson here. You can teach him the ropes. You'll both need to be here as soon as the doors open, first bell, every day. Dennis?"

Pickles nodded. "No problem."

Eddie wasn't sure how he felt about this. On the one hand, it was exciting to be paired with a famous person. On the other hand, it was a little scary, too. Eddie couldn't imagine himself telling the great Pickles Johnson what to do. Suppose he got nervous and forgot something? Suppose Pickles wanted to raise a pickle instead of the flag?

Mr. Brimlow got up and walked to the file cabinet, on top of which sat the glass tank with the hamster. "Does anybody know where this critter came from or who it belongs to?"

Salem raised her hand, and against his better judgment he let her speak. She told about the eighth-graders chasing it in the hallway, and how she lured it into her book bag because, "as a writer, one of your most important skills is to put yourself in other peoples' places, so you can understand them and therefore write better about them, which is precisely what I did in this case, except it was a hamster and not a person, of course. I asked myself, Now, if I were a hamster being chased down a hallway, remembering that a hamster is a rodent, what — "

"Okay, Salem" — Mr. Brimlow jumped in — "got the picture. Now, here's what I'm going to do. I'll make announcements, today, tomorrow. If nobody comes forward to claim the critter, well" — he smacked the cabinet — "then we'll keep it right here. Miss Wyler?" The girl looked up. "How would you like to be keeper of the critter?"

She crinkled her face. "Do I have to?"

Mr. Brimlow smiled. "Yes. Be here after school tomorrow."

The bell rang. They were getting up. He held out his hands. Ideas were rushing. "Hold it a second, gang. Thirty seconds, tops. You won't be late. Two quick things. On September eighteenth for the opening assembly we're going to present

Plumstead's new mascot. The students will vote for it. Three choices, one from each grade. I want you guys to come up with the nomination from sixth grade. You'll be a committee of four. Salem, you've just volunteered to be chairman — excuse me, chairwoman."

Outside, the hallway was bustling.

"And let's do this again next week, Wednesday, right here, lunch. Got it? Okay, outta here!"

12

"I *hate* it!" grumbled Sunny. "Even worse than I thought I would."

"My school's okay, I guess," said Hillary. "But it would be a lot better with you there."

The two best friends were in Sunny's room after dinner.

"I messed up every chance I got," Sunny went on. "Math class, English. Then I got a note, 'Report to the principal's office.' "

"Wow!" went Hillary.

"Yeah, wow is what I figured. I'm history, right? Expelled. Sayanara, Dumbstead — Cedar Grove, here I come."

"Yeah . . . so?" gasped Hillary. She was chewing on the ear of her teddy bear. Hillary slept over so often that the teddy bear had become a permanent resident of Sunny's bedroom.

"So, you know what it was?"

"What?"

"Lunch."

"*Lunch?*"

"Yeah. I was invited to *lunch* with the principal."

"The *principal?*"

"Yeah. In his office. He's as dorky as the school. He wears a bow tie."

Hillary switched to the bear's other ear. "So why'd he invite you? He friends with your parents or something?"

"Not that I know of. I don't know why. He knew my name. He knew my real middle name."

"Sunshine?"

"Yeah, you believe it?"

"He must have looked you up."

"Yeah, but why? Why me?"

They thought about it, but no answer came.

"And that's not all," said Sunny. "There were three others at the lunch, too."

"Kids?"

"Yeah, three dipsticks — oh — and you know who one was?"

"Who?"

"That Pickles kid."

"Pickles *Johnson?* The one with the skateboard?"

"Yeah. He brought it to school, and the gumball principal gets on it and goes down the hall and crashes into a classroom."

Hillary was goggle-eyed. "You're kidding."

"No. It's all over school."

Hillary edged closer. "Is Pickles cute?"

"*Cute?*" snorted Sunny. "Is *any* boy cute? Besides, he wears green sneakers, like he painted them or something, even on the rubber part, so how cute could he be? He's a meat loaf."

"I hear he does some crazy things," said Hillary. "Did he do anything at lunch?"

Sunny shrugged. "He caught an animal, is about it."

"*What?*"

Sunny told Hillary about the hamster's escapades and capture. "And you want to know the worst of it all? I got the job of taking care of the thing."

Hillary shook her head. "I don't know, your school sounds pretty exciting compared to mine. Maybe I should be getting myself transferred to Plumstead."

"Yeah, right, and have rodents running through your lunch."

The phone rang in the hallway. Sunny raced for it. She returned muttering about dingbats and dipsticks.

"Who was it?" said Hillary.

"Some girl named Salem. You believe that name? She was at the lunch, too. Really weird. The principal made her chairwoman of this committee we're supposed to have to pick the mascot for the school. She wants to have a meeting at her house on Saturday, so we can all get to *know* each other better and get the creative *juices* going. You believe it? She thinks she's thirty-eight years old."

"So," said Hillary. "are you going?"

Sunny sneered. "No way. I told her I will, but I won't. She can get to know the dodo better."

"What dodo?"

"Some little jerk that keeps talking to me and looking and grinning. He thinks I flicked a real snotball at him. What a moron."

Hillary hugged her bear. "Sunny — maybe he likes you!"

Sunny snorted. "Yeah? Well, he can like *this*." She flipped off her shoes and held her feet in Hillary's face. Hillary recoiled. "See these socks? I'm gonna wear them every day till they transfer me, just like the shirt."

"I don't believe I let you talk me into not washing my hair till you're transferred," said Hillary.

Sunny clapped. "We'll reek together!"

"They can use our hair to grease cars!"

The girls knelt face to face, mussing each other's hair.

"We can grow vegetables up there!"

"Cooties!"

"A cootie farm!"

"Eewwww!"

When first bell rang next morning, Eddie Mott went straight to the office and picked up the flag. Back outside, he found Pickles waiting at the pole.

Pickles was holding a brown paper bag. Uh-oh, thought Eddie, what could that be? Some new invention? A funny flag? He hoped Pickles wasn't going to mess things up. To Eddie, raising the flag was a serious, patriotic business.

"Okay," said Pickles, "what do we do?"

Eddie held out the flag. "Take this." Pickles put down the paper bag and took the flag. "Watch me," said Eddie, surprising himself that he had the nerve to give somebody an order.

Eddie unwound the rope from the two-pronged cleat on the pole. He fixed the rope to the two corner holes of the flag. "Okay," he said, "I'm gonna pull it up now. Just let it come out of your hands. Whatever you do, don't let it touch the ground."

Pickles nodded. "Take 'er away."

Eddie began to pull, slowly, as he was taught. When the trailing red-and-white-striped edge of the flag lifted clear of Pickles' hands, Eddie saw him reach down for the paper bag. Well-trained flag-raiser that he was, Eddie kept his eyes respectfully on Old Glory as she rose, but he begged Pickles in silence: *Please, don't mess up.* He heard the bag rustle, and then he heard — could it be? — the notes of reveille: the wake-up song he recognized from army movies.

Keeping his face to the sky, Eddie dragged his eyeballs downward. Pickles was playing a bugle — an old, dented, tarnished horn. Pickles was at attention, facing the school, his cheeks puffed and round as baseballs.

Eddie looked back to Old Glory, heading for the pole top. He got the chills. Patriotism surged through him.

The flag was at the top. Reveille ended. Eddie tied the rope to the cleat. He felt relieved, he felt good. Pickles hadn't messed up, he had made it better. Eddie was on the verge of telling him so when someone burst from the school and headed toward them.

The man was running, waddling actually. He was sort of old and very short, though it was hard to tell how tall he truly was, since he waddled with a stooped-over form. As he got closer, Eddie could see that his eyes were blazing, and then he saw the lips — or more specifically, the lower lip. It was huge. It drooped halfway down his chin, giving the man's face the appearance of a pouting baby. It looked as though his gum had been rolled outward. It looked as though it could be slapped in a roll and mistaken for a short, plump hot dog. And it was shiny, wet and shiny. And it jiggled as the man waddled up to them.

13

The waddling figure was Arnold Wolfgang Hummelsdorf, or — as he was known to generations of Cedar Grove music students — Lips. Lips Hummelsdorf was a lifelong resident of Cedar Grove, and in fact had attended Cedar Grove Junior High before it became a middle school. A look at school photographs from the years 1942 to 1945 would reveal an Arnold Hummelsdorf with a perfectly ordinary-looking mouth.

Neither heredity nor accident of birth was responsible for Hummelsdorf's knockwurst lower lip. Nor was it the woodwinds, and certainly not the percussion. No, it was the brass. Forty years of teaching the trumpet, the trombone, the French horn, and his favorite, the tuba. Forty years of snatching students' instruments and demonstrating. Forty years of kissing mouthpieces that had been spit, sniveled, and slurped into by forty years of coughing, sneezing, wheezing, flu-infested STUDENTS!

Forty years.

Bitter?

Why should he be bitter? Because all he had to show for forty years of teaching musical klunkheads was a lower lip that hung out like a plum, a salami? Because it presented to the wind a surface as broad as a sail, so that he was in constant danger of getting chapped gums? Because of which he had to continually moisten the lip, making it gleam? Because sometimes students would come up close to him and whip out their combs, believing they could use his lip as a mirror?

No.

The fact is, Hummelsdorf seldom gave his lower lip a thought. To him, it was no different than anyone else's lip.

The source of Hummelsdorf's bitterness could be found five blocks away, in Cedar Grove Senior High School. After many years of glory and prizes and even an appearance in the Orange Bowl Parade, the high school band had fallen on hard times. Last year only fourteen members marched out for the halftimes of football games.

"A disgrace!" blared the newspaper.

"It's embarrassing!" wailed the alumni.

"There's not enough music in the middle school," proclaimed the president of the school board.

And so the blame was dumped on Lips Hummelsdorf. He was called too old, out of step. A young stud music major fresh out of college was brought into Cedar Grove Middle School, and Lips was bumped over to the new place, Plumstead. Not the bargain it appeared to be. Improve the instrumental music program, he was told. Beef up the numbers, he was ordered. They bought new instruments for the college stud and left Lips with the horns and drums he'd been using for half a century.

That is why Lips was waddling out to this young bugler. He hadn't actually heard anything from inside, for his hearing, of all things, was going bad. He simply happened to be looking out a window and saw the boy, ramrod-straight like a private in boot camp, with the bugle to his lips. And now, as he hurried outside, the last few notes lingered in his imperfect ears like the music of the gods.

"You play the trumpet?" he asked the boy, gasping.

"No," the boy answered.

"You play the bugle, you can play the trumpet," Lips said. "Where'd you learn to play?"

The boy shrugged. "Just did."

Hummelsdorf's heart chimed. A born talent. Maybe genius. "You're coming out for band," Lips told him.

"I am?"

"Everybody is coming out for band."

* * *

Eddie thought he was kidding. During second period music, he found out he wasn't.

As Eddie walked into the music room, Hummelsdorf dropped a trombone into his arms. Eddie tried to return it. "I'm sorry, sir, but I don't play this."

"You will," said Lips, pushing it back. "Next."

Eddie took a seat. Salem Brownmiller and Sunny Wyler came in. The teacher gave Salem a drum and Sunny a clarinet. Sunny didn't move. She scowled at the clarinet. She held out the mouth end. The reed was chipped and splintered and pink from lipstick. "I'm not putting my mouth on this," she said, setting the clarinet down. "I'm not playing anything I have to put my mouth on."

"Fine," said Hummelsdorf. He reached into the box by his side. "Here." He handed her a pair of cymbals.

Sunny snatched them and headed for a seat. She was still wearing the DEATH TO MUSH-ROOMS T-shirt, now with the sloppy joe hamster paw print.

Salem spotted Eddie and took a seat next to him. In amazement they kept their eyes on the front of the room. To the kids now coming into class, Hummelsdorf was handing out kazoos and metal buckets and spoons and empty soda bottles and whistles and washboards. To the last bunch he gave long, thick rubber bands.

Eddie noted that Mr. Hummelsdorf was no

taller standing still than he had been waddling out to the flagpole. His head jutted forward, his back curved, his shoulders drooped, and his potbelly pouted over his belt like a second lower lip. His shape reminded Eddie of . . . "Kidney bean," he whispered to Salem.

Salem frowned in confusion; then she looked at the music teacher, and the frown gave way to a broad grin. "If people were vegetables — "

At that moment a shrieking blast paralyzed the room. Hummelsdorf had put a trumpet to his lips and blown a call to doomsday. Thirty sixth-graders froze in mid-motion, mid-word.

"That's how I bring a class to order," Hummelsdorf told them. "And now I will tell you what we are going to do with the instruments I handed out. As you know, a short time from now we will have our first assembly. Mr. Brimlow, the principal, has asked me to provide music for the occasion. Well, I will provide the music — and *you* will provide the music." He stretched out his arms. "We will *allll* provide the music."

He went on to tell them he was being blamed for the puny size of the high school band, and that he had been ordered to beef up the music program. "Well," he said, "we are going to do better than that. When the curtain opens for the music that day, *every single student* in this school will be onstage. For the first time in history, a whole school will be in the band."

He paused to observe their reaction. Nobody seemed too impressed.

He told them he had composed a special piece of music for the event, and that he would teach every student in Plumstead how to do one or two things on their instrument, no matter what it was.

For the rest of the period, Hummelsdorf went from student to student, demonstrating a twang here, a bang there, a toot, a bonk, a tweet.

With Salem, he showed her how to stutter the stick on the drumskin. "Hold it loose," he told her, "that's the secret. Pretend your wrist is rubber." He showed her: *Brrrrrrr-rrp*. On the third try, she did it.

With Eddie, he ignored the trombone at first and worked on Eddie's face like a sculptor with clay. He molded Eddie's cheeks and shaped his mouth till Eddie was sure he looked like a guppy. Then he put the horn in Eddie's hands and pressed the mouthpiece to his lips and said, "Okay, blow."

Eddie blew. Nothing happened but a faintly metallic gasp.

Hummelsdorf shaped Eddie's lips around the silvery circle of the mouthpiece. "Bring the air up from your feet," he said. "This is not a mouth. It's a nozzle. Squirt the air out. Blast it. Blow!"

Eddie blew. The sound that he heard, and that the rest of the class heard, was the death moo of a constipated cow. But to Hummelsdorf's declining ear, it was a perfectly acceptable note.

"Fine," he said, and moved on.

When he came to Sunny Wyler and told her to beat the cymbals, she replied, "No."

Hummelsdorf blinked. "What?"

"No."

"N-O? *That* no?"

"Right."

Hummelsdorf felt the room fall still and silent about him. He looked her over. She didn't seem to have a physical problem. The T-shirt with DEATH TO MUSHROOMS and a tiny orange paw print was no more ridiculous than most kids' clothes these days. The only really remarkable thing about her was that surly face. It could crack a mirror.

"Why not?" he asked her, holding his temper. "Is it against your beliefs or something?"

The girl stared right back at him. "I don't want to."

This was truly a new one. Not that he had never encountered uncooperative students before, but usually they were sneaky, behind-your-back types. Eyeball lasers from thirty sixth-graders scorched his skin. He could not allow her to win.

"Well," he said, aiming for a tone that was both calm and firm, "unfortunately, it's not up to you, young lady. It's up to me. I have music for the program" — he pointed to a stack of paper on his desk — "and somewhere in there, toward the end, it says 'Cymbals.' Cymbals is you. When we are up on the stage on September eighteenth and I point to you, you will bang the cymbals. Do you understand?"

"No," she said.

"You *will* do it," he said.

"I won't do it," she said.

Amid the barely breathing class they stared at each other. The music teacher changed colors: his neck reddened, his lower lip acquired a bluish tint.

They were like that for perhaps a full minute, then the bell rang. The girl stood. The music teacher jabbed a finger in her face. "You will."

She jabbed a finger at him — "I won't" — and walked out.

14

Salem Brownmiller and Eddie Mott were walking to lunch together.

"Do you *believe* what Sunny did?" said Salem.

Eddie shuddered at the memory. "I thought I was dreaming."

"I think Mr. Hummelsdorf did, too. Did you see, after she did it, he just stood there?"

"Like he was shell-shocked."

"He's probably *still* standing there."

They laughed.

"Want to know something else?" said Salem.

"What?"

"He likes her."

Eddie stopped in his tracks. "*What?*"

"Yeah, I think so." She grabbed his arm and pulled him along.

"How *can* he?" Eddie asked. "After *that*?"

Salem shrugged. "I don't know, I just feel it." She tapped her chest. "Here. I'm practicing listening to my instincts. You don't write just from

76

up here, you know." She patted the top of her head. "See, the best stuff comes from down below, in the subconscious. They don't even look like words, or ideas. I pretend they're little fishes, like with little neon feelers 'cause it's so dark down there. And what I do, see, is *oof!* — "

Salem was so preoccupied that she walked into a teacher standing outside his room. "Excuse me, sir, a thousand pardons," she bowed and backed away and continued on with Eddie. "What I do — this is especially true when I'm writing poetry — I pretend like the top of my brain is a beach, and I'm dropping my fishing line into the water of my subconscious, and if I'm lucky, one of those little fishes will bite, and I pull it up onto the beach. Then it dries out and becomes a word. 'The best words are the bones of visitors from the deep.' Isn't that incredible? I read it in one of my writing books."

You're pretty incredible, too, thought Eddie, who wasn't sure he understood all of that. He said, "I still don't see how Mr. Hummelsdorf can like Sunny."

Salem sang, "Time will tell. And I have another instinct about Sunny and somebody else." They were coming downstairs to the cafeteria hallway. She looked at him. "Want to hear it?"

She said this with a sly grin that warmed Eddie's face and made him afraid to say yes.

As they reached the bottom of the stairs, two

boys who had been standing there turned abruptly and blocked their way. One was skinny, one was fat. Both were nickelheads. Their hair had been cut to less than a half-inch all over, and then nickel-sized circles had been shaved down to the scalp. The result was a polka-dotlike haircut.

The skinny nickelhead pointed to Eddie's brown bag and said, "Lunch tax."

"Huh?" said Eddie.

"Lunch tax. Open your bag."

"Why?" said Eddie. He had thought that after yesterday, he was done with eighth-graders.

"Protection," said the skinny nickelhead. "You pay up, and we see to it that nobody bothers you."

"Right," sneered Salem, who had no bag, "until when?"

The nickelheads grinned at each other. "Till tomorrow."

"Come on, Eddie." Salem pulled him away, but the brown paper bag stayed behind, snatched by the skinny nickelhead, who opened it and began checking out the contents. He pulled out a chocolate pudding cup.

"I'm calling a teacher," said Salem, but before she took a step, the bag was snatched again — this time by Pickles Johnson, who had appeared as if from nowhere.

"You don't want this kid's lunch," Pickles told the stunned nickelheads. "He lives in a pigpen. Rats. Roaches. Garter snakes. I used to deliver

78

papers there. Once a week I had to go inside to collect. I quit my job just so I wouldn't have to. His parents are geeks."

As he spoke he folded the top of the paper bag and handed it back to Eddie. Then, in a blur of handspeed, he snatched the pudding cup from the skinny nickelhead. "You think this is pudding? This isn't pudding. It's probably mashed roaches with bathtub scum. Look — " He tore off the aluminum foil lid, turned the cup upside down, and dumped the contents onto the nickelhead's purple, red-and-white, gold-tongued, transparent bubble-soled, trampoline-treaded sneakers. "Oops," said Pickles. "I guess it *was* pudding."

He dropped the empty cup. Before it landed he was taking off. Before the nickelheads lit out after him, he was up the stairs.

Eddie stared at Salem. "I think my life just got saved."

Principal Brimlow made the intercom announcement once on Thursday, twice on Friday: "We have a lost hamster in the main office. If it belongs to anyone, you may come and claim it."

No one came.

Not even Miss Elizabeth Sunshine Wyler, despite direct orders to report after school.

Teachers were already talking about her. What was her problem? Apparently she knew exactly what she wanted, to get kicked out. Why not give

79

it to her? Punt her over to Cedar Grove, let them deal with her.

Mr. Brimlow brought the hamster tank from his file cabinet to the outer office. The trip sent the animal fleeing to a corner. "I'm taking you home for the weekend, little guy." The hamster stared at him, two black eyes in a ball of caramel-colored fur.

It was nearly five. Everyone else was gone. Two days. Plumstead Middle School was two days old. Someday, with luck, she would be fifty years old. Someday, these kids would bring *their* kids by and say, "See, that's where I went to school."

Would Wyler be one of them?

He looked at the hamster. He spoke to it. "She will, if I can help it."

He walked down the hallway toward the library.

15

Salem took one step back from the dining room table. She smiled. She nodded. "Perfecto."

It was 1:30 Saturday afternoon. She had told the mascot committee to come at 2:00, but you never knew when people might show up early. Besides, she was simply too excited to let it go until the last minute. Except for the food, the table had been set since ten o'clock.

Salem Brownmiller could no more host an ordinary meeting than Madonna could wear an ordinary outfit. Salem strove, whenever possible, to make every episode of her life an "occasion." Her mother had vetoed use of the elegant lace tablecloth, so she had had to settle for the pale yellow one. Though she was not allowed to use the silverware, she did win her argument to set the table with stainless steel instead of plastic, and with real plates instead of paper.

For the hundredth time she reviewed the sheet

that she had composed and printed out the night
before with her father's desktop publisher:

* MASCOT COMMITTEE MEETING *
Saturday, September 5
2 p.m.

ORDER OF EVENTS
BUFFET
BUSINESS MEETING
("Nominating a mascot
for Plumstead Middle
School")
SOCIAL HOUR
* * *

MUSIC: *Autumn*
by George Winston
* * *

MENU
Potato Chips
Onion Dip
Cold Vegetables (for dipping)
Cheese (cheddar, brie)
Pepperoni Slices
Pickles
Pigs in a Blanket
Grey Poupon
Mints
Periwinkle Punch

Salem had considered phrasing such as "Chips of Potato" and "Dip of Onion," but had rejected them as a little too uppity for this group. And anyway, there was enough elegance in the last item to cover everything.

During the past year Salem had developed the punch herself: a positively exotic blend of five fruit juices, two sodas, and rainbow sherbet. She called it Periwinkle Punch simply because she liked the sound of the two words together. Remembering that made her think of Pickles Johnson at lunch the other day, saying he hated how pickles tasted but liked how they sounded. Apparently he agreed with her that when it came to naming things, whether punch or people, sound could count for more than sense. It was interesting to discover this little tidbit that they had in common.

Salem was even prouder of the punch bowl than the punch. It was colossal, it was crystal, it sparkled like diamonds, it had been in the family for more than a hundred years, and her mother had promised to feed her to the garbage disposal if anything happened to it. The bowl sat regally in the center of the table, no fewer than eighteen matching crystal cups dangling from its rim.

She had chosen the music after trying out a dozen of her parents' tapes. *Autumn* was all piano, pleasant. It would do nicely as background during the buffet and social hour segments.

At precisely 1:45 she poured two large pitchers

of Periwinkle Punch into the crystal bowl. The punch had spent the night in the fridge. She wanted it cold, but not diluted with ice. Then, scoop by scoop, came the rainbow sherbet.

1:50.

Salem paced, sat, looked out the window, looked at the clock, paced, paced . . .

At 2:01 the doorbell rang. She ran, opened the door.

"Eddie! Hi!" She could have hugged him. "Come in."

Eddie came in. They sat in the living room. Salem talked. They waited for the others.

No one came.

By 2:30 Salem was still talking, but her eyes were glistening. "Well," she sighed, "I guess the others couldn't make it. You did tell Pickles, like I asked you, didn't you?"

Eddie stared at her, mouth open. "Uh-oh."

"You forgot."

"Uh-oh."

Salem sighed again. She stood. She inserted the *Autumn* tape. She forced a smile. "Ready to eat?"

"Sure!"

Name tags perched like little white roofs at the four place settings. Salem had tried every possible combination around the table before settling on one. As she had hinted in the hallway the day before, she suspected Eddie had eyes for Sunny.

84

Though she had since decided not to make him uncomfortable by mentioning it again, she did feel that the least she could do for Eddie was to seat him in the best place relative to Sunny. It boiled down to a question of basic romance: Is it better to seat the girl where the boy can see her best (across the table) or where he can be closest (next to him)? She finally decided on nearness over vision, and placed Sunny's card to Eddie's right.

Of course, none of that mattered now. "There's your name card," she said, pointing, "but you can sit anywhere you like." She poured him some punch and went to the kitchen to microwave the pigs in a blanket.

When she returned, half the potato chips were gone and half the dip.

"Like the dip?" she said.

He nodded with a mouthful and said something that vaguely resembled yes.

"Well," she said, passing the steamy plate of tiny, dough-wrapped hot dogs under his nose, "if you like that, you're gonna *love* these."

Each pig had a toothpick sticking out. It looked like a forest of toothpicks. Eddie chose one. He looked around. "Any mustard?"

Salem set down the plate of pigs. "Right in front of you."

Eddie looked again. "Where?"

Salem pushed a small side dish toward him. "There."

He made a face. "*That's* mustard?"

"The best. It's Grey Poupon."

"Gray — " Eddie went into a sudden spasm. He clamped his hand over his mouth, but not before several bits of potato chip had fired out and sunk into the sherbety foam of his punch. With the mouth cut off, the rest of the spasm exited through Eddie's nose in the form of a rippling, nostril-flapping snort. "Gray" — he croaked — "*poop?*"

Salem rolled her eyes and gave a parental sigh. "No, you goof" — she gave it her best French pronunciation — "Grrrrey Poo-*pawh.*"

She maintained her dignity while the boy suffered through a series of after-snorts. At last he calmed down enough to say, scratchily, "So where's the mustard?"

"It *is* mustard!" The "*is*" came out as a screech.

He held the toothpicked pig shoulder-high, as though the stuff in the side dish might leap for it. "It doesn't *look* gray."

"It's *not.*"

"But it *does*" — he giggled — "it *does* look" — another spasm was rising, his voice was cracking, his nostrils were fluttering — "a little like — "

Salem's patience vanished with an exasperated "Ohhhh!" She snatched the dish away and stomped off to the kitchen. In a moment she stomped back and slammed a jar of bright yellow French's mustard onto the table. "*Here.*"

16

Salem glared at Eddie for a while, but he just went on blissfully chomping. She picked a piece of broccoli from the cold vegetable dish and scooped up some dip. "You should try this." He nodded and reached for another pig. Then he reached for the mints.

"Mints are for afterward," she told him. "They're the last thing you eat."

Eddie looked at her, looked at the mints in his hand. He started to put them back. She stopped him. "Oh, never mind. Go ahead." He didn't argue.

Eddie's crystal cup was still almost full. "What did you think of the punch?" she asked him.

He chewed for a second. "Mm," he nodded. "Good."

"I call it Periwinkle Punch. I just kind of like the way it sounds. Do you?"

Eddie had been scanning the toothpicks for the

plumpest pig. "What was it?" he said, making his choice.

"Periwinkle."

He dipped the pig into the French's yellow mustard, clamped it respectfully in his teeth, and drew it from the toothpick. "Yeah, neat."

"Want to know what goes into it?"

"Mm," he nodded, chewing. He really likes those pigs, Salem thought.

"Well, I can't tell you *exactly* what goes into it, because that's a chef's secret — me being the chef — but I can tell you there are five different kinds of fruit juice and two kinds of soda, plus the sherbet. I'll let you guess what kind of sherbet it is."

Eddie popped a pepperoni slice into his mouth. "Rainbow."

"That's right." Salem sunk a carrot into the dip. "But don't even *try* to guess what the other ingredients are."

"I won't."

"Because I wouldn't tell you if you were right, anyway. You know why?"

Eddie made a sandwich of two potato chips and a pepperoni slice. "Nope."

"Mystery," she said. "Mystery is the hidden ingredient. It's probably one of the reasons you like it so much. Mystery is supposed to make things appealing, because people are attracted to things they don't understand. You ever notice that?"

Eddie nodded, munching. "Mm."

Salem chewed on a broccoli stalk, thinking. "Yeah, me, too. Like when this kid came to my house last Halloween. I was already in for the night, so I answered the door, and there was the neatest costume I'd ever seen. I mean, I didn't have the foggiest idea *what* he was supposed to be. I didn't even know if it was a he. All I knew was I was fascinated by the costume, probably 'cause it wasn't like any other costume I ever saw. And then the person took off the mask — and it was Donald, my cousin from up the street. Zap" — she waved a carrot stick — "fascination gone."

She ladled herself some more punch. "C'mon, drink up, before I guzzle it all." His punch was still riding high in his cup. "You *sure* you like it?"

"Mm," said Eddie.

"Well, how come you're not drinking it?"

Eddie stopped chewing. He stared at her. He blinked. He stared at the cup. He picked up the cup. He looked into the cup. He raised the cup to his lips, closed his eyes, and drank it down in three fast, rather noisy swallows. He put the cup down. He couldn't seem to stop looking at it.

Salem started to giggle.

"What?" he said.

"You have a rainbow sherbet mustache."

While he wiped away his mustache, Salem ladled him another cupful of Periwinkle Punch.

"So anyway," she went on, "where was I?" She crunched a carrot stick. "Oh yeah — mystery. So . . . sometimes I read grown-up books and magazine stories, you know, so I can get a little preview of what I'm going to be reading when I'm in my twenties. And you know what one of the most mysterious things around is? You want to guess?"

Eddie scooped out the last of the onion dip with the last potato chip. "Uh — black holes?"

"Nope. Women." She studied his face for a reaction, but all she found was a mouth devouring another pig in a blanket. "Yep — women. Of course, we're not mysterious to ourselves. We're only mysterious to men. Men have a hard time figuring us out."

She cut the triangular tip off the wedge of brie. She worked the soft, almost gooey cheese in her mouth and closed her eyes, trying to glimpse a hint of mystery within herself. She opened her eyes, tilted her head. "Do you think I'm mysterious?"

Eddie looked at her. His face was a total blank. Had he continued to look at her for a thousand years, his face would still have been a total blank. "Never thought about it," he said at last.

Salem pulled up the hem of the pale yellow tablecloth till it covered her face below the eyes. "How about now?"

Eddie looked again. He shrugged. "A little, I guess."

"You sure? You're not just saying it?" She kept the veil up.

He picked a pig. "No, really."

"What exactly is it?" she persisted. "My eyes?" She leaned toward him, opening her eyes as wide as she could. If Eddie hadn't known better, he would have thought she was seeing a ghost. "When you look into them, do you feel yourself being drawn into the eternal mysteries of the female? Do you feel yourself falling in a bottomless void?"

He looked as directly as he could at her eyeballs. It was a little hard to focus, she being so close. The pig slid silently from its toothpick into his mouth. He nodded. "Uh-huh." Then burped.

A small wind of pepperoni, mustard, hot dog, onion, potato chip, and mint blew through the pale yellow veil. Salem backed into her chair and dropped the tablecloth. She did not have her notepad at hand, but she made a mental note on the many personalities of Eddie Mott:

4. Glutton

The mints were now as gone as the chips and dip. Three pepperonis lay on their plate like beefy half-dollars. The last of the pigs in a blanket was disappearing into Eddie's own bottomless void.

His cup was full.

"You hate the punch," she said.

His head snapped toward her. "No, really, I *like* it."

"All that stuff makes people thirsty. You should've drunk most of that bowl by now."

"I drank a lot before I came over today, that's all."

She got up. "I'll get you something you'll like. A nice old-fashioned Coke."

"No — " he called, but she was already in the kitchen.

She returned with a glassful. She set it in front of him. "Classic. Only the best."

He looked at it for a moment, then pushed it away. "Really," he said, "look." He grabbed the punch cup and downed it straight away. He wiped off his sherbet mustache and sucked it from his finger as he would a taffy. He closed his eyes and smiled. "Mmm."

Salem slumped into her chair, not sure if she had just won or lost.

The two talked for almost another hour. By the time Eddie left, most of the pickles were gone.

Salem was cleaning up the table when she happened to glance at the printed program. She gave the floor a crystal-tinkling stomp. "Drat!" They —

or at least she — had talked about everything *but* what they were *supposed* to talk about: a mascot for Plumstead.

Not wanting to be a pest, Salem waited until seven that evening to give Eddie a call. They could discuss it for five minutes over the phone; then at least they'd have something to report to Mr. Brimlow.

A woman's voice answered. Pleasant.

"Hello? Mrs. Mott?"

"Yes."

"This is Salem Brownmiller. Eddie's friend? He was over at my house this afternoon?"

"Oh, yes. How are you, Salem?"

"Fine, thank you. I was wondering if I could speak with Eddie."

There was a short delay before Mrs. Mott answered. "Oh, I'm sorry, Salem. Eddie's in bed. I'm afraid he's not feeling too well."

17

When Sunny Wyler arrived in homeroom Monday morning, a note was waiting for her:

> *Report to the principal's office.*
> *AT ONCE!*

Mr. Brimlow did not smile when she walked in. The hamster tank was on his desk. Besides the hamster, there was now a carpet of wood shavings and a plastic exercise wheel.

The principal said, "You were supposed to be here after school on Friday. Did you forget?"

She nodded. "Yeah."

"No," he said, "I don't think you forgot. I think, for some reason, you just want out of here, and you're doing everything you can to make me kick you out." He pointed at her nose. "Well, I have news for you, Sunshine. If you do *not* take care of this animal, I will make certain that you do *not* leave this school until your three years are up."

Outside, the notes of reveille signaled the flag's ascent. The principal and the sixth-grader stared at each other, Sunny wishing she had the nerve to tell him how much she hated being called Sunshine.

The principal held out a pair of books. "Here." She took them. "These are from our library. Read the parts about hamsters and how to care for them."

He pointed to a shopping bag in the corner. "There's everything you'll need. Food. Wood chips. I'm going to set it up on a table right outside the office. This will be everybody's pet. And you will be the petkeeper. Every day. After school. Here. Got it?"

She nodded.

"Okay, on your way."

Sunny wandered off to first period wishing Hillary were there to talk to about this. What exactly did he mean? He had said he would not kick her out if she did not take care of the beast. Did that mean he definitely *would* kick her out if she did? Did that mean she did not even have to be bad anymore?

By third period music, she decided she couldn't afford to take that chance. She would take care of the beast *and* continue to be bad. She would leave the principal no choice.

On this day Lips Hummelsdorf began actual preparations for the assembly presentation. He spent time with each group of instruments, working on their notes. The rubber band section, for example, was fifteen strong. Though the rubber bands were huge, each one by itself made only a puny twitter. But a whole chorus of them, said Lips, would be another story. The audience would hear a twang they wouldn't soon forget. The secret was to pluck them all at precisely the same instant.

On this first day of practice, the twangers were decidedly ragged. As was every other group. Salem's drum section sounded like furniture falling down stairs. And together, Eddie and his trombone-mates sounded like a herd of constipated cows.

There was only one cymbalist — Sunny Wyler. When Hummelsdorf walked right past her to the buckets and spoons, you could almost hear the class gasp in amazement. After what had happened at the last class, they had expected a confrontation at least; maybe, if they were lucky, an all-out fistfight.

And then, when the period was over and Lips called, "Cymbals player, stay a minute," half the class found reasons to hang around the hallway just outside. But Lips closed the door.

"You don't like it here, do you?" he said.

Sunny shrugged.

"Sometimes I don't, either. Especially with all this blame coming down on me now, and they leave me with all the oldest instruments." For once, Sunny found herself staring at a puss as sour as her own. "So," he went on, "you say you won't play the cymbals, and I say I won't let you be the only student not in the band that day. What are we going to do?"

Sunny shrugged.

"Will you play something else? Rubber band?"

"No."

"Bucket?"

"No."

He stared at her. "What's your name?"

"Wyler."

"First."

"Sunny."

His eyebrows shot up. *"Sunny?* You sure it's not Cloudy?"

She let her glare be her answer.

He sat back. He gave a what-did-I-do-to-deserve-this sigh, which pushed out his lower lip even more. Sunny wondered if it was true, that you could see your reflection in it. It *was* shiny.

"Okay then," he said, "if you won't play anything, you can't be on the stage. But you also can't be in the audience. I will *not* have you make a mockery of me by being the only student in the audience. So you know what that means, Wyler?"

"No."

"That means you'll be sick that afternoon. You'll have to go see the nurse, stay in the infirmary. You won't show up. Agreed?"

Sunny was about to say okay, but then she thought: Hey, wait a minute, why should I agree? If the last thing he wants is for me to be in the audience, then that's exactly what I *should* do. So she said, "I don't feel sick."

"Well," he said, "it's almost two weeks away. That's plenty of time to suddenly come down with a nice stomachache."

"I don't get stomachaches."

"Well, *get* one."

"That would be lying."

Sunny then saw the last thing she expected: Mr. Hummelsdorf laughing. It seemed like he laughed forever. She was glad the door was shut. When he finished, he shook his head and looked at her as if he actually liked her.

"I'm old," he said. "I don't need this. I used to think, by now I'd be directing a major college band. Michigan State. Oklahoma. Two hundred members." He wagged his head. "Are you always this belligerent?"

"Huh?"

"A pain. Are you always such a pain?"

"No," she said. "I used to be good. I just started being a pain when I came here. I think I must be allergic to this school."

That set him off laughing again. "Oh, my . . .

98

okay, here — " He scribbled out a late note for her next class. "Maybe I *do* need this," he chuckled as he sent her on her way.

Eddie Mott had hoped to avoid Salem at lunch that day, but there was the voice that could only be hers, behind him: "Hey, Eddie, wait up."

Maybe he could draw her attention away. He said, as she caught up to him, "What do you think Lips said to Sunny in there today?" In spite of his mood, it made him feel a tiny bit bad and a tiny bit older to call a teacher "Lips."

Salem grinned deliciously. "I don't know. Wish I were a bug on the wall."

Before he could say anything else, she spotted the absence. "Hey, where's your lunch bag?"

He shrugged. "Uh . . . I'm buying today."

One glance at his face and she knew. She made him stop just inside the door of the cafeteria. "No, you're not. It got stolen, didn't it?"

He stared at her with what he hoped was his best I-haven't-the-slightest-idea-what-you're-talking-about face. "No," he said.

"That nickelhead jerk, right? He got you when Pickles wasn't around, and this time he took your whole lunch."

Eddie's eyes began to itch. "No, I'm buying today." *Don't look down*, he pleaded silently. *Please.*

She looked down. "Oh, no."

He had tried to wipe the pudding off in the bathroom, but you could still see traces of chocolate between his sneaker laces.

She looked back up. "He did to you what Pickles did to him."

Eddie tried to stare at her, but he couldn't. What a curse! To be a kid and not be able to tell a convincing lie. His mother said he wore his heart on his sleeve, whatever that meant. All he knew was that the whole world always seemed to know what he was feeling inside.

Salem stared at him until he blinked, then slumped, and she knew that she had gone too far.

She steered him toward the nearest table. They sat down. Half the school was mobbing past them for the lunch lines.

"I'm sorry," she said.

He shook his head. He stared down at his balled fist. "I'm a wimp."

"No — "

"I'm the world's biggest wimp."

"Eddie, you're only a sixth-grader." She touched his arm. He jerked it away.

"They throw me around like a football. They spit on me. They steal my lunch. They drop pudding on my shoe . . . and I don't do *nothin'*. And on toppa all that, I can't even *lie* right. What kinda kid *am* I? I know that story you're writing is about me. You can call it 'Eddie the Wimp.' I'm *worse* than a wimp. I'm a *disgrace*."

Kids going by were staring. A few eighth-graders snickered.

Salem's left hand had been resting in her book bag, touching her notepad. Suddenly she felt crummy. She now saw that in her own way, she, too, had mistreated him. She had tried to divide him into so many personalities. She had tried to reduce him to pages in a notepad. How insulting to him. Eddie Mott was not a subplot, as Mr. Brimlow would say, or even a main plot. He was a person. He was her friend.

18

This time T. Charles Brimlow was properly ready for lunch. He had brought a tablecloth from home and his hand-carved, hand-painted wooden dandelion to serve as a centerpiece. For the sake of easy cleanup, the plates, cups, and utensils were paper and plastic, but they were best quality and coordinated nicely with the tablecloth. He even felt a little proud when Salem entered, looked the table over, and pronounced it *"verrry* nice."

As the others came in, he updated his mental files.

Eddie Mott: faithful, competent flag-raiser; still looks like he wants to disappear, except when he's looking at Sunny Wyler.

Elizabeth Sunshine Wyler: still the sullen face and DEATH TO MUSHROOMS T-shirt; problems with Maestro Hummelsdorf; hair — did she dunk it in molasses?

Dennis Johnson: the pickle boy, as Mrs. Wilburham calls him, is a patriot; hasn't missed a morning blowing reveille.

He waited till they had been served before addressing them.

"First of all, I'm going to give you an official name — the Principal's Posse." They seemed to approve. "Now, schoolwise, it looks like we're on our way. We just finished our shakedown cruise. One week, and we didn't sink. I think we're going to make it."

He turned to Salem. "So, do we have a nominee for mascot yet?"

Miss Brownmiller briefly glossed over a mention that she had forgotten to convene a meeting — shifting eyes told Mr. Brimlow this wasn't quite true — and went on to offer her own views on the subject. "Whatever we nominate, let's not pick wildcats. Or lions or bears or dragons. For one thing, they're so common. Everybody has them. And for another thing, they're all, like, violent and . . . *growly*. Why does a mascot have to be a flesh-eating carnivore? Why can't it be something more original?"

She stopped, waited. The principal knew a cue when he heard one. "For example?" he said.

Salem waved her hand. "Oh . . . vegetables."

Eddie Mott sprang to life. "The Plumstead *Onions*!"

Everybody laughed, even Sunny Wyler.

Suggestions flew, laughter grew.

"The Plumstead String Beans!"

"The Plumstead Cauliflowers!"

"The Plumstead Plums!"

"Pancakes!"

"Bran Muffins!"

"Buttonholes!"

"Hamsters!"

Everyone stopped. For the first time in two lunches, Sunny Wyler had voluntarily spoken. All eyes swung to her.

Mr. Brimlow whispered it: "Hamsters." He pronounced it louder, his head tilted, testing, tasting the sound of it: "Plumstead Hamsters." He looked around the table, his eyes bright: "The . . . Plumstead . . . *Hamsters*."

"I love it!" chirped Salem.

"Shall we vote?" said Mr. Brimlow.

"Yeah!" came several voices.

"Okay, Posse, all in favor of the sixth-grade nominee for school mascot being the Hamsters, say 'Aye.' "

"Aye!"

"Opposed, 'No.' "

Silence.

"Hamsters it is!"

Cheers and slaps on the back to Sunny Wyler, whose face had regained its usual pout.

That day, Wednesday, was clean-the-hamster-house day. Sunny went to the lobby later than usual. She wanted to be sure no kids were still around to see her do the dirty work.

From the main office, where Mr. Brimlow had left them, she got the newspapers, paper bag, rag, and tennis ball can. Before today, she really hadn't had much to do with the animal. She just dumped some food in and, once, filled the water bottle. She never even really looked at it, except when she reached down to put the pellets in the bowl and found the animal looking up at her. She had yanked her arm out, fearing the beast had a mind to scurry up her sleeve. But she kept thinking of those pure black shiny eyes, so big. She had been remembering those eyes when *"Hamster!"* popped unexpectedly from her mouth at lunch a couple hours earlier.

She took off the screen that served as the cover of the glass tank. She reached in and took out the exercise wheel, food bowl, salt wheel, and water bottle. Now, the animal itself. It had to be removed so she could clean the tank. That's what the tennis ball can was for, so said one of the books she had read.

She removed the cap from the can and laid the can on the floor of the tank. Sure enough, within seconds, the animal went sniffing into it, exploring this new piece of furniture. Sunny clamped the cap on the can, lifted it out, and set it on the floor. Mr. Brimlow had punched an air hole in the cap.

She then proceeded to dump the old wood shavings onto the newspaper, which in turn she folded and stashed in the paper bag. She cleaned the inside of the tank with a rag, dumped in new shavings, replaced the furniture, and finally, holding the opened tennis can at a sliding board angle, dumped the animal back home.

Suddenly the beast stood on its hind legs, its paws on the glass walls. Was it going to leap? Quickly, she replaced the screen. In less than two minutes she was on her way home.

"So," Hillary asked that night, "is it a boy or girl hamster?"

"A boy," said Sunny.

"How do you know?"

"Some science teacher said."

"So who's gonna take care of it when you're gone, after you get kicked out?"

Sunny snapped, "I don't *know*. I don't *care*. I hate that . . . *rodent*."

Hillary scowled back. "Well, don't go hollering at me. *I* didn't make you take care of the thing. Look at my hair." She grabbed a handful on top of her head and pulled it up straight. When she released it, it stayed up: a thin, greasy, hairy, foot-tall spike.

Sunny laughed.

"Yeah, laugh," growled Hillary. "My father laughs, too. He says it looks like string cheese.

My sister says seaweed. My mother's ready to kill me. I keep telling her it's *not* grease, it's *mousse*. I tell her it's my new style. Every night I come out of the shower with a towel around my head and pretend I just washed my hair. You gotta get kicked out soon!"

Sunny pulled her own hair into spikes, till her head resembled a medieval weapon. "See — you're not the only one. I'm working on it."

"Well, you better work faster." Hillary scratched her head furiously. "I'm itching like mad. I think I already have cooties."

"C'mere," said Sunny. She led Hillary to her dresser. "Kneel down." The two girls knelt in front of the dresser. "Ready?"

"Ready for what?"

Sunny grinned faintly and opened the bottom drawer. Hillary, unaware that Sunny was holding her breath, peered into the drawer, but it was not her eyes but what reached her nose that knocked her backward as smartly as if she had been punched. *"EEEWW!"* she shrieked, clamping her hand over her face and gagging, scrambling to the farthest corner of the room.

Sunny closed the drawer, moved away, took a small breath.

"What — ?" gasped Hillary.

"My socks. I've been wearing them for a week now. I keep them in their cage here, by themselves. I moved everything else out."

Hillary, pinching her nose, oinked, "How can you *stand* it?"

"I hold my breath and put on my shoes *real* fast." Sunny grinned as she peeked into the future. "Any day now . . . "

19

Principal Brimlow made the announcement next morning: "We now have the candidates for school mascot. Eighth-grade nominee is . . . the Demons! Seventh-grade nominee is . . . the Wildcats! Sixth-graders nominate . . . the Hamsters! We will vote next Thursday. The winner will be announced the following day during opening assembly."

By lunchtime every sixth-grader in Plumstead Middle School had managed to stop by the hamster house and say hello. The greeting usually took the form of a fingernail tapping upon the glass wall and waking up the occupant, who was trying to take a nap. The result was a hundred happy sixth-graders and one very cranky hamster, who profoundly wished that one of those tapping fingertips would come within reach of his teeth.

Sometime, somehow, during the day, the hamster also acquired a name: Humphrey.

By the following week, Sunny Wyler found herself longing for the "old days," when it was just her and the hamster after school. Now, when she came to feed him, he was in such a foul mood from being kept awake by tapping fingernails all day, he was no fun at all to be with. "What a grouch," she muttered to him every day.

Sometimes when she arrived after school, she found food on the table on which the hamster house rested. Left by well-meaning sixth-graders, the food was usually unhealthy for hamsters: M&M's, brownies, pickle chips, raviolis.

Sometimes, too, she found things that were more than unhealthy: bubble gum, old soap, dirty erasers. These things, Sunny knew, were from some seventh- and eighth-graders, kids who wanted the mascot to be a demon or a wildcat. Once, in fact, she found a sign propped in front of the tank:

MENU FOR THURSDAY
HAM(STER)BURGER

Thursday was the day of the vote. Sunny ripped the sign in half. She ripped the pieces again and kept ripping in frustration and anger. She was mad at the hamster for being so cute. Mad at herself for having feelings for it. Mad at the principal for not kicking her out. And mad at the whole school for butting in between her and Hillary.

She threw the pieces, practically confetti now, into a basket. She would have to make her move soon.

20

For the most part, Lips Hummelsdorf was satisfied, even pleased. Counting today, Wednesday, only two days of practice remained, and yet he felt confident they would do it.

The rubber bands were lagging, but he would have them up to speed by Friday. The washboards and drums were coming along. The kazoos were better than expected, and the buckets and spoons — well — they lent his music a surprisingly primitive power.

Only one question remained: Would he become the first bandmaster to direct a whole school — or a whole school minus one?

Miss Wyler. She of the sunny disposition. She was still refusing to bang the cymbals and still threatening to be the only student in the audience. He feared she meant it.

As he worked with the soda bottlists that day, coaxing a mournful, flutelike note from them, he noticed that Miss Wyler was not only her usual sullen self today, she was also something of an island. The chairs directly before and behind her and the chair to her left were all unoccupied. Only the Mott boy, a trombonist, sat near her.

Within the next minute, two students slipped away into seats even farther from her. Below the bottlists' note, he sensed an undercurrent of whispers, from which erupted an occasional cough or muffled squawk. Another student moved. Something like a tide was receding from Wyler. Suddenly a kazooist popped up and staggered to the back of the room, his hands to his face.

Hummelsdorf wandered a step into the now vacated space around Wyler and Mott, and he knew. And then he knew why — her shoes were off. And he knew, without asking, that it wasn't for lack of soap. It was deliberate.

She had won.

"Wyler," he thundered, "out! Principal's office! Now!"

Sunny padded down the hallways in her stocking feet, holding her breath as best she could, taking in air through her mouth, in tiny sips. Along the way one teacher, two teachers, left their blackboards, took a look, took a whiff, and shut their classroom doors. Later that day, a number of students would report to their parents that a skunk had been loose in the school.

As Sunny approached the office, she slowed

down. The hamster house . . . something was different . . . *wrong*. She rushed up to it. The screen was off, leaning against the tank.

The hamster — Humphrey — was gone!

Moments later, Sunny was in the office, hysterically telling Mrs. Wilburham and Mr. Brimlow what had happened. They hurried out to see for themselves, leaving Sunny alone in the office. She looked down. Her shoes were on her feet. She could not remember putting them on.

The principal made announcements. He wasn't after punishment, he said. If you took the hamster, just put it back in the tank when no one was looking. No questions asked.

Accusations flew. Sixth-graders accused seventh-graders of hamsternapping. Seventh-graders accused eighth-graders. Everyone accused the nickelheads. The nickelheads gestured innocently and pointed out that the animal itself could have nudged the cover off and climbed out.

The usual Wednesday lunch meeting of the Principal's Posse was replaced by a schoolwide search.

In the cafeteria that day, several sixth-graders, recalling the sign propped in front of the tank, looked at their hamburgers and screamed.

After school, Sunny gave the tank its usual

114

Wednesday cleaning. There was no need for the tennis ball can.

Tears came to her eyes as she looked at the lobby wall above the tank. A sixth-grade English class had taped a dozen sheets of paper together to make a banner. It read:

HUMPHREY — COME HOME!

The school was locked up and closed down at nine that night. The hamster house was still empty.

21

Mrs. Wilburham took her job as school sec-retary quite seriously. She had her own key and usually opened up the building before the custodians arrived.

Thursday morning was no exception. Upon arriving, she turned on the coffee maker in the teachers' lounge and headed for the kitchen. On the side of one shelf in the big stainless-steel food freezer she kept her frozen muffins. With boxes of blueberry, corn, and bran, she looked forward each morning to her tasty dilemma: which flavor to choose.

Some days she could not make up her mind until she took each package off the shelf and studied the pictures of the muffins within. This was one of those days.

First she took the bran muffin package from the shelf and considered it. Then the corn. Then the blueberry. So intent was she on the muffins that at first she failed to notice the hamster. It was on the shelf below the muffins and more to the center of the freezer. It was lying on a box of twenty-four Mister Mario's Delux cheese pizzas. It was on its back, its four legs straight in the air. Its eyes were closed. It wasn't moving.

Blueberry, decided Mrs. Wilburham. She removed a single muffin and replaced all three boxes. That's when she saw it. She screeched, thinking it was a mouse. Then she realized it was the hamster. What was its name? Hubert? Harry? Mrs. Wilburham never had cared much for this hamster business. This one was either dead or it was impersonating a dead cockroach. With a corner of the blueberry muffin box, she nudged one of the stiff, upraised legs. The beast rolled onto its side like a wooden toy.

What to do with a dead hamster in the food freezer? First, close the door, you're wasting electricity. She shut the door. But she knew she couldn't leave it in the freezer one second longer than necessary. Suppose the dietician came in early today. Suppose the Board of Health dropped by. Suppose the beast had romped around the freezer going to the bathroom before it died. Suppose there were little frozen hamster pooplets all over. Suppose . . . she looked at the muffin in her hand . . . of *course* they were blueberries. Nevertheless, she tossed the muffin into a trash can.

She searched through the utensil bin and came up with the largest spatula she could find, a real

117

he-man pancake flipper. She pulled the trash can in close. She reopened the freezer, scanned the interior — good, no pooplets. Carefully, as if she were turning a fried egg, she slid the spatula under the corpse. Her plan was to dump it into the trash can, cover it with papers — get it out of sight — then wait for Mr. Brimlow, and tell him.

Slowly, carefully, she lifted the spatula. As the body rose on the silvery surface, it gave the impression of a tiny, vanquished warrior borne from some arena of combat on its shield. Swinging the spatula around toward the trash can brought the front end of the animal into view. She saw the frost then, a white dusting on the animal's nose and whiskers and closed eyes, as though it had been sniffing powdered sugar when it expired.

Mrs. Wilburham's heart sank. This was not, after all, a half-eaten hot dog. It was not garbage.

She placed the body back on the box of Mario's pizzas, shut the freezer door, and hurried back to the office. To her delight, she saw the pickle boy waiting by himself outside the front door. She let him in.

22

Pickles took it from there. He retrieved the body from the freezer. He found a box of pencils in the office. He emptied out the pencils. From the infirmary he obtained cotton balls. He pulled them shapeless and laid them together in the bottom of the pencil box, making a soft, white bedding. Upon the bedding he placed the body. He then set the box next to the glass tank in the lobby. He did not disturb the tank or the empty exercise wheel.

He completed this by the time Mr. Brimlow arrived. Pickles related to the principal what had happened.

Buses began to pull up. Students crowded outside the door, awaiting the bell. Those in front peered in, making a bridge between the dark glass and their eyes.

When the students poured in, they found the hamster lying in state and Pickles Johnson at rigid attention by the casket. There were cries of surprise and grief as the students paused, then moved on.

With everyone in homeroom, the principal called for a moment of silence. In the farthest reaches of the school, from the teachers' lounge to the cafeteria kitchen, could be heard a bugle playing taps.

Motorists on their way to work slowed down to 15 m.p.h. and wondered why the Plumstead Middle School flag was flying half-mast.

All day long students went to classes by way of the lobby. Not just sixth-graders, but many seventh- and eighth-graders as well.

The votes for school mascot were cast and collected in homeroom after last period. The ballots were brought to the main office.

Upon leaving school, few of the students were surprised to find the casket empty. They asked among themselves where he was buried. No one seemed to know. Nearly everyone called him Humphrey now. Seldom was he referred to as "the hamster."

Among the last to leave the lobby that day were Salem Brownmiller and Eddie Mott and Sunny Wyler and Pickles Johnson.

For quite a while, no one said a word. Then Sunny cleared her throat and spoke to Pickles. "Did you bury him?"

Pickles turned, his eyes wide. "No, didn't you?"

23

Seated onstage along with the principal and other school administrators, Maestro Hummelsdorf tapped his baton nervously on the side of his chair. His hands were clammy.

Had he bitten off too much? Was he about to make a fool of himself? For the past two weeks he had rehearsed the students as much as he could in their separate music periods. For the most part, they had learned their limited parts well. But not once had they practiced together, all 340 of them. This time, following the announcement of the mascot, would be the first.

Would they follow his directions? Would he prove that a whole school, musicians or not, could perform as a band? Would it in fact *be* the whole school, all 340 of them? Or 339?

He scanned the auditorium for Wyler, but could not locate her. Backstage, behind the curtain, the cymbals sat alongside the other instruments. The clash of the cymbals would bracket his tuba solo, which would be followed by the Johnson boy playing reveille — a late addition to the score. Reveille: wake up: a new beginning: a new school year: a new school! The perfect finale. He loved it.

Would they?

" . . . and the winner *is* . . . " the principal was saying, holding up a slip of paper, " . . . the Plumstead . . . *Hamsters!*"

The place went wild. The little sixth-graders were joined by older ones yelping and jumping in their seats. Obviously, it was a sentimental choice, a memorial to the dead. Who knows how many votes the animal piled up just by croaking?

Personally, Hummelsdorf detested the choice. Marching bands tended to take on the names of their schools' mascots. He cringed at the thought of the Strawberry Festival parade next spring . . . someone at a microphone announcing as they passed the review stand: " . . . and here they come, ladies and gentlemen . . . the famous Plumstead Middle School Mmmmarching *Hammmmmmm-sters!*"

And now the principal was saying it's time for the music, and the curtain was whooshing open, and the audience was getting up. While the principal and other assembly speakers pulled their chairs from the stage, Hummelsdorf took his place at the podium front and center. Only scattered teachers remained in the seats now, as the students poured down the aisles and out to the wings. He felt a small surge of power.

He turned to face the students clomping onto the stage. He had given them all diagrams, so they knew where to stand or sit. All instruments waited except for the whistles and rubber bands, which were supposed to be in their players' pockets.

Hummelsdorf turned to the auditorium, seeking and again failing to find Wyler. When he turned back, he almost jumped. There she was, in front, a few feet to his left, holding the cymbals by her sides, as he had shown her. She wore a different shirt, and a different face. Her hair looked . . . normal.

The students were testing their instruments, producing a jumbled junkyard of toots, tweets, bams, and twangs. The maestro mounted the single step. He tapped his baton on the podium. The band fell silent.

Hummelsdorf stood as erect as his hunched, five-feet-four-inch frame would allow. Whenever he stood at the podium, all those eyes looking up, waiting for him, he felt he was the tallest person in the world. He raised his arms. At his back, the vast, expectant stillness swelled like a balloon to the bursting point.

He turned to the twenty whistles. "Ready," he mouthed silently, and prayed they were. He brought the baton down. Twenty whistles — well, nineteen — tweeted in unison, four quick notes. They were off!

For the first time Hummelsdorf was hearing what before he had only imagined in his inner ear. He was pleased, even surprised. By Beethoven, this wasn't bad! Even his defective hearing could tell that. Sure, it was jangling and raucous, but in a quirky sort of way. Sure, it was amateurish, but in an honest, genuine sort of way. The dueling kazoos and soda bottles. The primitively happy clamor of the buckets and spoons. The washboards' stirring racket that made him want to march. The perfectly comical *TWANG!* of the rubber bands. Behind him he thought he heard outbursts of laughter and clapping. In his band's faces he saw the approval of the audience. Maybe they weren't the Philharmonic, but they were entertaining.

The last part was coming up. He nodded to Wyler. She brought the cymbals up from her sides, her eyes fixed on his. With a brisk downbeat, he snapped off the washboards' final roll. His arms aloft, he held the silence — he held the world — for one second . . . two . . . three . . . he turned full face to Wyler and gave the downbeat a sledgehammer blow. Wyler's hands leaped together, letting the force of the collision drive them apart, turning the cymbals outward, like a broad brass-petaled flower, letting the sound bloom over the auditorium. *Just as he had taught her*.

Almost forgetting himself, he laid down the baton and took up his tuba. He worked his lips briefly, cleared his throat, took a deep breath, and blew. The first thing that came out was a strangulated belch of a note such as Hummelsdorf had never heard, much less produced, before. The second thing was a hamster.

"Humphrey!" cried several voices as the animal clung momentarily to the tuba's massive rim, then dropped to the stage floor.

"Rodent!" bawled a voice from the audience, and a dozen teachers screamed and jumped onto their seats.

The stage was in tumult: 340 band members and one conductor lunging and shrieking at once.

"There he is!"

"There!"

"There!"

"Stuff your pants in your socks! They crawl up legs!"

"EEEEEEEEEEEE!"

Chairs clattered, buckets clanged. Who was chasing whom, it was hard to tell. So loud was the commotion that no one heard when Sunny Wyler started screaming: "Stand *still*! You'll *step* on him!"

The tumult was fully into its third minute and Sunny still screaming in vain when Eddie Mott came up to her, grinning as usual. One hand covered the mouth of his trombone.

"I stuck it in front of him," he said, "and he scooted right in."

Gaping in disbelief, Sunny meekly obeyed when he said, "Put your hand over mine." He pulled his hand away, leaving hers to cover the trombone.

"They have it!" someone shouted. "Look!"

The commotion ceased. All eyes turned toward the sixth-grade girl holding the trombone.

Eddie nodded. "Go ahead."

Carefully Sunny reached into the mouth of the instrument. When she withdrew with a tiny, furry, caramel-colored bundle in her fingers, a full-school cheer erupted from the stage. And for the first time since she had arrived at Plumstead, looking straight at Eddie Mott, no less, Sunny smiled.

Along with chants of "Humphrey! Humphrey!" the notes of reveille filled the auditorium.

24

"It's like . . . hibernation, I guess," Sunny was explaining to Hillary that night. "When the temperature goes below forty-something, they go into this kind of coma. Their heart only beats about once a minute. It's just like they're dead. So it must've thawed out and woke up and climbed out of its own coffin."

"And into a *tuba*?" marveled Hillary, pulling a brush again and again through her newly washed hair.

"Yeah," chuckled Sunny. "You shoulda seen the conductor's face when he heard his first note."

"So how did the hamster get in the freezer in the first place?"

Sunny shrugged. "Who knows? Probably some jerk eighth-grader."

There was a minute of silence.

"So now you're gonna stay."

Sunny looked away from her friend. She picked up her own brush and began stroking her hair. She nodded. "I guess."

Hillary walked around the room, touching things. She went to the bedroom window and stood there, looking out.

She did not see Sunny pull off her shoes, then her socks. She did not know Sunny was sneaking up behind her, reaching over her shoulder, until she saw the socks dangling in front of her nose. She screamed, flailed at the socks, and steam-rollered over Sunny on her way to the closet.

Sunny followed, bent with laughter. At the closet entrance, she extended the socks into the darkness. "Hillary, here, take a whiff."

"No!"

"Hill, come on. Just a little one. You'll live, I promise."

From the darkness came a short sniff; then another, longer one; then a long, deep breath. A hand snatched the socks. Hillary came out, grinning.

"It's better if I'm happy at my school, right?" said Sunny.

"Right," agreed Hillary, breathing deeply. "Right!"

On Saturday morning Eddie Mott watched only half his usual dose of cartoons. He turned off the TV and went outside, looking for someone to play with. He walked one block, two blocks. A few grown-ups were outside doing chores, but not a kid in sight. Cartooning, Eddie figured.

He was ready to give up when he heard the sound of a skateboard clacking down the sidewalk cracks behind him. Then a voice calling: "Yo, Mott!"

He turned just as Pickles Johnson wrapped him with a curl-and-stop.

"Hi," said Eddie, staring at the pickleboard. He had never been this close to it.

"What's up?" said Pickles.

Eddie shrugged. "Not much. Nobody's out."

Pickles spread his arms. "Hey — do I look like nobody?"

Eddie laughed.

Pickles pushed the pickleboard over to Eddie. "Try it."

Eddie goggled. "You kiddin'?"

"No, go ahead, step on."

"I might crash it."

"You won't. It's a tank."

"I'm not a good skateboarder."

Pickles lifted Eddie's right foot and set it on the board. *"Go!"*

Eddie went.

He couldn't believe he was actually riding the famous pickleboard. It was much larger than he had realized. It was like riding a giant green slipper. And smooth — wow! — it took the ground like whipped cream melting over his tongue.

The sidewalk was level here. Eddie coasted easily along while Pickles trotted at his side.

129

"Waddaya think?" said Pickles.

"Wow!" was all Eddie could answer.

They went along like that for a block or so; then Pickles hopped aboard in front of Eddie and said, "Pull your foot in and *hang on!*" Eddie grabbed onto Pickles' waist, and away they went on a rollicking ride. Eddie couldn't have been prouder if he had hitched a ride on Superman's cape.

Ten minutes later, in a neighborhood Eddie did not recognize, Pickles swung up a driveway and into a backyard. "My house," he said. He parked the pickleboard. "Come on. I have something to show you."

Pickles steered Eddie down a set of steps into a basement. "This is my workbench," he said, pointing to a long wooden table busy with tools, containers, and scraps of every sort. He led Eddie to the end of the bench, where he picked up an old jelly jar. It was half full of a greenish-gray goop.

"Ugh," said Eddie. "What *is* it?"

"Mashed garbage," said Pickles, "mixed with rotten milk and dead fish juice." He held out the jar. "Want a taste?"

Eddie jumped back.

"I don't blame you. It could be fatal. The secret is the fish juice. My father uses it to fertilize his tomato plants in the spring."

"So what's it for?" said Eddie.

Pickles gazed proudly at the goop. "Anti-nickelhead booby trap."

"What?"

"They attacked your lunch two times so far, right?"

"Right."

"So, as soon as I get this all worked out, you can have a surprise ready for them next time. I have to figure out something to put the stuff in. I'm thinking about a Rice Krispie bar." Pickles' eyes were bright as he explained. "Cut it in half. Hollow out the middle. Put in the stuff. Stick the two halves back together. You take it to school each day. Nickelhead swipes your lunch. Nickelhead bites into Rice Krispie bar. Nickelhead — "

They finished it together: *"dies!"*

"Or thinks he's gonna," grinned Pickles. "And that's the last time anybody ever takes *your* lunch."

They laughed. Eddie was almost giddy. First a ride on the pickleboard, and now this. Who would have thought Pickles Johnson would one day turn his genius on Eddie Mott?

And that's what touched Eddie most of all — not the anti-nickelhead booby trap itself, but the fact that Pickles had done it for him. Eddie knew then that Pickles had become more than a flag-raising partner or lunch-bag rescuer. He was a new friend.

25

As far as Eddie knew, there was no mail delivery on Sunday, so what was a white envelope doing in the mailbox? He took it out. There was no stamp, no address even. Only his name.

He took it up to his room and opened it. There were three sheets of paper, stapled together in the upper left corner, typewritten. Or maybe computer printed. At the top it said:

The Wimp Who Wasn't
by
Salem Jane Brownmiller

He let it fall to his bed. He closed his door. He got out his mini-basketball set and fired up about fifty three-pointers. He dropkicked the nearly weightless, foam ball into his closet. He returned to the bed. He sat down, picked up the papers, and began to read.

It was a story. About a kid named Perry T.

Winkle. This kid has all kinds of problems as a new sixth-grader in middle school.

After being flung around by some big football players on the way to school, he refuses to leave the bus until the principal coaxes him off. Everywhere he turns — bathroom, cafeteria, hallways — he gets terrorized by eighth-graders.

The kid, Perry, soon gets disgusted with himself. "I'm a wimp!" he cries out. He believes he has no guts. He wants to stay in bed forever. He doesn't deserve to appear in public. He's nothing but a human beanbag.

And then Perry goes to a girl's house for lunch. Her name is Susan, and she serves him all this good stuff to eat. But there's one thing that isn't good: her homemade punch. In fact, it's abominable. But Susan thinks her punch is great, and she keeps pestering him to drink more, *more*.

Well, the thing about Perry is, he's a goodhearted kid. He sees how proud Susan is of her punch, and he doesn't want to hurt her feelings. So he keeps drinking it, and what's more, pretending he likes it.

He goes home and gets sick. When Susan finds out, she tells herself it's because of all the food he ate. But deep inside, she knows better. It was the punch. And now she realizes that he sacrificed himself for her feelings.

In the end Susan sits in her room wondering how she can thank Perry. And wondering how she can convince him that he's not a wimp at all, but in his own little way, he's a hero.

Eddie just sat there for a while. Then he put the story away in his special drawer where he kept his most valuable stuff. He went back to shooting mini-ball baskets.

He thought about his first horrifying days at Plumstead Middle School: flung around the bus, nickelheads after his lunch, spit at, lost. He shuddered just to remember. Then he thought of recent days: catching the hamster, Sunny Wyler smiling at him, Pickles' friendship, Salem's story.

It suddenly occurred to Eddie that something was missing, had been missing for several days now. He no longer wished he were back in grade school. In fact . . . he looked at his clock. It said 3 P.M. That would be nine . . . plus seven . . . sixteen hours and fifteen minutes till he would catch the bus to school next day.

He couldn't wait.

About the Author

Jerry Spinelli is the author of several novels, including *Fourth Grade Rats*, *The Library Card*, *Picklemania*, and the Newbery Medal–winning *Maniac Magee*. He lives in Phoenixville, Pennsylvania, with his wife and fellow author, Eileen Spinelli, and their children.

Any Way You Look At It,
LOUIS SACHAR'S
Books are Hilarious

___ 0-590-45726-8	**Sideways Arithmetic from Wayside School**	$4.99
___ 0-590-47762-5	**More Sideways Arithmetic from Wayside School**	$4.99
___ 0-590-46075-7	**Sixth Grade Secrets**	$4.99

Available Wherever You Buy Books or Use This Order Form